Stealing Lincoln's Body

Stealing Lincoln's Body

Thomas J. Craughwell

THE BELKNAP PRESS OF
HARVARD UNIVERSITY PRESS
Cambridge, Massachusetts
London, England

First Harvard University Press paperback edition, 2008.

Library of Congress Cataloging-in-Publication Data
Craughwell, Thomas J., 1956–
Stealing Lincoln's body / Thomas J. Craughwell.
p.   cm.
Includes bibliographical references and index.
ISBN 978-0-674-02458-8 (cloth : alk. paper)
ISBN 978-0-674-03039-8 (pbk.)
1. Lincoln, Abraham, 1809–1865—Tomb.   2. Grave robbing—Illinois—
Springfield—History—19th century.   3. Crime and the press—United States—
History—19th century.   4. Lincoln, Abraham, 1809–1865—Family.   5. Grave
robbing—United States—History—19th century.   6. Counterfeits and
counterfeiting—United States—History—19th century.   7. Irish American
criminals—History—19th century.   I. Title.
E457.52.C73   2007
973.7092—dc22   2006050842

For Lizzie and Thanial
with all my love

Acknowledgments

More than forty years ago my parents, Marilyn and Ambrose Craughwell, took me and my sister Karen to see the Lincoln sites in New Salem and Springfield, Illinois. Outside the Lincoln Monument my dad told me how a gang of grave robbers had tried to steal Lincoln's body but were stopped at the last minute. It's a great story, and I'd never forgotten it, but it never occurred to me to write about the grave robbery—until a couple years ago when I was talking with my family about possible book ideas. My father said, "Why don't you write something about the Civil War. Or better yet, something about Lincoln." His suggestion jogged my memory, and suddenly the story he'd told me in Oak Ridge Cemetery so many years before came back to me. A few weeks later I started researching the plot to steal Abraham Lincoln's body. I owe this book to my father; it is just the latest in a lifetime of debts to my mom and dad that I can never repay.

All authors need allies, and I have been especially fortunate in mine. Dr. Wayne C. Temple, chief deputy director of the Illinois State Archives, and the dean of Lincoln scholars, shared his expertise with me and spent countless hours hunting down forgotten documents. Kim Bauer, Glenna Schroeder-Lein, Debbie Hamm, Mary Ann Pohl, and the rest of the staff of the Abraham Lincoln Presidential Library in Springfield, and Mark L. Johnson, Springfield's historic sites historian, offered me advice, and leads, as well as introductions to experts, and friendship. Jon Austin and Jason Meyers at the Museum of Funeral Customs in Springfield threw open their archives and gave me an intensive crash course in nineteenth-century embalming techniques. Nan Wynn, site manager of the Lincoln Tomb, and her friendly staff at the Lincoln Monument provided me with a clear, concise history of the tomb and the multiple removals of the Lincoln family's remains.

For many of the images that appear in this book, my thanks to Jennifer Ericson, Mary Michals, Roberta Fairburn, and Jim Helm at the Abraham Lincoln Presidential Library; Jason Kendrick, Thomas Grupski, and Michael Sampson of the U.S. Secret Service; and R. Emmett Tyrrell, Jr., the great-great-grandson of Patrick D. Tyrrell.

I am especially grateful to Loyola law student Laurence Acker, who tracked down old Illinois statutes on grave robbing; Prof. James Carey of Chicago's Loyola University Law School, who offered insights into how prosecutors think; Jennifer M. K. Kittlaus, library assistant at George Washington's Mount Vernon Estate and Gardens, who located a pile of original sources and answered all my questions about the attempt to steal George Washington's bones; Terry Tatum for his expertise on Chicago neighborhoods in the nineteenth century; and my friend Candis LaPrade, who discovered wonderful items in the *News Orleans Daily Picayune*.

My thanks to the staff of the New York Public Library, the

Acknowledgments

Chicago Historical Society, Grace Dumelle of the Newberry Library in Chicago, Cindy VanHorn and Joan Flinspach of the Lincoln Museum in Fort Wayne, Indiana, and the staff of the National Archives in College Park, Maryland—especially Wayne DeCesar.

I am indebted to the Carlson Family, Msgr. Richard Soseman, Kevin and Ellen Donovan, and Bob and Jeanne Tyrrell for their hospitality. For their generous help and advice I thank Kathleen Drummy, Joseph Cummins, Cormac O'Brien, Mariah Fredericks, George Foster, Amy Thomas, Dianna Baldwin, Lance Bodrero, Rev. Joseph Ponessa, and my sister and brother-in-law Kathy Craughwell-Varda and John Varda.

Finally, my heartfelt thanks to four people I could not have done without: my sister and copyeditor, Karen Jeffreys; my friend Molly Kennedy, the gold standard among researchers; and my editors at Harvard University Press, Kathleen McDermott and Susan Abel.

Mariae gratias.

Contents

Illustrations follow p. 180.

Stealing Lincoln's Body

Prologue:
"Lay My Remains in
Some Quiet Place"

At 7:22 on the morning of April 15, 1865, a twenty-three-year-old United States Army surgeon felt the last tremor of life leave the body of Abraham Lincoln.

All through that long night, as at least fifty-seven visitors passed in and out of the tiny back bedroom of the Petersen family's house on Tenth Street in Washington, D.C., Dr. Charles A. Leale, a stranger to the dying man, had stood beside the comatose president, holding his hand, "to let him in his blindness know," as Leale explained later, "that he had a friend."[1] By seven in the morning Lincoln was barely breathing. Knowing the end must be near, Leale kept one finger of that comforting hand on the president's pulse. The minutes ticked by. The pulse weakened. Leale detected a faint throb, then—nothing. The young doctor waited almost a full minute before releasing Abraham Lincoln's hand; then, raising his head, he looked across the bed at Dr. Joseph K. Barnes, surgeon general of the United States. Barnes understood. Reverently, he folded the dead man's hands across his chest. To the hushed little crowd of about a dozen mourners Barnes whispered, "He is gone."[2] Twenty-one-year-old Robert Todd Lincoln, the Lincolns' eldest son, put his head on the shoulder of Senator Charles Sumner and sobbed.

No one in that tiny back bedroom moved. No one spoke. Finally, Secretary of War Edwin Stanton broke the silence with words that would become Lincoln's unofficial epitaph, "Now he belongs to the ages."

But James Tanner heard it differently. Tanner, a twenty-one-year-old corporal who had lost both legs below the knee at the Second Battle of Bull Run, was not part of Lincoln's inner circle or a member of the president's staff, or even a government employee. He boarded at the house next to the Petersens'. About midnight, when General Christopher C. Augur called out to the crowd gathered in front of the Petersen house, asking whether there was anyone present who could write in shorthand, Tanner shouted back that he could. The crowd cleared a path for the young man, and Augur brought him into the house. All night the young stenographer alternated between formally recording the testimony of witnesses who had been at Ford's Theatre and jotting down his private impressions of what was occurring in the room where President Lincoln lay dying. According to Tanner's notes, Stanton said, "He belongs to the angels now."[3] As aphorisms go, Tanner's version does not scan well; nor does it reflect what we know about Stanton's personality. Given the secretary of war's stern, unsentimental nature, it is more likely that Stanton would have spoken of ages than of angels.

Mary Todd Lincoln was not in the room at the moment of

her husband's death: she had made her final visit to him about thirty minutes earlier. Kneeling beside the little bed, too short for Lincoln's six-foot, four-inch body, she had cried, "Love! Live but one moment to speak to me once—to speak to our children." When no response came, Mary Lincoln gave way to a fit of hysterics so violent that the sad and solemn men gathered around their chief's deathbed could not bear it. Friends half carried Mary to the front parlor of the house, where she could vent her awful grief in private.[4]

Outside, a steady rain was falling. Elizabeth Dixon, one of the First Lady's confidants, had spent all night at the Petersen house, trying to console her desperate friend. She remembered that morning as so dark and dreary it seemed the sun "was struggling with dim candles" and making no headway.[5]

The Lincoln family pastor, Rev. Dr. Phineas D. Gurley of the New York Avenue Presbyterian Church, had offered a prayer at the moment of the president's death. Now, accompanied by Robert Lincoln, Dr. Gurley made his way to the president's widow. As Mary lay on a sofa moaning, Dr. Gurley knelt and prayed for her. Then the two men lifted the grief-stricken woman and escorted her out of the house. At the curb a carriage was waiting. As she was about to climb in, Mary Lincoln paused, looked across the street at Ford's Theatre, and spat out what for her amounted to a curse, "Oh, that dreadful, dreadful house!"[6]

Another hour and a half would pass before President Lincoln's body was taken from the Petersen home. On Stanton's orders, the bedroom was locked up and a guard posted at the door. Only after the secretary of war had conferred with several members of the cabinet about what must be done next was Lincoln's body prepared for removal. Soldiers from the Veteran Reserve Corps entered the bedroom, pulled back the bed-clothes, wrapped their dead commander in an American flag, and placed his body in a plain pine coffin. As the name implies, the Veteran Reserve Corps was made up of Civil War veterans—in this case, men whose wounds or some other medical condition made them unfit to return to the front lines. Although they remained on the active list, they were assigned light duties. On this morning their duties also bore a weighty historical significance.

The pine box had been procured by assistant quartermaster General Daniel Rucker, a man who understood the importance of delivering what was needed to the right people at the right moment. For nearly the entire length of the Civil War he had been in charge of funneling massive quantities of supplies to the Union armies in northern Virginia and around Richmond. At that point, when what was needed most urgently was a pine box, Rucker had managed to find a coffin maker.

Carefully, the veterans carried the coffin down the curving staircase outside the Petersen house, then slid it into the back of the waiting hearse. With a small cavalry escort, the little cortege set off for the White House, arriving just as Elizabeth Dixon, physically exhausted and emotionally drained, was leaving. She had settled her friend in a spare second-floor bedroom. Mary Lincoln had refused to use her own room, where she would be overwhelmed by memories of her husband. Elizabeth Keckley, an ex-slave and dressmaker who was Mrs. Lincoln's most intimate friend, would tend to her now. As Mrs. Dixon descended the staircase, she met several soldiers carrying up the flag-wrapped body of Abraham Lincoln. She thought, as she later wrote to her sister, that the soldiers were taking "the remains of the murdered President . . . into the great State bedroom." She was mistaken. The guard carried Lincoln's body to a guest room in the northeast corner of the second floor of the White House. There some boards were laid across trestles to form a makeshift table, then covered with sheets and towels in preparation for a cranial autopsy.[7]

Two army assistant surgeons, J. Janvier Woodward and Edward Curtis, performed the autopsy. Also present were Surgeon General Barnes; the Lincoln family physician, Dr. Robert Stone; army surgeons Charles Crane, Charles S. Taft, and William M. Notson; General Rucker; and one of the Lincolns' friends from Illinois, Orville H. Browning. Dr. Curtis wrote an account of the autopsy:

> Dr. Woodward and I proceeded to open the head and remove the brain down to the track of the ball. The latter had entered a little to the left of the median line at the back of the head, had passed almost directly forwards through the center of the brain and lodged. Not finding it readily, we proceeded to remove the entire brain, when, as I was lifting the latter from the cavity of the skull, suddenly the bullet dropped out through my fingers and fell, breaking the solemn silence of the room with its clatter, into an empty basin that was standing beneath. There it lay upon the white china, a little black mass no bigger than the end of my finger—dull, motionless and harmless, yet the cause of such mighty changes in the world's history as we may perhaps never realize.[8]

Once the autopsy had been completed, Lincoln's body was turned over to the undertakers, Charles D. Brown and Joseph B. Alexander, the same men who in 1862 had arranged the funeral of the Lincolns' eleven-year-old son Willie. In 1860, before the outbreak of the Civil War, the city directory for Washington and Georgetown listed thirteen undertakers, but no embalmers.[9] Embalming, of course, has been practiced for thousands of years, in different countries following differing practices, with varying degrees of success. The ancient Egyptians turned the preservation of the dead into an art that is still a source of wonder. At the opposite end of the spectrum was the rough-and-tumble method of embalming favored in early America, in which the body was disemboweled, the cavity packed with charcoal, and the corpse wrapped in a sheet that had been soaked in alum.[10]

For the sake of convenience, one can say that modern embalming was born in 1836, when a French chemist, Jean Nicolas Gannal, developed a formula that would revolutionize funeral customs. Gannal's method of preservation involved injecting six quarts of acetate of alumnia into a corpse through the carotid artery. Originally, Gannal had developed his process to preserve the cadavers that medical schools required for the study of human anatomy. Very quickly, however, he realized that his embalming method would also find a market among funeral directors. Throughout the early decades of the nineteenth century in France there had been a movement away from the traditional swift burial after death, in the interests of leaving the body on display for a few days—perhaps in imitation of burials for royalty and important churchmen, whose bodies always lay in state for several days before the funeral. This new fashion in funerals created a demand for a method of embalming that would keep the corpse looking fresh and natural all during the wake. To prove the effectiveness of his method, Gannal published reports in which he asserted that he had tested his fluid by embalming several bodies and then exhuming them thirteen months later. When their coffins were opened, the dead embalmed by Gannal looked as fresh as the day they had been buried.

Gannal's method made him a celebrity; indeed, he became the founder of a French embalming dynasty. His sons, Adolphe, Antoine, and Felix, became the embalmers for some of the most celebrated men and women in France, including Ferdinand de Lesseps, the engineer who had dug the Suez Canal and tried, unsuccessfully, to dig a canal across Panama.

At the same time that Gannal was promoting the preservative qualities of acetate of alumnia, another Frenchman, J. P. Sucquet, began experimenting with zinc chloride. He found that five quarts of a 20 percent solution of zinc chloride injected through the popliteal artery not only preserved a body for a minimum of two years, but also wrought a wondrous transformation, giving the body the appearance of luminous white marble. Recognizing that he had come upon a potential gold mine, Sucquet hired an agent to sell the rights to his discovery. About the year 1845, the agent sold the American rights for Sucquet's method to the undertakers Brown and Alexander.[11]

The Civil War created an unprecedented demand for embalming. The idea that a fallen loved one might be dumped into a mass grave or left lying among thousands of casualties in a far-off place, without any of the traditional funeral rites, troubled many families. They wanted the body of their father, son, or brother returned home for a proper funeral; and the new methods of embalming made that possible. Undertakers opened embalming "parlors" in military camps, from which they then shipped embalmed bodies back to the soldiers' hometowns. During the war Brown and Alexander ran an advertisement in a Washington newspaper offering "the practice of their art upon such of their fellow countrymen who may be so unfortunate as to fall by wounds or disease while struggling for freedom in the great civil war now raging." The ad went on to assert that unlike other American undertakers, Brown and Alexander did not use "arsenic or other poisonous chemicals . . . but rather a preparation which in a short time renders the body hard and marble-like in character."[12]

It was Sucquet's zinc chloride that had been used to embalm Willie Lincoln. The little boy looked so lovely that the *Sunday Morning Chronicle* reported, "The embalmment was a great success, and gave great satisfaction to all present."[13] Neither Brown nor Alexander personally embalmed Willie; that job fell to their master embalmer, Henry P. Cattell. On Saturday morning, April 15, 1865, Cattell was sent to the White House again, this time to embalm the body of Abraham Lincoln. On the same trestle table used for the cranial autopsy, Cattell made an incision in Lincoln's right upper thigh and pumped in the zinc chloride. As was customary at the time, he did not drain the body of blood. Once again, the embalming formula worked its miracle, and the dead president took on the appearance of a marble sculpture.[14]

Next, Cattell shaved Lincoln's face, leaving a short tuft of beard at the chin. He arched the eyebrows and set the mouth in a slight smile. He pulled a white sheet over the president's body and laid a white cambric handkerchief over his face. As a final touch, he scattered green leaves and white flowers over the deceased. Later that afternoon, Secretary of War Stanton would supervise the dressing of the body—in the black Brooks Brothers suit the president had worn at his second inauguration, a black bow tie, and white kid gloves.[15] Brown and Alexander charged $260 for their work—$100 for the actual embalming and $160 for sending embalmers along on the Lincoln funeral train to tend to the body during its long journey home to Springfield. When Benjamin B. French, commissioner of public buildings (the government agency that paid for the Lincoln funeral), approved Brown and Alexander's bill, he wrote across it, "This was done and well done."[16]

April 16, 1865, was Easter Sunday, yet workmen took no notice of the holy day as they streamed into the East Room of the White House to begin building the platform and catafalque for the president's coffin. The cavernous East Room—eighty feet long, forty feet wide, with a ceiling twenty-two feet high—would be an impressive setting for the first stage of Abraham Lincoln's seemingly endless funeral. Laboring for two days, the army of carpenters built a structure sixteen feet long and ten feet across; it stood four feet off the floor and was crowned by a soaring canopy so tall that to accommodate it the workmen had to take down the central chandelier in the East Room Then upholsterers came in and swathed the entire structure in yards of black and white silk, satin, and velvet fabric. People who saw it called the catafalque the Temple of Death.

Upstairs the president's body had been laid at last in a proper coffin. It was a coffin maker's masterpiece—solid walnut, its exterior covered entirely in black broadcloth and embellished with silver tacks, its interior lined with overstuffed quilted white satin. The top third of the coffin lid could be removed, to permit mourners to look upon the face of Abraham Lincoln. Four massive silver handles stood out along the two sides of the coffin; and on the lid, an engraved silver shield read:

Abraham Lincoln
16th President of the United States
Born February 12, 1809
Died April 15, 1865

By the evening of Monday, April 17, everything was in readiness in the East Room. Before creeping upstairs to the spare room that held the president's body, the eight pallbearers removed their shoes. They did not want Mrs. Lincoln to hear the heavy tread of men carrying a great burden and realize what was passing just outside her door. As quietly as possible, they bore Lincoln in his ornate coffin down to the "temple" in the East Room. Outside the White House gates an immense crowd, lined up seven abreast, waited to see their president for the last time.

At last, at 9:30 on Tuesday morning, the gates of the White House swung open and the crowd surged forward. The East Room would be open to the general public for only eight hours. Nonetheless, twenty-five thousand people passed by Lincoln's coffin before the viewing ended at 5:30 in the afternoon. Thousands more were shut out; they would have to wait until the next day, when Lincoln would lie in state at the Capitol. The public viewing once concluded, a private viewing began. From 5:30 until 7:30 that evening, the East Room was reserved exclusively for four hundred of Lincoln's friends and colleagues from Illinois.[17]

No one knows whether Mary Lincoln ever left her room to

view her husband's body. It is not likely. Since the morning Lincoln had died, Mary had remained in the guest room she had made her own, overcome by grief. Friends and acquaintances who called to comfort her were turned away. She would see no one except her immediate family and her personal servants. Her most trusted friend, Elizabeth Keckley, remained almost constantly at her side. Years later Keckley recalled what she witnessed in that room. "I shall never forget the scene," she wrote in her autobiography, "the wails of a broken heart, the unearthly shrieks, the terrible convulsions, the wild tempestuous outbursts of grief from the soul."[18] The only one who could get through to Mary was her youngest surviving child, Tad. "Don't cry so, Mamma!" he begged. "Don't cry, or you will make me cry, too! You will break my heart."[19]

Since the death of her three-year-old her son, Eddie, Mary Lincoln had found it very hard to accept the grim fact that once a loved one was dead, she must move on. Mary's way was to mourn as one who would not be comforted; often her sorrow was so total that it degenerated into hysteria. She was a churchgoing woman, yet Mary could not bring herself to submit to the will of God. After the death of eleven-year-old Willie, his mother's and father's favorite child, Mary Lincoln came to believe that she could see the spirits of her dead sons. She confessed to her half-sister, Emilie Todd Helm, "Willie lives. He comes to me every night and stands at the foot of the bed with the same sweet adorable smile he always has had. He does not always come alone. Little Eddie is sometimes with him." To supplement these ghostly visitations, Mary attended séances, even inviting mediums to the White House (perhaps as many as eight times) to summon the spirits of her dead children. Emilie Todd Helm regarded with horror these attempts to contact the dead, but her half sister found them reassuring. They gave her the strength to continue as Abraham Lincoln's wife, as Robert and Tad's mother, as First Lady of the United States.[20]

If Mary Lincoln's grief at the death of her husband was out of all proportion, it was because the loss was so much worse than even the deaths of her two little boys. The couple's happiness had been at its height—the Civil War was over; the Union had been preserved; the slaves were free. Just when all their anxiety and suffering had been vindicated, an assassin came up from behind and murdered the president—as his wife sat beside him, with her hand in his. It was more than Mary Lincoln could endure.

At dawn on Wednesday, April 19, the citizens of Washington awoke to the boom of cannon fire from the siege guns on the outskirts of town. Every fifteen minutes another volley thundered across the city in tribute to the martyred president. Soon bells tolling from church steeples and firehouses added to the clamor. It was to this grim accompaniment that six hundred invited mourners rose from their beds, dressed, and headed to the White House for the funeral of Abraham Lincoln. Robert Lincoln had drawn up the list of guests, probably with the assistance of Edwin Stanton, who simultaneously oversaw the arrangements for the president's funeral and organized the manhunt for Lincoln's assassin, John Wilkes Booth.

By eleven o'clock, the East Room was beginning to fill. Robert Lincoln took a seat at the foot of his father's coffin with two of his uncles from Springfield, Ninian W. Edwards, the husband of Mary's oldest sister, Elizabeth, and Clark M. Smith, the husband of Mary's youngest sister, Ann. The bond between the Lincolns and the Edwardses was especially close. In 1842

Abraham Lincoln and Mary Todd had been married in the parlor at the Edwardses'; in 1882 Mary Lincoln would die in an upstairs bedroom of the same house. Abraham Lincoln and the Smiths appear to have gotten on well too. It is said that Lincoln wrote his first inaugural address on an unused bookkeeper's desk above the Smiths' dry goods store. The relationship between the sisters, Mary Lincoln and Ann Smith, was less happy, owing to childhood rivalries that had matured into full-blown adult resentments.[21]

Two of the Todd cousins also took their places with Robert Lincoln—Dr. Lyman Beecher Todd and General John Blair Smith Todd, both highly regarded by the Lincolns because, when so many Todds had given their allegiance to the Confederacy, these two men had remained loyal to the Union. Filling out the intimate group of mourners were Lincoln's two private secretaries, John G. Nicolay and John Hay. At the opposite end of the coffin, seated alone, was General Ulysses S. Grant. Mary Lincoln, too distraught to show herself in public, remained upstairs in bed.[22]

At ten minutes past noon, the religious service began. Abraham Lincoln had never declared his religious affiliation; it is unlikely that he was ever baptized. Since he was a man without a church, clergymen from several denominations were assigned parts in Lincoln's funeral. Rev. Dr. Charles H. Hall of Washington's Episcopal Church of the Epiphany read portions of the burial service from the Book of Common Prayer. Bishop Matthew Simpson, a Methodist, came down from Philadelphia to offer a lengthy prayer. A long-winded funeral oration was delivered by Phineas D. Gurley, the Lincoln family's Presbyterian pastor. After two hours, the service concluded with the offering of a mercifully brief prayer by Rev. Dr. Edwin H. Gray of the E Street Baptist Church and chaplain of the United States Senate.[23]

After the lid of the coffin had been closed, twelve sergeants of the Veteran Reserve Corps stepped forward. Four, with swords drawn, served as a guard of honor, while the remaining eight lifted the casket to their shoulders and carried it out of the White House to the street, where an impressive hearse drawn by six magnificent white horses stood ready to receive it.[24]

As the hearse turned toward the Capitol, the cannon, which had been firing at fifteen-minute intervals, boomed every sixty seconds—in a traditional signal of distress recognized by military men.[25] The bells of the city still tolled, joined now by muffled drums that set a steady, solemn cadence for the marchers, while thirty marching bands played competing dirges. Such a cacophony of mournful noises must have been dreadful to hear.

At the head of the procession marched the Twenty-second U.S. Colored Infantry, newly arrived in Washington that very day from the scenes of fighting around Richmond. Behind them came a cortege that numbered in the thousands: workers from the various offices of the federal government, from the railroads, from the docks, from the Navy Yard; members of church groups and fraternal lodges; schoolchildren; convalescing veterans from Washington's many military hospitals; and bringing up the rear of the procession, thousands of African American mourners representing a host of benevolent, religious, and fraternal organizations.[26]

Thousands more, many of whom had come into Washington in the last few hours aboard special trains, crowded the sidewalks, perched on rooftops, hung out the windows of homes and shops and offices. All along the route, buildings were shrouded in black bunting. Even the columns of the Capitol were enveloped in black. "The city of Washington," Dr. Leale recalled, "was wrapped in a mantle of gloom."[27]

Once Lincoln's hearse arrived at the Capitol, the pallbearers carried the coffin up the stairs of the east front and into the Rotunda, where a raised dais covered in silver-trimmed black cloth stood ready to receive it. All the paintings and sculptures in the vast circular hall were shrouded in black. Only Houdon's statue of George Washington had been left uncovered, but it wore a black sash draped over its shoulders.[28] Before a small handful of Lincoln's family and friends, Gurley offered a prayer from the Presbyterian burial service: "It is appointed unto men once to die. The dust returns to the earth as it was, and the spirit to God who gave it." Outside the Capitol, the cannon and the bells and the bands fell silent.[29]

The public was not admitted until the next morning at eight. It was raining, yet thousands had waited for hours to file past Lincoln's bier. Noah Brooks, a reporter for the *Sacramento Union* assigned to Washington and a friend of president (he was one of the dozen who had declined an invitation to accompany the Lincolns to Ford's Theatre), managed to talk a guard into letting him climb up to the gallery of the Rotunda, 365 steps above the floor.[30] He later described the sight below as "weird and memorable" from his vantage point. "Directly beneath me lay the casket in which the dead President lay at full length, far, far below; and like black atoms moving over a sheet of grey paper, the slow-moving mourners . . . crept silently in two dark lines across the pavement of the rotunda, forming an ellipse around the coffin and joining as they advanced toward the eastern portal and disappeared."[31]

Before seven o'clock the next morning, a smaller procession, composed almost exclusively of military men and government officials, came to the Capitol to escort the body of Abraham Lincoln to the Baltimore & Ohio Railroad train station on New Jersey Avenue. By chance, the cortege reached the depot just as the coffin of eleven-year-old Willie Lincoln arrived from its vault in Georgetown's Oak Hill Cemetery. The Lincolns had always said that when they left Washington, they would take Willie's body back to Illinois with them; now the bodies of father and son would be making the journey back to Springfield together. At 8:00 A.M. precisely, the special nine-car train lurched out of the station to begin the first leg of its 1,654-mile journey.[32]

Before it came to rest in Springfield, Lincoln's body would be removed from the train for processions, public viewing, and funeral ceremonies in ten cities: Baltimore, Harrisburg, Philadelphia, New York, Albany, Buffalo, Cleveland, Columbus, Indianapolis, and Chicago. Yet many more cities had hoped to honor the martyred president. James H. Thomas, mayor of St. Louis, telegraphed Mary Lincoln, saying, "The authorities of St. Louis have made the most elaborate arrangements" to receive the body. C. W. Chapin, president of the Western Railroad Corporation, pleaded for the train to stop in New Haven or Hartford, because "in no portion of our common country do the people mourn in deeper grief than in New England." Sadly for Thomas, Chapin, and their counterparts in Pittsburgh, Cincinnati, and many other cities, they would have to endure disappointment. By eleven o'clock on the night of April 19, Mary Lincoln had given her final approval for the itinerary of her husband's funeral train.

Towns and cities that would not enjoy the privilege of honoring Lincoln formally were determined nonetheless to show their grief and respect, even if only for the few minutes it took the train to pass through the city limits. Consequently, the announcement of the train's route set off a frenzy of preparation in whistle-stops and urban areas all along the way. No fewer than twenty-seven towns erected memorial arches over the train tracks. Herkimer, New York, and Michigan City, Indiana, were just two of many towns to create a living tableau of the Union, with thirty-six young women, representing the thirty-six states, dressed all in white except for a black mourning sash.[33]

There were so many memorable moments along the way that it would be the labor of a lifetime to catalog them all. Pennsylvania congressman Thaddeus Stevens had been one of Lincoln's bitterest political opponents, damning the president as an incompetent rube and a lukewarm opponent of slavery.[34] Yet Stevens came out in a driving rainstorm to wait beside the tracks for the funeral train to go by. As it passed, the old fire-eater raised his hat.[35]

In Philadelphia three hundred thousand mourners tried to view Lincoln's body as it lay in state in Independence Hall. Anxious that they would not get a chance to approach the coffin, the crowd, pressing in tighter and tighter around the historic building, crushed or trampled hundreds of people, mostly women and small children. The city police lost control of the situation, and even soldiers with bayonets failed to keep the panicky throng in order.

In New York City seventy-five thousand marchers escorted the coffin in a massive procession through the streets of the city.[36] A photograph of the procession passing through Union Square shows two small boys watching from a second-story window; they are six-year-old Theodore Roosevelt and his four-year-old brother Elliott.[37]

When the funeral train arrived in Illinois, Lincoln's home state, the crowds became enormous. In Chicago, wooden fences and wooden sidewalks collapsed, unable to bear the weight of so many spectators. It was midnight when the train rolled into Joliet, Illinois, yet twelve thousand people were waiting to receive it. Just as the train came to a stop at the depot, a meteor shot across the night sky, to the amazement of the onlookers.[38]

At 8:40 on the morning of May 3, the Lincoln funeral train arrived in Springfield, inching its way through an immense but silent throng that lined both sides of the railroad track.[39] Springfield's regular population of 12,000 was overwhelmed by more than 150,000 visitors, all eager to witness the funeral and, if they were lucky, view the body. Such an outpouring of affection for Abraham Lincoln was deeply touching, but Springfield did not have anywhere near sufficient accommodations for so many people. The committee charged with the funeral arrangements now urged the people of Springfield to "throw open their homes and exercise the most liberal hospitality to strangers." Committee members sent urgent pleas to farmers outside the city to come into town with wagonloads of "good dry straw" for bedding and with cooked food that could be sold at curbside. A Chicago reporter telegraphed his editor at the *Chicago Tribune*, "[Springfield] is so crowded that it is impossible to procure lodging in a bar-room or on a pool-table." Just at that moment, as if Springfield did not have enough to contend with, a party of pioneers in twenty wagons headed for the Oregon Territory rolled into town.[40]

The procession from the depot that escorted Lincoln's coffin to the statehouse, known today as the Old Capitol, passed through a town drowning in grief. The Lincoln family home, Lincoln's law office, and the Presbyterian church the family had attended were all hung with mourning bunting. The exterior of the statehouse, where Lincoln had delivered his "House Divided" speech, was almost entirely wrapped in black—including the little dome that crowns the brownstone building.

Most homes in the city hung a mourning wreath on the door or nailed a swag of black cloth to the lintel. The businesses of Springfield, however, put on a more elaborate show. The First National Bank displayed a large portrait of Lincoln with the motto "He left us upheld by our prayers. He returns embalmed in our tears." The Smith & Bros. store displayed a bust of the president within an evergreen wreath and an inscription that read, "How we loved him." Over the doors of Wolf & Bergmann hung a panel inscribed with a bit of heartfelt doggerel: "An honest man now lies at rest, / As ever God with his image blest; / Few hearts like his with virtue warmed, / Few heads with knowledge so informed."[41]

Before the public was admitted to the Hall of Representatives, where the former president would lie in state, Charles Brown, the funeral director who had accompanied the body all the way from Washington, and Thomas Lynch, a local undertaker, locked the chamber doors, then raised the coffin lid for a routine examination. They found that Lincoln's face had darkened considerably, so much so that Brown couldn't imagine letting Lincoln's friends and neighbors see him in such a state. Lynch had a solution to the problem. He slipped out of the chamber and pushed his way through the great crowd that packed the corridors and stairway of the statehouse. Once outside, Lynch headed for a neighborhood drugstore, where he bought rouge chalk, amber, and a few brushes. Lynch recorded what he did back in the Hall of Representatives: "I at once set about coloring the President's features, placing the materials on very thick so as to completely hide the discoloration of the skin. In half an hour I had finished my task and the doors were thrown open to the public."[42]

The discoloration of Lincoln's face was not the result of decomposition or a side effect of the embalming fluid. It was a phenomenon, common with gunshot wounds to the head, known as contrecoup. In such cases the bones opposite the point of the bullet's impact break, causing severe bruising of the skin and attendant discoloration of the face.[43] It was a phenomenon understood at the time of the president's death. An article published in the *Chicago Tribune* reported, "[Lincoln's] face was somewhat discolored, as might have been expected from the character of his wound, but not more than we remember to have seen in cases of gunshot wounds."[44]

Meanwhile, at Oak Ridge Cemetery, two miles from the statehouse, workmen were rushing to refurbish the small receiving vault where the bodies of Lincoln and his son Willie would lie until a permanent tomb was completed. In the minds of many Springfield residents, the question whether that permanent tomb would be in Oak Ridge, in downtown Springfield, or even back in Washington was still unresolved.

Almost from the moment the president died, members of Congress lobbied for Lincoln to be buried in Washington. They suggested a resting place in the vault directly beneath the Capitol dome that had been built originally for the remains of George Washington. By chance, Illinois governor Richard J. Oglesby happened to be in Washington at the time of the assassination; supported by Senator Richard Yates and other Illinois politicians, Oglesby began the delicate task of advancing

Springfield's claim to the president's corpse. Robert Lincoln and Judge David Davis, one of Abraham Lincoln's closest political advisers, agreed that Springfield ought to be the site of the president's tomb. By April 17, just two days after her husband's death, Mary had made up her mind: her husband would be buried in Oak Ridge Cemetery on the outskirts of Springfield.[45]

Oak Ridge was Springfield's nod to a trend that has come to be known as the rural cemetery movement. Traditionally, both in Europe and in the United States, burials had taken place in churchyards or burial grounds within the city limits. As cities grew (between 1775 and 1820, the population of Boston tripled, for example) these small graveyards filled up quickly. Sanitation became an issue—it could not be healthy to have so many bodies decomposing right in the heart of town. Finally, from an aesthetic point of view, urban burial grounds were often an eyesore. Writing of a typical Massachusetts graveyard in 1831, William O. Peabody described the place as "the most neglected spot in the region, distinguished from other fields only by its leaning stones and the meanness of its enclosures, without a tree or a shrub to take from it the air of utter desolation."[46]

While Peabody lamented the condition of traditional burial grounds, another Massachusetts man, Jacob Bigelow, was imagining a radically new type of cemetery. Bigelow, a physician, a professor at Harvard College, and the founder of the Massachusetts Horticultural Society, counted many Boston Brahmins among his friends. He proposed designing an exquisitely landscaped garden cemetery outside the Boston city limits.[47] Inspired by Romanticism, which fostered idealized notions about the splendors of the natural world, Bigelow saw his cemetery as part botanical garden, part arboretum, and part outdoor art museum.[48]

In 1831 Jacob Bigelow's dream was realized, and America's first garden cemetery opened ten miles from the noise, congestion, and smells of central Boston. The seventy-two-acre site was named Mount Auburn, and it was everything Bigelow and his supporters hoped it would be—a little Eden where fresh air, natural light, and lovely landscaping created an atmosphere of peace and optimism—the polar opposite of the aura of gloom and despair that hung over those neglected city graveyards. Bostonians responded enthusiastically to Mount Auburn; they saw in the parklike setting a fitting resting place for the dead and a pleasant place for grieving families to visit. Almost immediately families began lining up to buy lots at sixty dollars apiece. Some families even bought multiple lots, large enough to accommodate the graves of future generations. It was not uncommon for lot holders to erect monuments before any member of the family had died and then to send professional gardeners to Mount Auburn to landscape the family burial site.[49]

Like Paul Revere's house and Bunker Hill, Mount Auburn became a popular destination for visitors to Boston. Soon committees in major cities and small towns were reviewing landscape designs for their own version of Mount Auburn. Springfield joined the trend in June 1855, when Councilman Charles H. Lanphier persuaded the city fathers to purchase seventeen undeveloped acres for a new cemetery two miles north of town. At the dedication of Oak Ridge, Springfield's former mayor James C. Conkling delivered an address that summarized the philosophy of the rural cemetery movement. "Here," he said, "with naught but the pure arch of heaven above us, and Nature in all her silent beauty and loveliness around us, we dedicate the City of the Dead." Present in the crowd that day were Abraham and Mary Lincoln.[50]

It was not fashion alone that prompted Mary Lincoln to choose Oak Ridge for her husband's final resting place. Years later Mary would claim that she was fulfilling Lincoln's express wish. In his 1885 biography of Lincoln, Isaac N. Arnold tells how, just a few weeks before the assassination, Abraham and Mary Lincoln took a carriage ride out into the country. As their carriage rolled along a peaceful lane beside the James River, Lincoln saw a small cemetery and ordered the driver to stop. It was a lovely, shady spot where the first wildflowers of spring grew upon the graves. As the Lincolns walked among the headstones, the president grew pensive. "Mary," he said, "you are younger than I. You will survive me. When I am gone, lay my remains in some quiet place like this." Arnold said Mary Lincoln told him this story in October 1874—long after the controversy over the burial place had been settled decisively in Mary's favor.[51]

Once Mary Lincoln had named Springfield as her husband's final resting place, Governor Oglesby went right to work. On April 24, 1865, while the funeral train was making its slow way westward, thirteen of Springfield's most prominent citizens (including Mary Lincoln's cousin John Todd Stuart) formed the National Lincoln Monument Association, selected a burial site, and began the business of raising money for the construction of a tomb that would, according to the founding document, "be a worthy tribute to [Lincoln's] fame and an honor to the nation."[52] Without consulting Mary Lincoln, the gentlemen of the association jettisoned the plans for a tomb in Oak Ridge. The cemetery was too far from downtown; the throngs of visitors that were certain to come to Springfield would surely prefer a location in the city center. The National Lincoln Monument Association had just such a site in mind: the centrally located hilltop on which the Mather home was situated.

The Mather Block, as the site was known, had been in the running from the beginning. Three days after Lincoln's death, the *Illinois Daily Journal* had reported: "The beautiful square now occupied by the residence of Mrs. Mather . . . will probably be selected [as the grave site], as the grounds are singularly well adapted to the purpose. It is suggested that the whole square be purchased and properly improved and beautified. It lies in full view of the Chicago and Alton Railroad, and would be convenient of access to visitors."[53] The site truly was splendid—the highest point in Springfield, the hill was covered with a lovely grove of trees. Fully satisfied with their choice, the association members entered into a conditional contract with Widow Mather for her property.[54] No money exchanged hands. In fact, no record survives to indicate that Hannah Mather and the members of the Monument Association ever arrived at a conditionally agreed-upon price.

How much was the property worth? A 1912 history of Sangamon County claims that Hannah Mather could have gotten $62,000 for her seven or eight acres.[55] Two years later, when the issue of where Abraham Lincoln would be buried had long been settled, Hannah Mather did sell her property. On January 18, 1867, she entered into a contract with the state of Illinois, selling her land for $45,000. The Mather Block and some adjacent parcels became the site of the new Illinois State Capitol complex.[56]

The members of the Monument Association, meanwhile,

wasted no time. They hired excavators and stonemasons and set them to work building a small but handsome tomb on the north side of the Mather property. Complete with ornamental urns flanking the entrance, it was ready to receive the body by the day of Lincoln's funeral.[57]

Back in Washington, word of the change of plans roused Mary from her grief. Furious that her neighbors had failed to respect her rights as the widow, she asked Secretary of War Stanton to send a telegram to the Monument Association insisting that Lincoln's body be interred at Oak Ridge. On April 29 John Todd Stuart sent Stanton this terse reply, "I have your telegram. The Committee instruct me to say that the wishes of Mrs. Lincoln shall be complied with."[58]

In the gravesite controversy, Robert Lincoln sided with his mother. On May 1 he sent his own telegram to Governor Oglesby: "There seems to be a disposition at Springfield to disregard my mother's wishes in regard to the interment— Both the temporary and final interment must take place in the Oakridge [*sic*] Cemetery. . . . We expect and demand that our wishes should be consulted."[59]

Bowing to the will of Mary Lincoln, the Monument Association sent a new team of workmen out to Oak Ridge to prepare the cemetery's temporary receiving vault for the funeral. "This decision [has caused] a feeling of profound regret among a large majority of our citizens," Springfield's *Illinois Daily Journal* reported, "in view of preparations of another character which had just been completed."[60]

On May 4, the final procession carried the remains of Abraham Lincoln from the statehouse for the final leg of the journey. Lincoln's coffin was borne through the streets in a magnificent hearse on loan from the livery stable of a Mr. Arnot of

St. Louis.[61] Immediately behind the hearse walked the president's horse, Old Bob, led by Rev. Henry Brown, a black minister who had supplemented the meager salary he received from his congregation by working as a handyman for the Lincolns when they lived in Springfield. In a carriage behind Old Bob rode Robert Lincoln and his mother's cousin, Elizabeth Todd Grimsley; Abraham Lincoln's cousin John Hanks walked a bit farther back in the procession; these three—Robert, Cousin Elizabeth, and Cousin John—were the only members of the president's family present at his funeral. Abraham Lincoln's seventy-eight-year-old stepmother, Sarah Bush Johnston Lincoln, was too feeble to make the journey from her farm at Goosenest Prairie in southern Illinois. When another Lincoln cousin, Dennis Hanks, had brought her the news of the assassination, she had said, "I knowed they kill him. I ben awaitin fur it."[62]

Out at Oak Ridge, a crowd of spectators stood waiting. Early in the day they had staked their claim to choice spots on the hillside above the receiving vault, the best location from which to view the entire proceedings.[63] Already in position inside the vault, on a newly cut slab of white marble, lay the coffin of Willie Lincoln. As soon as the president's hearse drew up before the vault, the pallbearers slid his coffin into place beside his son's. Then came the closing prayers and the last hymns, with a lengthy final eulogy delivered by Philadelphia's Methodist bishop Matthew Simpson, who had also preached at the president's White House funeral service. Standing before Lincoln's coffin, the bishop delivered the last farewell. "Hushed is thy voice," he intoned, "but its echoes of liberty are ringing through the world, and the sons of bondage listen with joy."[64] Moments later, with a clang, the heavy metal doors of the vault were closed and locked, and the key given to Robert Lincoln. As he planned to return to Washington, Robert passed the key to his mother's cousin, John Todd Stuart, for safekeeping.[65] With nothing more to see, the thousands of mourners turned away from the little tomb and made their way back to their homes.

After three weeks of lying at the center of uproar, emotional outbursts, and frenzied planning, the body of Abraham Lincoln was finally at rest. But not quite. In the days since John Todd Stuart had fired off his curt telegram to Secretary Stanton acceding to Mary Lincoln's wishes regarding Oak Ridge, the gentlemen of the National Lincoln Monument Association had renewed their resolve to bury the president in the center of Springfield. On this point they had the Springfield press on their side. Only days after the funeral, any pretense regarding Oak Ridge was shattered when the *Illinois Daily Journal* praised the members of the Monument Association who had "wisely resolved to retain the 'Mather Block' as the site for the proposed Monument. . . . A more beautiful and appropriate site could not be found."[66]

At no stage did any member of the Monument Association advise Mary Lincoln that they had decided to override her objections and bury Abraham Lincoln in the center of town after all.[67]

But Mary learned about their plan anyway—from the same newspaper articles celebrating the good sense and good taste of the Monument Association. She had left the White House on May 23 and taken up residence in Hyde Park, a suburb on Chicago's South Side. She had barely unpacked when she issued her first warning. Her mouthpiece was one of her husband's old political supporters, Jesse W. Fell. Writing to Shelby Cullom, one of the Springfield men who had escorted Lincoln's body home to Springfield, Fell expressed his hope that the Monument Association would build a tomb for Lincoln at Oak Ridge. "Would it not better accord with Lincoln's tastes," he asked, "to be buried in a quiet, pleasant place, among his old friends, rather than by himself, in the heart of [a] crowded, dusty city." There was, of course, another consideration. Fell warned that if the Monument Association insisted on the Mather site, "Mrs. L and many others will make violent efforts to carry [Lincoln's] remains to Chicago."[68]

On June 5 Mary Lincoln issued an ultimatum to Governor Oglesby: "I feel that it is due to candor and fairness that I should notify your Monument Association, that unless I receive within this next ten days an official assurance that the Monument will be erected over the Tomb in Oak Ridge Cemetery, in accordance with my oft expressed wishes, I shall yield my consent, to the request of the National Monument Association in Washington & that of numerous friends in the Eastern States & have the sacred remains deposited in the vault, prepared for Washington, under the Dome of the National Capitol, at as early a period as practicable."[69]

Unnerved by Mary's threat, Oglesby announced his intention to travel up to Chicago to persuade Mary that the center of Springfield truly was the best location for her husband's tomb. In a calculated effort to win over the widow, he planned to bring along Ozias M. Hatch, one of the Lincoln's closest friends and a personal favorite of Mary's. But Mary Lincoln got wind of this scheme, too. When Ogelsby and Hatch stepped off the train in Chicago, Robert Lincoln met them with word that his mother would not let them inside the house. She had, however, written a letter, which Robert delivered by hand.[70]

On the subject of burial in Oak Ridge she wrote, "My determination is unalterable." She gave the Monument Association five days to comply with her terms in writing or she would make good on her threat to take Lincoln back to Washington.[71]

Mary Lincoln got her way. On June 15 Governor Oglesby issued a public statement that the Lincoln tomb would be built at Oak Ridge, "in accordance with the wishes of Mrs. Lincoln."[72] On June 19 the Monument Association passed a resolution to adopt "the proposition of Mrs. Lincoln . . . in relation to the erection of a Monument over the remains of her lamented husband." In a follow-up resolution, the association members voted to send Mary Lincoln a copy of their formal acquiescence to her demands.[73]

I

The World of the Counterfeiters

In 1647 the General Court of Rhode Island ordered the confiscation of all counterfeit wampum. The counterfeiters were Indians, members of the Algonquian nation, a large group of
tribes that dominated what is now the northeastern United
States. Their currency was wampum, strings of beads made
from white whelk shells and purple-black quahog shells. In the
Indian economy, the quahog shells were worth about twice as
much as the whelk. It was an unfamiliar form of money to Europeans; but since the gold and silver coins of the Old Country
were scarce in the New World, the English colonists of Rhode
Island and the Dutch colonists of New Netherlands agreed
among themselves to adopt wampum as legal tender. It wasn't
long before the Indians realized that here was an opportunity to take advantage of the newcomers. They hoarded the
valuable quahog shells for themselves, dyed the cheaper white
shells a dark purplish black, then passed them off as the real

thing to the undiscerning Europeans. (The record is sketchy, but it is probable that Europeans also manufactured counterfeit wampum.) It took some time, but eventually the white men discovered that they had been had. Soon thereafter, the colonists went off the "wampum standard" and returned to conducting their business with gold and silver coins.[1]

But hard money was still in short supply, so in 1652 the government of Massachusetts authorized the first mint in British North America. The Massachusetts mint issued a series of silver coins, some stamped simply "NE," for "New England," others engraved with images of oak, pine, or willow trees. Today, collectors covet these coins as the first examples of American-made money. But coins from Massachusetts bear another distinction—among them were the first coins counterfeited in America, beginning around 1674, when John du Plessis was found guilty of turning out pewter imitations.[2] Alas, the du Plessis case was not an isolated incident. Very quickly, counterfeiting became rife in the colonies.

In 1682 William Penn complained that he could not bring his "holy experiment" in Pennsylvania to fruition when half the coinage in his colony was phony. Counterfeit shillings were so common in Connecticut in 1721 that the colonial government despaired of ever getting them out of circulation. Delegates from the lower house of the Connecticut legislature suggested they accept the bogus coins as legitimate currency and assign them an actual value of two pence. In 1735 the governing council of South Carolina conceded that the colony's paper money was so debased by counterfeits that the colony had no choice but to recall all the fifteen-, ten-, four-, and three-pound notes. Making the matter worse was the English custom of transporting felons to America. In 1770 the convict ship

Trotman docked in Maryland. Among the exiles were a number of counterfeiters, who within days of coming ashore were back in business.[3]

Poverty and illiteracy allowed counterfeiting to flourish. Since few colonists had ever seen a gold coin, they would accept any shiny, circular, gold-colored piece of metal as the genuine article. In the case of paper currency, so few colonists could read that sloppily printed counterfeit currency bearing such absurd spelling errors as "Instice" for "Justice," or "Two Crowes" for "Two Crowns," passed undetected through the hands of the unlettered. Consequently, colonists who were barely scraping by suffered the most from bad money, while the literate and well-to-do spotted these crude jobs at once and refused to accept them.[4]

Initially, the courts treated counterfeiting as a misdemeanor. A New York silversmith caught producing false coins in 1703 was punished with a small fine. But as counterfeit money took a greater toll on America's economy, the judges' sentences became harsher. In 1720 a Philadelphia counterfeiter was hanged, and in Newport, Rhode Island, a counterfeiter had his ears sliced off as a prelude to being sold into indentured servitude. To show that it meant business, New Jersey's colonial government adopted a motto for its three-shilling note: "To Counterfeit is Death."[5]

In spite of the shoddy coins and paper money in circulation, some ambitious counterfeiters understood that they would realize greater profits by turning out a superior product. In the early part of the eighteenth century two of the most successful counterfeiters in America were women. In 1712 Freelove Lippencott, the wife of a Rhode Island sailor, traveled to England, where she had plates engraved, patterned on the paper money of Rhode Island, Massachusetts, and Connecticut. Back home she recruited a gang of men known as shovers to put her false currency into circulation.[6]

The most ingenious of the eighteenth-century American counterfeiters was Mary Butterworth, the wife of a prosperous house builder in Rehoboth, Massachusetts. She was thirty years old and the mother of seven children in 1716, when she started making paper currency in her kitchen. Butterworth's method was breathtakingly original. First, she placed a piece of damp muslin over the bill she planned to counterfeit, then ran over it with a hot iron—the one she used to press clothes. The heat, by causing some of the ink to adhere to the muslin, created a pattern. Next, Butterworth laid the pattern on a blank piece of paper and ran the iron over the muslin again, a process that transferred the ink to the paper. With a fine pen she filled in the rest of the details of the bill, then burned the muslin pattern, thereby eliminating the evidence. It was a brilliant method, one that worked so well that Mary Butterworth turned her counterfeiting into a cottage industry employing three of her brothers, Israel, Steven, and Nicholas Peck, as well as Nicholas's wife Hannah, to help her produce high-quality forgeries of Massachusetts, Rhode Island, and Connecticut currency. Mary Butterworth sold her product (she never used her bogus money herself) at half its face value to her shovers, among whom were a neighborhood innkeeper, some of the carpenters who worked for her husband, and the local deputy sheriff.

For seven years Mary churned out her bad money without attracting the attention of the law. Then, in 1723, she came under suspicion of counterfeiting. The authorities searched her house, but they found not a scrap of evidence against her. After all, there is nothing incriminating about a clothes iron and a fine pen. Nonetheless, the episode unnerved Mary; she gave up counterfeiting and lived quietly until her death in 1775 at eighty-nine years of age.[7]

The undisputed king of eighteenth-century American counterfeiters was a Morristown, New Jersey, engraver named Samuel Ford. In the 1760s and 1770s he produced imitations of New Jersey, New York, and Pennsylvania currency so good that even the provincial treasurers of those colonies could not tell the difference between a forgery by Ford and the real thing. Small wonder that he was never caught.[8]

With the outbreak of the American Revolution, the Continental Congress authorized a national paper currency—popularly known as continentals—backed by the credit of the United States. This was a problematic claim, for no European power had recognized that the American rebellion marked the birth of a legitimate new nation, let alone that the rebels possessed the type of credit international bankers would respect. There was also the matter of the American treasury—in essence, none existed. The thirteen states collected customs duties and taxes, and precious little of what they took in made its way to the congressional coffers in Philadelphia. Realizing that the new American currency had an unstable foundation, the British concluded that it would not take much to depreciate it. So around January 1776 a printing press was hauled out to the warship HMS *Phoenix* in New York harbor; the ship became a British-sanctioned counterfeiting workshop. The British counterfeits of continentals were excellent—so good, in fact, that in April 1777 the king's counterfeiters ran an ad in a New York newspaper offering to sell their false currency to loyal subjects of the Crown at a rock-bottom price—the cost of the paper it was printed on. The counterfeiters boasted about their bills: "[They] are so neatly and exactly executed that there is no Risque . . . it being almost impossible to discover, that they are not genuine."[9]

The British found an indigenous distribution network for their phony money among the Tories, Americans who remained loyal to King George. One such loyalist, Colonel Stephen Holland, operated a network of shovers that extended from his home in New Hampshire down to the colonies in the South. Two other distributors, David Farnsworth and John Blair, were arrested by supporters of the American cause in Danbury, Connecticut, with ten thousand dollars' worth of false continentals on their persons. They tried to excuse themselves, saying that they were petty criminals compared with other members of their gang, who had passed forty thousand or fifty thousand dollars in bad currency elsewhere.[10]

The British lost the war, but they won the campaign to undermine America's finances. By 1779, less than three years after it was first issued, the continental currency was so debased that Congress declined to print any more. Fortunately for the new United States, its finances were rescued by the timely arrival of loans from France and the creative accounting of Robert Morris, the financial wizard of the Revolution.[11]

After the continental currency debacle, the general trend after the Revolution was toward establishing a monetary system based on gold and silver coins, a movement that gained momentum in 1792 when Congress authorized the establishment of the U.S. Mint. This did not stop the counterfeiters, however: they simply acquired new equipment to manufacture coins. A story has come down to us of an English counterfeiter named Peach who set up shop in the basement of a house on

James Street on Manhattan's East Side, in what is now China-town. Peach manufactured "gold" Spanish doubloons, which had been esteemed good money in America since colonial times and were still in circulation in the 1820s. He was a man who took pride in his work; his false doubloons were of exactly the same weight and stamped with precisely the same design as authentic doubloons. Peach even took the trouble to "age" his coins. He churned his finished product in a barrel of sawdust, which rubbed the shine off the new coins and gave them a much-handled appearance. Next, he scattered the coins on a sheet of iron, then held the iron over a fire until the dou-bloons were slightly tarnished around the edges. This was a nice, authentic touch, because genuine doubloons really were tarnished, as a result of the coins' soaking in bilgewater in the hold of the Spanish treasure ships that distributed doubloons to Spain's colonies in the New World.[12]

Although the United States shied away from instituting a national paper currency, individual banks issued their own pa-per money known as banknotes. Unlike a national currency, the banknotes had no uniform design—bankers adopted what-ever style they found appealing. This absence of a single, uni-versally accepted banknote proved a bonanza for counterfeit-ers. By 1859, the eve of the Civil War, nearly four thousand different types of counterfeit bills were in circulation. Some were authentic banknotes whose denomination had been tam-pered with—a one-dollar bill became a ten; a five-dollar bill became a fifty. Others were outright counterfeits, ostensibly drawn against real or imaginary banks.[13]

Like all criminal professions, counterfeiting had its own vo-cabulary. *Coney* and *queer* were terms for counterfeit currency. The person who manufactured the false money was a *coney man* or a *koniacker*. *Boodle* meant bundles of counterfeit bills. A *boodle carrier* sold the counterfeit currency to distributors known as shovers. *To shove* meant to pass counterfeits in public as real money. As for real currency itself, that was *rhino*, *nails*, *putty*, or *spondulics*.[14]

In the years before the Civil War, counterfeiters began to congregate in carefully selected urban areas. Before 1820 counterfeiters had set up shop in any place that suited them; some were in small towns, others out in rural areas. Some even operated out of Canada. After 1820 almost all counterfeiters relocated to cities—especially cities that had a substantial printing industry and were major transportation hubs. Since there were more printing and engraving businesses in the lower Manhattan neighborhood bounded by Broadway, the Bowery, Houston, and Chatham Streets than anywhere else in the country, this area became the unofficial capital of American counterfeiting. St. Louis did not have many printing businesses, but it enjoyed two other assets that counterfeiters prized. First, its location on the Mississippi River and its proximity to the Ohio and Missouri Rivers made it a natural distribution center for channeling the queer into the Midwest and the Far West. Second, Missourians hated banks. Time and again voters had rejected proposals to charter a state bank. As a result, the only paper currency in Missouri was banknotes from out-of-state banks, a situation that made the citizens of St. Louis and the rest of the state especially easy marks for counterfeiters.[15]

Yet in the years before the Civil War, as counterfeiting spread across the United States, it met with only haphazard resistance from local law enforcement. Certainly arrests were made: nineteen counterfeiters were arrested in New York City in 1830; thirty-one were picked up in 1840. Arrests dropped, inexplicably, to thirteen in 1850, then skyrocketed to ninety in 1860. In spite of these statistics, neither New York nor any other American metropolis ever launched an all-out campaign to eliminate counterfeiting from its jurisdiction. City police forces of the pre–Civil War era were not designed to fight counterfeiters. City cops were not trained as detectives. They were patrolmen who walked an assigned area of the city, the rationale being that the presence of a uniformed officer on the streets would make the criminals of the neighborhood think twice. A different type of lawman was required to track down counterfeiters, someone who had informants among the criminal underclass, who perhaps could work effectively undercover, and whose duties permitted him to spend months closing in on a suspect. No such crime-fighting organization existed in the United States of the 1860s. It took the crisis of civil war to bring such an agency into existence.[16]

From the moment the first artillery shell was fired at Fort Sumter in Charleston harbor, the finances of the United States slid into a crisis. The Union's largest immediate expenditure was for recruiting a vast new army, equipping it, and keeping it well supplied. In April 1861 the U.S. government had sixteen thousand regular troops, most of whom were deployed out West against hostile Indians. By December 1861, the number had exploded to six hundred thousand men in the Union army. The cost of weapons, ammunition, uniforms, equipment, food, and salaries for such a force was staggering, but government income was not keeping up with it.[17]

During April, May, and June of 1861—the first three months of the Civil War—the federal government's revenue amounted to $5.8 million; its expenditures for the same period totaled $23.5 million.[18] And it only got worse. On October 2, 1861,

Salmon P. Chase of Ohio, the newly appointed secretary of the treasury, wrote to his friend Judge Simeon Nash, "The expenditures everywhere are frightful. . . . The average daily drafts on the Treasury for two weeks past have been a million and three-quarters at least." Faced with such enormous outlays of cash, the U.S. government went into "slow pay" mode, holding back payments to merchants, manufacturers, and other suppliers. Of course, this caused cash-flow headaches for the suppliers, who responded by raising their prices.[19]

Chase attacked the problem on several fronts. He issued more than $414 million in bonds and treasury notes. In early July he went to Capitol Hill, where he assured Congress that since the war was certain to be over in a year, the $80 million that would derive from customs duties, sale of public lands, and such taxes as Congress might approve, plus $240 million in loans, would be sufficient to cover the government's expenses.[20] A few weeks later, in August, Chase negotiated a loan from a consortium of New York, Philadelphia, and Boston banks— $150 million in gold to be delivered to the treasury in three installments between August and mid-November 1861.[21]

The New York, Philadelphia, and Boston bankers assumed that they would be following the standard practice of opening a line of credit against which the government could draw funds as the need arose. Chase, however, insisted on receiving the three $50 million installments in gold coin, a demand that strained the resources of the banks, drained their gold reserves, and made the bankers very uneasy. If the public lost confidence in the North's ability to win the war, it would start hoarding gold coin and stop buying treasury notes. In other words, the gold the banks had lent to the federal government would not return through the usual method of payments, deposits, and investments, and the shortfall would place in jeopardy the ability of the banks to meet their obligations.[22]

The bankers' fears proved well founded. The autumn months brought the defeat of General Ulysses S. Grant at Belmont; Great Britain appeared poised to enter the war on the side of the South; and in his annual report, Chase conceded that, given the financial burdens placed upon the government, the treasury could expect a deficit of approximately $260 million. The public panicked, responding to the rash of bad news exactly as the bankers had said it would—Northerners hoarded their gold coins as a hedge against political and economic disaster and stopped buying treasury notes.[23]

On December 28, 1861, representatives of the banks of New York met to discuss the looming financial crisis. Rather than deplete their gold reserves further, the New York bankers voted, twenty-five to fifteen, to suspend making payments to the treasury in gold coin. A few days later, the bankers in Philadelphia and Boston passed the same resolution. Once gold ceased flowing in from the banks, the treasury could no longer pay its bills with hard currency. With the gold supply drying up, the nation's powerbrokers in Washington began discussing what many perceived as their only option—the authorization of a national paper currency.[24]

Such an alteration in the administration of the nation's finances would require an act of Congress. The legislators on Capitol Hill, recognizing that the country was on the verge of a serious economic crisis, acted with surprising speed. On February 24, 1862, the Legal Tender Act authorized the treasury to issue $150 million in paper currency, to be recognized throughout the country as legal tender. The next day President Abraham Lincoln signed the bill into law.[25] It was a farsighted piece of legislation, but one element was missing—Congress failed to charge any law enforcement agency with safeguarding the integrity of the new national currency.[26] Any thought of counterfeiters appears to have been far from the minds of the congressmen. Like everyone else in Washington, they were anxious to see how the buying public would respond to paper money.

In April 1862 the *New York Times* announced that the paper currency had won "almost universal confidence" across the country. Three months later a jubilant and relieved Secretary Chase boasted, "Not a single requisition from any department upon the Treasury remained unanswered. Every audited and settled claim on the government and every quartermaster's check for supplies furnished which had reached the Treasury had been met."[27]

Like the rest of the American public, counterfeiters adjusted to the new national currency quickly. In fact, they preferred it to the old banknotes. A Philadelphia shopkeeper who would have studied a fifty-dollar banknote from the Planter's Bank of Tennessee would accept a U.S. fifty-dollar bill without a second thought. Even loyal sons and daughters of the Confederacy were eager to get hold of the new Yankee dollars, since their own government's paper currency was losing more of its value with each passing day. To meet the demand in Dixie, enterprising shovers carried bags of false currency down South, where no one was familiar enough with the new Yankee money to be able to distinguish between the real and the counterfeit.[28]

Nonetheless, it was in the North that counterfeit currency caused the most trouble. By 1864 approximately half the paper money in circulation in the North was counterfeit. And if the American public lost faith in the value of the new paper money, the federal government would not be able to finance the war. With the economy teetering on the brink of disaster, Secretary of the Treasury Chase asked Secretary of War Edwin Stanton for a favor—would he relieve William P. Wood of his duties as superintendent of the Old Capitol Prison, so that the Treasury Department could employ him in tracking down counterfeiters?[29]

Wood was an interesting choice. A tall, square-jawed man, he was a hero of the Mexican-American War, in which he had distinguished himself through acts of daring that some celebrated as swashbuckling and others derided as half-mad. Once back in the United States, however, Wood had earned a reputation as a shady character. In 1854 Edwin Stanton was a member of a prestigious Washington legal team involved in an important patent-infringement case; Wood, who as a young man had been trained as a model-maker, was brought in as a consultant. Thanks to his expertise, Stanton's firm won the case. But it was whispered around town that Wood had doctored the evidence in Stanton's favor.

Wood's appointment as superintendent of the Old Capitol Prison at the start of the Civil War gave Washington gossips even more material. Some claimed he was spying for the South. Persistent rumors had it that Wood had exceeded his authority by negotiating prisoner-of-war exchanges with the Confederate government. And there were stories of Wood's sending counterfeit currency to Union prisoners of war, so that they could buy food, clothes, and other necessities from their clueless Confederate guards.[30] That last rumor may have been true. What other reason could Chase have had to select Wood, a prison warden, as his point man for a new law enforcement agency, unless Wood already knew the world of counterfeiting intimately?

Technically, Chase and Stanton should have sought the approval of Congress, or endorsement from President Lincoln, before they created what was in essence a new government bureau. But counterfeiting had reached crisis proportions, and neither man had the patience at that moment to drag the new idea through the usual government channels. Instead, they just turned Wood loose. "I was permitted to use my own methods," Wood said later.[31]

Wood was not working alone. In 1864 he hired three men to assist him, all of them rough characters. He found his first recruit, Henry O. Wright, in a Chicago jail; the Chicago police suspected that Wright was involved in a counterfeiting ring. Virgil Barlow, another of Wood's early picks, had been making counterfeit money in New Jersey. Wood's third man, George Hyer, was under arrest for forgery and was suspected of murdering five men.[32] Given the backgrounds of these recruits, it came as no surprise to anyone that they played fast and loose with accepted law enforcement procedures. One typical case was a February 1865 raid on a den of counterfeiters. While searching the premises, operative John Eagan, an ex-cop from St. Louis, found $14,500 in false currency and $600 in legal tender. The counterfeit $14,500 he turned over to his superiors, but the $600 in good money he kept for himself.[33]

Wood's men ran a variety of scams. They offered suspects immunity, even protection, in return for a fee. Sometimes they kept a portion of the counterfeit currency they confiscated, sold it to shovers, and pocketed the proceeds. A counterfeiter who had earned—or bought—the goodwill of Wood and his

men could count on having at least one Secret Service operative show up in court to testify on the crook's behalf.[34]

Wood's unorthodox methods might have been scandalous
but they were also effective. "In eight months," Wood bragged,
"I rounded up counterfeiters in nearly every state east of the
Alleghenies."[35] And he was not exaggerating. Within a year of
his appointment, Wood and his band of unlikely agents of the
law had seized over two hundred counterfeiters and confiscated an enormous amount of counterfeit currency, as well as
engravers' tools, plates, and other essential materials.[36]

Chase and Stanton's ad hoc agency became an official part of
the United States government in July 1865. Hugh McCulloch,
the man who replaced Salmon P. Chase as secretary of the treasury in Lincoln's second term, claimed to have discussed the
counterfeiting problem with the president on April 14, 1865,
just hours before the Lincolns left the White House for Ford's
Theatre. McCulloch laid out the problems for the president—
the spate of fake money that was undermining the American
public's confidence in the national currency and the ineffec-
tual efforts of local and private law enforcement agencies to
fight counterfeiters. McCulloch recommended the creation of
a permanent, aggressive organization of government operatives trained to target counterfeiters. After hearing McCulloch
out, Lincoln said, "Work it out your own way, Hugh. I believe
you have the right idea." The assassination of the president and
the arrest, trial, and execution of the conspirators occupied official Washington for the next three months, so it was not until
July 5, 1865, that William P. Wood was sworn in as the first
chief of the United States Secret Service. Almost immediately,
Wood hired more men; by the end of 1865, he had thirty Secret Service operatives in the field.[37]

Wood and his men are often remembered today for their scams, but they were adept at persuading counterfeiters to turn on each other. On one occasion the operatives had captured a boodle carrier who went by the name of the Flying Dutchman. The Dutchman's territory included Indiana, Ohio, and parts of Pennsylvania. But he had a rival—Lewis "Mysterious Bob" Roberts—who made monthly road trips by mule through the Midwest, selling $50,000 in counterfeit currency each time to his distributors. As the Dutchman sat in jail, he resolved that if he was going to prison, he would take Mysterious Bob with him. Once Bob and the Dutchman were both in custody, however, the two rivals teamed up to cut a deal with the Secret Service: in exchange for a lesser charge, they agreed to reveal the identity of thirty fellow counterfeiters.[38]

Police and other law enforcement officers, not to mention the general public, regarded the methods employed by Wood and his crew as underhanded, even downright unethical. But there was no denying that by making up its own rules, the Secret Service had done serious damage to counterfeiting rings in the North. In 1869, when Wood was succeeded by Hiram C. Whitley, the new chief defended Wood's unorthodox methods. In an open letter to the American public Whitley wrote, "The system of using one counterfeiter against another has created greater distrust and caused more alarm among [counterfeiters], as a class, than the untiring labor of the most skilled detectives. It is impossible for them to guard against this kind of treachery." Adopting a mocking tone, Whitley wondered what the critics of the Secret Service would like his operatives to do. Should they treat counterfeiters as gentlemen, approaching them "in a differential [*sic*] manner, with hat in hand and with many apologies for the intrusion, announce themselves as detective officers and request the suspected criminal to furnish the evidence necessary to convict and send him to the State Prison"?[39]

Very quickly, Secret Service men became skilled undercover agents. Cincinnati in the late 1860s was a mecca for counterfeiters, and the hottest spot in town was the home of a shapely widow who went by the name of Mother Roberts. She had a reputation for selling counterfeit currency out of her house and taking her favorite clients to bed. An operative who passed himself off as a Missouri farmer and occasional shover insinuated himself into Mother Roberts's circle and eventually became one of her lovers. On a day when the widow and the "farmer" planned to combine business with pleasure, he showed up at Mother Roberts's house with some friends in tow. While the friends—all of them Secret Service operatives in disguise—made themselves comfortable, Mother Roberts invited the farmer up to her room, where she opened the front of her dress and began a seductive striptease. When she got to her bustle, she opened it, revealing an enormous stash of counterfeit money. Calling to his friends for help, the farmer seized Mother Roberts, while his fellow agents nabbed two other counterfeiters who happened to be in the house. Mother Roberts went to prison, and her counterfeiting ring was destroyed.[40]

Whitley may have defended the freewheeling methods of his predecessor, but when it came to recruiting new operatives, the new chief of the Secret Service was looking for a different caliber of person. Wood had had a penchant for jailbirds; Whitley preferred such solid, dependable men from the middle class as Thomas E. Lonergan. Intelligent and courageous, Lonergan had dropped out of Notre Dame, the little Catholic college he had been attending in South Bend, Indiana, to fight for the Union. Not long after he enlisted, Lonergan's superiors recognized his natural leadership abilities and sent him to West Point. Thomas Lonergan proved to be one of Whitley's finest recruits; in time he would serve as superintendent of a succession of the most important offices of the Secret Service, including Chicago and New York.[41]

One of the minor players among Midwest counterfeiters was James "Big Jim" Kennally. He had been born in Ireland in 1839; it is unknown when he emigrated to the United States. By the early 1860s he was in the counterfeiting business. His earliest arrest record dates to January 15, 1865, when he was picked up in St. Louis for dealing in and passing counterfeit currency.[42] In April 1870 he was arrested in Peoria, Illinois, for having in his possession $102 in counterfeit bills. The court found him guilty and sentenced him to eighteen months at the Illinois State Penitentiary in Joliet.[43]

In the nineteenth century the Joliet prison authorities kept the Convict Register, in which they recorded a host of personal details about each convict, including physical traits, religion, profession, and place of birth. From the Convict Register we learn that Kennally stood nearly five feet, eleven inches tall. He had a fair complexion, light-colored hair, and gray eyes. He stated that his parents were dead and that he had no wife or children. He also said he had no religion. The admitting officer recorded that Kennally could read and write and that he drank. Under the column heading "Habits of Life" is the notation "Intemp.," an abbreviation that tells us Kennally was not abstemious with alcohol. He gave his profession as "Railroader."[44] When the collector for the 1870 United States Census visited the Joliet penitentiary, he put Kennally down as a U.S. citizen.[45]

After serving his sentence in Joliet, Big Jim Kennally traveled to St. Louis, where he opened a livery stable that would become the front for his counterfeiting ring. By 1876 he was also a silent partner in a saloon and billiard hall called the Hub on Chicago's Near West Side.[46] Although Kennally was a small-timer among counterfeiters, he had one extremely valuable asset—Benjamin Boyd, one of the best engravers of counterfeit plates in the country, worked for him.

Benjamin Boyd had been born in Cincinnati, Ohio, in 1834. His father was a master engraver—the honest kind—and Boyd learned the rudiments of the art from him. Young Benjamin showed promise, so his father arranged for him to study for a year with James Edward Smith, one of Cincinnati's finest engravers. Although he was still a teenager, Boyd's skills were impressive—so much so that he attracted the attention of yet another Cincinnati engraver, Nat Kinsey, who offered to teach Boyd his particular area of expertise. Kinsey had been born in Delaware in 1828, and his legitimate profession was engraving landscapes. William P. Wood, the first chief of the Secret Service, commented on Kinsey's "gentlemanly appearance." His one physical flaw was that he had lost all his upper teeth; he compensated by wearing a set of dentures.[47] At what juncture Kinsey made the transition to counterfeiting is unknown, but he became one of the best. The high point of his career came in 1864, when he engraved the plate for a bogus hundred-dollar greenback that became a counterfeiting classic; it escaped detection for years.

Encouraged or at least inspired by Kinsey, Boyd cut his first counterfeit plate when he was only twenty-one years old.[48] By then he had reached his full height—five feet, nine and a half inches. He was a stout, round-shouldered young man with a dark complexion, dark gray eyes, and a head of hair that would turn prematurely gray. He did not drink, and he belonged to no church.[49]

At the same time that he apprenticed himself to Kinsey, Boyd met Pete McCartney, one of the best-connected counterfeiters in the Midwest. Nearly thirty years old at the time, McCartney was a strong, handsome man, just shy of six feet tall, with a charming personality. Even Secret Service operatives admired his "quiet, gentlemanly manners."[50] McCartney, an itinerant scholar of the counterfeiting arts, traveled from one skilled engraver to the next, with an eye toward becoming a master engraver himself. He stayed for a time with Kinsey and Boyd in Cincinnati, then moved on to Indianapolis to continue his education under a German immigrant named Aikman, whose two daughters, Martha and Almiranda, were themselves promising novice counterfeiters. During McCartney's visit old Aikman died; but the widow Aikman did not mourn long. In less than a year she married John B. Trout, a much-admired Missouri counterfeiter. As for McCartney, he married the Aikmans' older girl, Martha.[51]

By now McCartney was engraving his own counterfeit plates and using Aikman and Trout's connections to distribute his false currency throughout the Midwest. Then he met a Prussian immigrant named Frederick Biebusch, the biggest distributor of counterfeit currency in the West and Southwest, who was famous among counterfeiters for having been arrested fifty times but never convicted.[52] He had begun his criminal career as a horse (and mule) thief. Around the time he was achieving

fame in counterfeiting circles, Wood described him as "a notorious villain . . . open for the transaction of any species of ras-
cality whereby he can make money illegitimately."[53] Impressed
by the quality of McCartney's counterfeit banknotes, Biebusch
became one of his biggest clients, buying bundles of boodle,
which he sold out West to his shovers—most of whom were
women and children. With Biebusch as an ally, McCartney
moved into the big leagues of counterfeiting.[54]

Then came the break every American counterfeiter dreamed
of. The federal government's decision in 1862 to issue a national currency gave engravers like McCartney, Boyd, and
Kinsey, along with distributors like Biebusch and Kennally,
an unprecedented opportunity to strike it rich. Boyd and
McCartney decided to pool their talents and set up shop in
Mattoon, Illinois—and that is where Secret Service agents ar-
rested them in 1865. It was two-pronged operation. While
Boyd and McCartney were being cuffed and hauled off to jail
in Mattoon, another squad of operatives had staked out the
Everett House, the Springfield, Illinois, hotel where Boyd and
McCartney's boodle carriers, Edward Pierce and Almiranda
Aikman, were staying. When the Secret Service burst into
Aikman and Pierce's rooms, they found a basket stuffed with
thirty thousand dollars in counterfeit bills.[55]

Pierce went to trial and was sentenced to prison, but Boyd
managed to win his own release and that of Almiranda Aikman
by cutting a deal—in return for his and Almiranda's freedom,
he agreed to turn over an engraved plate for printing counterfeit fifty-dollar bills. The confiscation of the plate was a coup
for the Secret Service but no hardship for Boyd—it was one of
McCartney's plates that he gave up.

Boyd was smitten with Almiranda Aikman. In 1865 the petite, slender brunette was about twenty years old.[56] Soon after their release, Benjamin and Almiranda were married in Marine City, Michigan. For the next ten years the couple stayed on the move, setting up shop in Des Moines and Le Claire, Iowa; Decatur, Clinton, and Fulton, Illinois; and Prairie du Chien, Wisconsin. Boyd kept busy engraving plates and passing queer. His masterpiece from this period was a five-dollar bill so accurate that it fooled most experts. Boyd was not only a great engraver, he was also a successful businessman. Even John S. Dye, the celebrated counterfeit-detector, praised Boyd as "sagacious, wary and fortunate in his selection of partners."[57]

Since his brush with the Secret Service in 1865, Boyd had had no more trouble with the Feds. His brother-in-law, McCartney, was not so lucky, but Pete took it in stride. Experience had taught him how easy it was to break out of most local jails. In fact, he thought jailbreaks were fun. He claimed that escaping from the St. Louis jail was "as easy as falling off a log!" After dismissing the Springfield lockup as "a mighty poor structure," he went on to explain, "It wasn't a comfortable place and I didn't like my quarters. So I stepped out early one morning and left."[58] But jailbreaks were not McCartney's only means of escape from tight situations. Counterfeiting had made him a wealthy man, and experience had taught him that a bribe could make almost any Secret Service operative look the other way. Toward the end of his life he claimed, "I have paid away over $70,000 to escape the clutches of the law."[59]

As for Boyd, his luck ran out when he came to the attention of Elmer Washburn, onetime Chicago chief of police and, starting in 1874, the new chief of the Secret Service. Washburn had been born in 1834 in Plymouth County, Massachusetts. For a time he was division superintendent of the Illinois Central Railroad. After the Civil War he was warden of the Illinois State Penitentiary in Joliet. In an age when the term *public servant* was often a synonym for "crook," Washburn was a man of integrity. Once he sold some surplus state land attached to the prison, made a tidy profit on the deal, then faithfully deposited the entire amount in the prison treasury. When the reform candidate Joseph Medill took office as mayor of Chicago in 1872, he appointed honest Elmer Washburn chief of police. Unfortunately for Washburn, Mayor Medill was almost his sole admirer in Chicago.

Even before Washburn arrived in town, Chicago's police commissioners decided they didn't like him. They felt it was their right to name the chief of police. Not only had Mayor Medill usurped their authority, but he had not even bothered to ask for their opinion about Washburn. They found Washburn self-important, haughty, and bureaucratic. An eyewitness recorded that after Washburn moved into Chicago police headquarters, "there was no longer any interchange of opinion between the chief and his captains. He would listen to no suggestions, simply waving his subordinates off." When Washburn wanted to communicate with the department, he issued a memo. And because he enjoyed issuing written orders to his officers, Chicago police headquarters was adrift in a blizzard of paper. "Written orders were a weakness with him," the same witness recalled. "A question which might have been answered by a nod of the head, was replied to with ponderous verbosity and a bombardment of officialisms over the length and breadth of a sheet of legal cap."[60]

Having alienated his police force, Washburn went on to antagonize almost the entire city. Medill tried to put into effect an old law decreeing that Chicago's saloons and beer gardens must remain closed on Sunday. Other mayors had tried to enforce the statute, always with disastrous results—particularly in 1855, when Irish and German workingmen and -women had rioted in the streets until the taverns were reopened.[61] Washburn, inflexible as ever, tried to enforce Medill's Sunday closing proclamation. This time the citizens of Chicago expressed their outrage at the polls. In the 1873 election, Medill was tossed out of city hall, and Washburn lost his job as chief of police.[62]

Washburn's unemployment was short-lived, however. His exacting standards, his unshakable integrity, and his experience running a big-city police department were qualities that recommended him to Bluford Wilson, the attorney who had been charged with reorganizing the Secret Service. He offered Washburn the job of chief of the Secret Service, with the understanding that he would reform and revitalize the organization. For Wilson, improved relations between the Secret Service and local law enforcement would be the cornerstone of the revitalized agency. The first two chiefs of the Secret Service had been dismissive, even contemptuous, of the police and U.S. deputy marshals. Wilson believed that rather than provoke the local law enforcement officers, it would be more productive if Secret Service operatives solicited their help.[63]

Then Washburn had an inspiration—the Secret Service really ought to be secretive. In a general order dated October 31, 1874, Washburn instructed all operatives to keep their names and their crime-busting activities out of the newspapers and to let the police take the spotlight instead. It was a brilliant idea that generated immense goodwill among local police officers, who became the heroes of every case. As for the Secret Service operatives, by keeping their names and activities secret, they could be even more effective in the struggle against counterfeiters.[64]

Washburn differed from his predecessors in another respect. Wood and Whitley had been hands-on Secret Service chiefs, often going out on cases with their operatives and collaring criminals personally. Washburn, by contrast, remained at his desk at the agency's new headquarters in Washington, D.C. It was just as well—Washburn always had been better at formulating policy than at working with people one-on-one. In fact, during his administration, Washburn introduced valuable new methods and regulations that improved the performance and enhanced the reputation of the Secret Service. He spelled out clearly what he expected. Operatives would "be judged by the character they sustain, by the results they accomplish and by the manner in which they accomplish them." With this single sentence Washburn intended to sweep away both the corrupt methods that had been common practice under William Wood and the pragmatic philosophy of Hiram Whitley, in whose view the ends justified the means. Washburn's operatives would be honest enforcers of the law.

But Washburn did more than hold his men to a lofty ideal; he demanded documentation of everything they were doing. And for once, at least, Washburn's love affair with paperwork produced a result other than clutter. He required his operatives to file written reports of their day-to-day activities. If they went undercover and bought counterfeit currency, they must say who sold it to them, where the transaction took place, how much bad money they bought, and how much they paid for it. Operatives who had informants on their payroll had to report each informant's name and address, how much the informant was being paid, and all related expenses.[65] The Secret Service files from this period show that Washburn's new procedures were put into practice immediately. And one of the most methodical operatives was a new Secret Service agent, Patrick D. Tyrrell.

Tyrrell was the kind of recruit Washburn looked for—honest, respectable, incorruptible. Not only was he a good detective, but he had a high tolerance for filing reports and filling out forms. Tyrrell was a handsome, beefy, broad-shouldered man with a high forehead, a prominent nose, and a cleft chin. He had been born in 1831 in Dublin, Ireland.[66] He lived with his wife and children in Chicago, in a handsome house at 867 North Clark Street, right at the corner of Centre (now Armitage) Street. From their front porch the Tyrrells enjoyed a beautiful view of the new park and the vast blue expanse of Lake Michigan beyond. But the area around North Clark and Centre Streets had not always been so pleasant.[67]

Before the Great Chicago Fire of 1871 this had been a shabby neighborhood. By the lakeshore had stood a poorhouse, and nearby had been an unkempt graveyard. The Great Fire burned the area clean, and in the rebuilding of Chicago the neighborhood experienced a new incarnation. The scruffy old burial ground was transformed into the lovely lakefront Lincoln Park. Attractive cottages and frame houses were built on the ashes of the old shacks and hovels. And as for the area's new residents—the Tyrrells and their neighbors—they were ambitious, hardworking Irish and German families, proud of what they had accomplished so far and relieved to have left the slums behind them.[68]

Unlike so many Irish immigrants in Chicago, Patrick Tyrrell

had moved rapidly into the middle class. Now Washburn was giving him a career-making opportunity. If Tyrrell nabbed Boyd, he would be a hero, and so, by association, would Washburn. The chief's instructions were simple: Tyrrell had free rein to use whatever methods he believed would result in Benjamin Boyd's arrest and conviction.

2

Big Jim Kennally's Big Idea

Among Irish immigrants of a certain type, Patrick Tyrrell was a role model. He had an honest profession that enabled him to support his family in comfort. He lived in a part of the city that was clean, respectable, desirable. In other words, within a few years of coming to America from Ireland, Patrick Tyrrell had successfully entered the American middle class. He was not alone; plenty of Irish immigrants in Chicago, as well as in other cities and towns across the country, were assimilating nicely as productive members of American society. Yet in spite of such success stories, many native-born Americans still regarded the Irish newcomers with loathing. And they had their reasons.

The Irish created Chicago's first slum. By the 1830s they were crowding in around Archer Avenue and Halsted Street on the South Side, in a neighborhood originally known as Hardscrabble but since renamed Bridgeport. From the beginning it was a rough, unappealing part of town. Chicago's first slaughterhouses opened there in the 1840s; and in the decades that followed, brickyards, meatpacking houses, and steel mills moved in. Street gangs with such colorful names as the Dukies and Ragen's Colts plagued Hardscrabble/Bridgeport, and the neighborhood was home to such notorious felons as "Smiling Jack" O'Brien, the last man hanged in the Cook County jail, and Martin "Sonny Boy" Quirk, who beat several murder raps, only to be murdered himself.[1]

Unlike the Famine Irish of the 1840s, who would flee to America to escape starvation at home, the Irish immigrants who arrived in the United States in the 1820s and 1830s had come looking for opportunity. A lucky few managed to make a comfortable life for themselves and their families. The majority, however, scratched out a miserable existence performing the dirty, dangerous, backbreaking jobs the native-born Americans didn't want. The Irish dug the canals, laid the railroad tracks, and did the heavy lifting at construction sites and on the docks.[2]

Pick-and-shovel men, fresh from digging the Erie Canal, were among the first Irish inhabitants of Chicago. Having heard of the plan to build the Illinois and Michigan Canal, a project designed to link Lake Michigan with the Illinois and Mississippi Rivers, they moved west, hoping for work.[3] By 1837 the Irish population of Chicago was considerable. That year 117 Irish men and women, all parishioners of St. Mary of the Assumption Church (the parish known today in Chicago as Old St. Mary's), signed a petition to their bishop, Joseph Rosati, in St. Louis, asking him to revoke the decree that reassigned their beloved parish priest, Father John Mary Irenaeus St. Cyr, and sent in his place a German priest, Father Bernard Schaeffer. "We have in this town," the letter read, "two thousand and perhaps more Catholics. . . . The attention therefore of a clergy-man speaking the English language will be indispensably necessary." The parishioners of St. Mary's did not question Father Schaeffer's zeal, only his language skills. They had met the man and found that he had, as they put it to Bishop Rosati, "an imperfect knowledge of the English language." Rosati, although he did not return Father St. Cyr to his former parish, did withdraw his appointment of Father Schaeffer and sent instead a priest he felt certain would win the hearts of the Irish of St. Mary's—Father Timothy O'Meara.[4]

In the six years that followed the St. Mary's petition, Irish immigrants poured into Chicago. By 1843 Chicago's population stood at 7,580, 10 percent of which was Irish. By 1850, 20 percent of Chicago's population was Irish-born. The 1870 census recorded that 39,988 Chicagoans had been born in Ireland and that 237,479 were first- or second-generation Irish Americans. Numerically speaking, Chicago's Irish community ranked fourth in the United States, after those of New York, Philadelphia, and Brooklyn.[5]

For the most part, the Irish clung to one of three neighborhoods—Hardscrabble below the south branch of the Chicago River, Kilgubbin on the northeast fork of the Chicago River, and the area between Kinzie and Erie Streets on the West Side. Hardscrabble became the largest of nineteenth-century Chicago's Irish ghettos, but the city's worst Irish slum was Kilgubbin. It was settled in the 1840s by refugees from the Potato Famine, most of whom had been tenants on the Kilgubbin estate in County Cork.[6] It was a neighborhood of miserable shanties huddled along muddy alleys where chickens, geese, and urchins ran loose.[7] The number of geese kept by the residents earned the area another name—Goose Island. Kilgubbin was slummy, but at least jobs were to be had there—the Irish found work in the shipyards along the Chicago River or in nearby factories, such McCormick's Reaper Works.[8]

All trace of Kilgubbin's squalor disappeared years ago. The only tangible holdover from the old neighborhood is Holy Name Cathedral on the corner of State and Superior. The parish of Holy Name was founded for the poor immigrants in 1849. Today's stone cathedral stands on the exact site of the original wooden frame church where the Catholics of Kilgubbin heard Mass more than 150 years ago.[9]

The native-born Protestant citizens of Chicago were not uniformly hostile to the Irish. In the late 1830s, when work on the Illinois and Michigan Canal was suspended, the Irish workmen lost their jobs. Because they had no skills and no other work available to them, their situation became so desperate that compassion moved Mayor Benjamin Raymond to contribute his entire annual salary for 1839 toward the relief of the starving Irish of his city. During the famine of the 1840s, Protestant benevolent associations in Chicago joined with Catholic charities to send food and money to Ireland.[10] But the goodwill generated by the ecumenical famine-relief effort unraveled quickly. The 1840s were a decade of religious revival among the leading Protestant denominations of Chicago. Preachers urged their congregations to be more zealous in the practice of their religion, and especially to put the principles of the Gospel into action through renewed evangelism, reform of the public schools, promotion of the temperance and antislavery movements, and enactment of legislation that would compel virtually every business in the city to close on Sundays.[11]

Read today, the goals of the Chicago revival seem tame; but at the time, the Catholics of Chicago—both Irish and German—perceived every one of them as a threat. The immigrants would be the object of Protestant missionary activity. Their children would be forced in public school classrooms to recite Protestant prayers, sing Protestant hymns, and read from textbooks that derided the Catholic religion. Especially popular in public school libraries of the time was a children's book entitled *The Irish Heart* about a deluded young Irish Catholic named Phelim Maghee. One of the objects of the book was to reveal to youngsters how the malformed Catholic conscience operated. "When Phelim had laid up a good stock of sins," it read, "he now and then went over to Killarney of a Sabbath morning and got relaaf by confissing [*sic*] them out o' the way . . . and sealed up his soul with a wafer and returned quite invigorated for the perpetration of new offenses."[12]

The temperance movement and Sunday closing laws may not have been as insidious as was proselytizing to Catholic children in public schools, but the Irish and Germans still regarded those strictures as a slap in the face. The Irish liked their men-only saloons, which reminded them a bit of the village pubs back in Ireland, and the Germans enjoyed their lively beer gardens, where they brought their families after Sunday Mass.[13] Why, the immigrants asked, could American Protestants not leave them to keep the Sabbath in their own way?

As for black slaves, poor Irish immigrants did not own any; but that did not make the Irish abolitionists. In fact, Irish laborers feared that if slavery were abolished, they would be competing for work with millions of newly freed black men and women from the South. Sometimes Irish anxiety over losing jobs to free blacks erupted in ugly incidents, such as the eight-day riot that took place in New York City in 1834.[14]

By 1850 Chicago was a polarized city. On the one side stood

fervent native-born citizens, mostly Protestants, who had a new vision for their city. On the other, fighting them every inch of the way, were the Irish Catholic immigrants.[15] Many Protestants in Chicago and elsewhere around the United States began to regard Catholic immigrants as more than simply an irritating obstacle to reform; they surely posed a genuine threat to American society. In 1855 Protestant voters backed the anti-immigrant, anti-Catholic Know-Nothing political party, electing as mayor of Chicago Lèvi Boone, great-nephew of the legendary pioneer Daniel Boone. In true Know-Nothing style, Boone used his inaugural address to issue a thinly veiled denunciation of the city's Catholic immigrants. "When," he said, "I come to count the true friends of our country and those to whom our institutions may be safely committed, I am frank to confess, gentlemen and I know many, both of native and foreign birth, who think with me, I cannot be blind to the existence in our midst of a powerful politico-religious organization, all its members owning and its chief officers bound under an oath of allegiance to the temporal, as well at the spiritual supremacy of a foreign despot, boldly avowing the purpose of universal dominion over this land and asserting the monstrous doctrine, that this is an end to be gained, if not by other means, by coercion and at the cost of blood itself."[16]

Nor did anti-Irish, anti-Catholic rhetoric disappear with the collapse of the Know-Nothing party. "Scratch a convict or a pauper," an editor of the *Chicago Evening Post* wrote in 1868, "and the chances are that you tickle the skin of an Irish Catholic at the same time—an Irish Catholic made a criminal or a pauper by the priest and politicians who have deceived him and kept him in ignorance, in a word, a savage, as he was born."[17] The *Post*'s editor may have been a bigot, but he was not entirely mistaken about the Irish criminal element. In the 1840s, 1850s, and 1860s, the Irish were overrepresented in America's prisons, reform schools, poorhouses, and lunatic asylums. A large number of Irishmen could be found running Chicago's saloons and gambling dens, and a significant number of Irishwomen served in the city's brothels. During the 1870s the city's top crime boss was Michael Cassius McDonald—Mike to his friends. Mike owned a saloon, of course, but he also operated a grand four-story stone gambling parlor known as the Store, and he ran the Cook County Democrats. He was a man with political muscle and the money to back it up—in fiscal year 1872–73 alone, the Store brought in a hundred thousand dollars in profits. Mike could have expanded his disreputable empire to encompass other forms of vice, but his scruples would not permit him to have anything to do with pimps or prostitutes. As one of his friends put it, "a crook has to be decent to work with Mike."[18]

Under Mike's protection, Chicago became a swindlers' paradise. Adroit con men—many of them Irish—targeted some of the city's prominent visitors. In 1882 "Red Jimmy" Fitzgerald bamboozled seven thousand dollars out of Charles Francis Adams, the brainy descendant of two U.S. presidents. That same year Oscar Wilde fell victim to a con run by "Hungry Joe" Lewis. When Wilde left Chicago, his pockets were lighter by several thousand dollars.[19]

When Mike McDonald was just a saloonkeeper who ran a gambling parlor on the side, he bought himself immunity from prosecution by paying off Chicago's cops and public officials. Now, as the head of Chicago's Democratic Party, he hand-picked the candidates, took the necessary steps to ensure that his men were elected, and, once they were office, told them exactly what to do.[20] By the late 1870s Mike was in a position to select a candidate to run for mayor. A less cunning man would have tapped an Irish Catholic, but Mike chose a Chicago Protestant blue blood named Carter Harrison. Of course, behind his mask of Anglo-Saxon respectability, Harrison was entirely the creature of the Irish political machine. To the dismay of the people in favor of good government in Chicago, he did nothing to restrict the spread of brothels and gambling parlors in the city. Members of the temperance movement were outraged when Harrison refused to close saloons on Sundays—but his Irish, German, and Bohemian constituents were delighted. And Harrison further ingratiated himself with Chicago's Catholic voters by sending his son to be educated by the Jesuits at St. Ignatius College on Twelfth Street. Harrison's subservience to the machine, combined with his shameless courting of Chicago's immigrant and working-class voters, paid off handsomely; he was elected to five terms as mayor.[21]

Not all Chicago politicians had Harrison's finesse. The office of alderman, especially, seemed to attract men who were as corrupt as they were colorful. During the 1892 election, Edward "Foxy Ed" Cullerton managed to win nomination by both the Democrats and the Republicans. Confident of victory, he once advised an audience that it would be wiser to reelect "a man who has stolen enough already"—meaning himself—"than send in Fred Rohde [his opponent] who is a new man."[22]

Equally shameless were Foxy Ed's contemporaries Mike "Hinky Dink" Kenna and "Bathhouse John" Coughlin. They were aldermen for the city's First Ward, which encompassed the business district and the vice-ridden "Tenderloin." Both types of commerce offered Kenna and Coughlin tremendous opportunities for graft, and they exercised them all, becoming obscenely wealthy in the process.[23] Every year, to finance up-coming campaigns, Kenna and Coughlin threw a mammoth Christmas party. Every pimp, prostitute, pickpocket, and bur-glar in the first ward was required to buy a ticket. Owners of the district's brothels, saloons, and gambling parlors were ex-pected to buy blocks of tickets. At the party itself, the most prosperous madams paid extra for boxes where, surrounded by their most attractive girls, they treated cops and city officials to bucket after bucket of champagne.[24]

Nonetheless, the aldermen and other local politicians of the old-time, big-city political machines worked hard to win—and keep—the loyalty of their constituents. They found jobs for the unemployed, supplied coal to the poor, delivered turkeys at Christmas and hams at Easter, and paid the lion's share of the expenses for countless baptisms, weddings, and wakes. Acts of philanthropy are heartwarming—and there is no denying that for families barely scraping by, those deliveries of food and fuel were most welcome. But in picking up the tab for a wedding reception or keeping a poor family's furnace going, thanks to a generous delivery of coal, the aldermen were not advancing the cause of the welfare state; they were buying votes.[25] No doubt the folks on the receiving end of this generosity voted happily, even gratefully, for Hinky Dink and Bathhouse John. As for the ward bosses, they regarded all those Easter hams and baptismal presents merely as the price of getting elected.

Certainly the Irish were not the only immigrants who made their way to America in the nineteenth century. How, then (with a few exceptions), did they come to dominate city politics within a few short years? Unlike other European immigrant groups, the Irish had three major advantages working in their favor. Almost all of them already spoke English. Centuries of living under English rule had made them familiar with British common law and British political institutions—both of which had been adopted in the United States. And wherever the Irish gathered together in America, they formed parishes, a natural foundation on which any would-be candidate could build a power base and launch a political campaign.[26]

Of course, plenty of Chicago Irish, like Patrick Tyrrell, stayed out of trouble and worked hard to join the American middle class. They found the shenanigans of corrupt pols like Kenna and Coughlin, like the squalor of Kilgubbin and Hardscrabble, deeply humiliating. By the 1870s first-generation Irish Americans had made progress. They took up such skilled trades as carpentry or bricklaying. Some founded small construction companies or opened little shops. Many others, attracted by the job security and the promise of a pension, joined the civil service or the police or fire department.[27] In 1860, of the 107 cops on the Chicago city police force, 49 were Irish.[28] And of course it was the Irish who dominated the Catholic Church in Chicago. Although by the end of the Civil War there were more German Catholics in Chicago than Irish Catholics, the Irish clergy retained their hold on the city's cathedral, the chancery office, and most of the parishes well into the twentieth century.[29] As Irish Americans prospered, they began to move into predominantly Protestant middle-class neighborhoods, where they bought large homes and built handsome Catholic churches and schools. An even more conspicuous sign, in its own peculiar way, that the Irish had arrived was the white marble mausoleums bearing Irish surnames that sprouted in Calvary Cemetery.[30]

Chicago's respectable, law-abiding, upwardly mobile Irish found their voice in William Dillon, editor of the *New World*, the newspaper of the Catholic diocese. "The Irish would have occupied a far higher position in America than they do today," Dillon claimed, "if, instead of manifesting an extraordinary genius for manipulating primaries and running ward politics they had devoted their remarkable brightness of mind and cleverness to the task of earning an honest living, outside of politics."[31] This tension between the Irish criminal underclass and the striving Irish middle class played out between the counterfeiters and would-be grave robbers Big Jim Kennally and his two Chicago henchmen, Terence Mullen and John Hughes, on the one hand, and the Secret Service Detective Patrick D. Tyrrell, on the other.

While it is true that Kennally, Mullen, and Hughes were all immigrants from Ireland, they were not representative of the counterfeiting industry as a whole. More often than not, counterfeiters were native-born Americans. Between the years 1830 and 1860, 59 percent of the counterfeiters arrested in New York City were American-born, while only 22 percent were immigrants from Ireland. After 1860 the number of Irish counterfeiters declined; those Irish who stayed in the business tended to serve as shovers. Passing counterfeit money, though not as glamorous as manufacturing the queer, was profitable, sometimes extremely profitable—witness an anonymous New York lemon seller who socked away between twenty-six and thirty-six dollars a day.[32]

Big Jim's counterfeiting ring was a small operation, but with Benjamin Boyd as his engraver he had a good chance of entering the big leagues. Boyd's partner at the time was Nelson Driggs, another talented manufacturer of counterfeit currency. There is conflicting information about Driggs's origins. Some sources say he was born in New York in 1802, whereas others report that he was born in Scotland in 1800.[33] Driggs was on the tall side and solidly built, weighing in at 180 pounds. In an age when beards and mustaches were popular, Driggs kept his face clean-shaven. His distinguishing feature was a large, flat nose. In middle age he lost almost all his hair; but like many bald men then and since, he tried to mask his baldness by growing the hair on the side of his head long and combing it over the top.[34]

As a young man Driggs had worked on the boats that made their slow way through the Erie Canal. By the early 1840s he was running a general store in Freeport, Ohio, where the word around town was that anyone who shopped at Driggs's store should look closely at the change—the shopkeeper had a reputation for passing counterfeits to his customers. About 1850 Driggs turned over his store to relatives and moved to Chicago. There, in 1854, he was arrested for counterfeiting; the police found thirty thousand dollars in bogus banknotes in his rooms. A court sentenced him to ten years in the state penitentiary, but a year later, for reasons unknown, the governor of Illinois granted Driggs a pardon. Next he went to St. Louis, where he teamed up with a counterfeiter named John Roe. Together the partners ran off spurious banknotes attributed to thirty-nine different banks.[35] When the St. Louis police raided Roe's house in March 1861, they found $285,000 in bogus paper money on the premises, as well as twenty-one plates for producing counterfeit lucre, plus paper, ink, and everything else necessary to keep a counterfeiting operation running.[36] Driggs received another ten-year sentence, but this time he served seven years of it before a pardon released him. He tried to go straight, setting up as a merchant in Louisville, Kentucky; but counterfeiting must have been in Driggs's blood. The year 1871 found him working with Benjamin Boyd.[37]

The two men were not operating out of the same location, however. Boyd and his wife, under the aliases of Mr. and Mrs. B. F. Wilson, were living in a large wood-frame house on Prairie Street in Fulton, a little place near the Mississippi River in the northwest corner of Illinois. At the other end of the state, 140 miles south of Springfield, Driggs, his wife Gertrude, and their associates had set up shop in Centralia. Washburn and Tyrrell did not want either man to get away, so they planned dual raids in which Boyd and Driggs would be seized simultaneously. The Feds sprang their trap at nine in the morning on October 21, 1875.[38]

Tyrrell, the assistant chief of the Secret Service, James J. Brooks, and Operative John McDonald all approached the Boyds' house at the same time but from different directions. They were all inside the fence when suddenly a man drove up in a carriage and asked in a loud voice if B. F. Wilson lived there. It must have been a warning signal prearranged by Boyd and his accomplices in Fulton, because a moment later a man darted out the front door. Tyrrell recognized him as Nat Kinsey, the Cincinnati engraver who had introduced Boyd to counterfeiting years earlier. Tyrrell had no warrant for Kinsey's arrest, so he let him escape.

Now the detectives moved quickly. Posting Brooks and McDonald in the yard, Tyrrell went around to the back door and, without knocking, walked in. In the dining room he encountered Almiranda Boyd. They had never seen each other before, but Almiranda must have had a good idea what Tyrrell was doing there, because she seized the collar of his coat and tried to prevent him from going any farther into the house. Grabbing the woman's wrist, Tyrrell wrenched himself free, yelling to Brooks to come inside and take custody of the lady. While Brooks guarded Almiranda, Tyrrell headed up to the second floor. At the top of the stairs he ran into Boyd, in his shirt-sleeves, about to come down. Frightened and confused, Boyd blurted out, "Who are you?" The Secret Service agent answered, "United States Detective Tyrrell." In a quiet voice Boyd replied, "I have heard of you, Tyrrell." The counterfeiter did not resist as Tyrrell locked handcuffs around his wrists.

From a window Tyrrell called to McDonald, ordering him into the house. McDonald relieved Brooks, so that he could go upstairs and take charge of Boyd. Meanwhile Tyrrell began searching the house for evidence. In a second-floor bedroom he found a workbench with engraving tools and an unfinished plate to produce counterfeit twenty-dollar bills. In the front room on the second floor, concealed in the false bottom of a wooden crate, he found more tools and another partially completed plate for printing counterfeit currency.[39]

Downstairs, Almiranda was trying to strike a deal with McDonald; she promised him a thousand dollars if he would let her collect whatever she wanted from the house and hide it. McDonald refused the bribe and reported it to Tyrrell.[40] Apparently conceding defeat, Almiranda offered to show the detectives where she and her husband kept their money. In the first-floor bedroom she pointed out a large, nondescript box near a window.[41] When Tyrrell broke it open, he found over seventy-eight hundred dollars in genuine currency. While he was occupied with the cash, Almiranda tossed a small rug over a second box. Tyrrell saw what she was doing, broke open the box, and once again discovered a secret compartment, in which were concealed engraved front and back plates for printing counterfeit hundred-dollar bills.[42]

For six hours Tyrrell searched the Boyd house, turning up finished, partially engraved, and blank plates, as well as a trove of engraver's tools. As Tyrrell's pile of physical evidence grew, Boyd made an astonishing confession to Assistant Chief Brooks—he had engraved the plates for a fifty-dollar bill and printed and sold six thousand bills to dealers in counterfeit currency. With that one plate Benjamin Boyd had single-handedly slipped three hundred thousand dollars in bad money into the U.S. economy.[43]

While Tyrrell rummaged through every room of the Boyd house in Fulton, about 325 miles away Chief Washburn and his men had succeeded in arresting Nelson Driggs at his home in Centralia. Inside the house the Secret Service men had discovered fifteen plates for counterfeit currency and more than $117,000 in queer.[44]

It was late in the afternoon when Tyrrell, Brooks, and McDonald took their prisoners to the Fulton depot for the ride back to Chicago. On the train Tyrrell asked Boyd what he would like him to do with the more than seventy-eight hundred dollars in good money he had found in the house. Ten years earlier a Secret Service detective might have pocketed the loot, but Tyrrell was an operative of the new school. Thinking ahead, Boyd directed that it be deposited in Fidelity Bank, so that he could pay his defense attorneys.[45]

Hiring good lawyers was secondary in Boyd's mind; what he really wanted was some way to get himself and his wife off the hook. So he promised Tyrrell to reveal everything he knew about his counterfeiting operation and that of his associates— but only if he could disclose that information personally to

Elmer Washburn. When he passed the offer along to Washburn, Tyrrell declared, "Boyd will squeal."[46]

Washburn was not the kind of man to pass up such an offer. He directed Tyrrell to move the Boyds from the Cook County jail and keep them under guard in comfort at Burke's Hotel. On October 26, five days after the raid on their home, the Boyds sat down in their hotel room with Elmer Washburn and began to talk. Boyd admitted that while still a boy, he had cut his first counterfeit plate in his parents' house in Cincinnati. He traced his connections to Pete McCartney and Nelson Driggs. And he told a story about a former Secret Service operative, John Eagan, that could not have struck Washburn as welcome news. In 1872 Eagan approached Driggs and a couple other counterfeiters, suggesting that "if they got up a good plate," and paid him a percentage of the profits, "he would and could protect them from arrest." Driggs and his friends agreed and commissioned Boyd to cut a plate for a $50 bill, from which $265,000 in false money was printed. As his share, Boyd received $40,000 of the counterfeit currency. But the deal with Eagan didn't last. A year later, when Driggs was arrested in Cincinnati, Eagan failed to come to his rescue. Nervous that he might be picked up, too, Boyd burned his $40,000. But even without Eagan's help, Driggs managed to evade the law—"he squared himself" with the Cincinnati chief of police by handing over Boyd's $50 plate, a pocketful of good money, and two gold watches. Boyd concluded his confession by listing all the plates he had cut recently, all of which were now in Driggs's possession. In passing, Boyd mentioned that Driggs still owed him $4,500 for his engraving work, a detail that helps explain Boyd's willingness to squeal. Washburn must have been pleased; but if he made any promise to the Boyds, Tyrrell did not record it. Instead, Washburn instructed Tyrrell to have the Boyds arraigned.[47]

The next day a grand jury indicted Benjamin Boyd on the charge of counterfeiting and Almiranda Boyd on a charge of aiding and assisting a counterfeiter. Bail was set at $30,000 for Benjamin, $15,000 for Almiranda.[48] The bail was more than the couple could raise, so they were taken to jail.

Two weeks after the Boyds' indictment, a man named Samuel Felker called on Tyrrell. Felker was linked to the Whisky Ring, a nationwide racket of distillers and crooked revenue officers who conspired to dodge the tax the federal government imposed on distilled spirits. St. Louis was the headquarters for the ring, but it had branches in Milwaukee, Chicago, Peoria, Cincinnati, and New Orleans. It was a formidable operation. In St. Louis alone, the Whisky Ring in 1874 successfully defrauded the federal government of $1.2 million in tax revenue.[49] Felker posed a hypothetical question: If Boyd should make bail, did Tyrrell have any other charges against him? Tyrrell saw through Felker and assured him that if Boyd made bail, he, Tyrrell, would rearrest him on some other charge.

Why a man associated with the Whisky Ring would be interested in a counterfeiter remains a mystery. Perhaps Felker was looking to explore new business opportunities. Perhaps he had ties to counterfeiters. In any case, Felker left Tyrrell's office disappointed.[50] Not long after Felker's visit, Boyd took matters into his own hands, trying to escape the Cook County lockup by making copies of the jailer's keys.[51]

November 21 was a slow day at Tyrrell's office, so he called at the jail to see Boyd. During their conversation Boyd expressed his anxiety about his wife's going to prison, at the same time admitting to Tyrrell that he would like "to get his wife out if possible."[52] In the days and weeks that followed, Tyrrell exploited Boyd's fretfulness by suggesting that the court would be lenient if the Boyds agreed to testify against Driggs. The couple took the hint.

On December 23, Tyrrell was in Springfield; before leaving town, he visited Driggs in his cell at the Springfield jail. Driggs had been thinking about deals, too. He offered to plead guilty to one of the six charges in his indictment. If Driggs had imitated Benjamin Boyd and promised more, Tyrrell might have been inclined to bargain with him; but on the basis of such a skimpy offer, Tyrrell declined to exert himself.[53]

The Boyds' trial opened in Chicago on January 21, 1876. The preponderance of evidence against them was so overwhelming that the best their defense counsel could do was argue that Boyd had engraved the counterfeit plates only after being pressured by his old mentor, Nat Kinsey, the man seen fleeing the Boyds' house the morning of the raid. In the case of Almiranda Boyd, the defense attorneys made better headway, arguing that the detectives' invasion of her home had startled the lady, and that it was only natural for a loving wife to try to defend her husband. Taking her cue from her attorneys, Almiranda did her best to appear pathetic by weeping frequently during the trial.[54]

In recognition of the Boyds' willingness to testify against their former business partner, the judge decided to be lenient. He instructed the jury to acquit Almiranda Boyd because, as Tyrrell explained in his report to Washburn, she "only did her duty to her husband by covering up his guilt as much as possible, as his wife was expected to do." As for Benjamin Boyd, it took the jury only twenty minutes' deliberation to find him guilty.[55] But Boyd's cooperation with the Secret Service worked in his favor—the judge gave him a reduced sentence of ten years at the state penitentiary in Joliet.

On February 5 Tyrrell and Brooks escorted Benjamin and Almiranda Boyd down to Springfield to testify at the trial of Nelson and Gertrude Driggs and their gang of counterfeiters. Between the testimony of the Boyds and the evidence seized by the Secret Service in the October raid on the Driggs house in Centralia, the defense had no hope of getting its clients acquitted. After ten minutes of deliberation, the jury found Nelson Driggs guilty of five of the six counts of counterfeiting listed in the indictment.[56] It was enough. The judge sentenced Nelson Driggs to fifteen years in the penitentiary at Joliet and ordered him to pay a fine of five thousand dollars. Whether Driggs would ever come out of prison alive was an open question—the day he was sentenced, Driggs was seventy-two years old.[57]

The arrest and conviction of Boyd and Driggs was a tremendous coup for the Secret Service, and Washburn rewarded Tyrrell with a promotion. On January 13, 1876, Patrick D. Tyrrell submitted his first daily report to Washburn in his new capacity as chief operative of the Chicago District. Tyrrell tackled the job with his customary energy. Two weeks later he reported to Washburn that four counterfeiters he had been pursuing for some time had been arrested and brought before a grand jury. One of them was a pathetic underachiever named James Rivers, who was charged with "Manufacturing Counterfeit 5 cent Nickels and passing the same on the Street cars in Chicago."[58]

With the Boyd-Driggs operation out of commission, the Midwest coneymen who had been their customers fell on hard times. They could still get their hands on counterfeit currency, but they had to go through middlemen, and doing that reduced their own profits. Worse still, the stuff being produced by lesser engravers was not up to the old Boyd-and-Driggs standard, and the decline in quality was making it much riskier to pass the queer money. Big Jim Kennally was just one member of the extended Boyd-Driggs family of counterfeiters who was feeling the pinch; he could see only one way to restore his fortunes: he had to get Benjamin Boyd out of prison.

Nelson Driggs was admitted to the state penitentiary in Joliet on February 16, 1876; Benjamin Boyd arrived two days later.[59] Within days of their incarceration, Kennally devised a scheme that was as daring as it was devilish. He would steal the body of Abraham Lincoln from its tomb in Springfield, conceal it in some safe place, then cut a deal with the governor of Illinois to ransom it. As soon as Ben Boyd was released from jail, Kennally would return the body of the Great Emancipator.

It is interesting that Kennally wanted only Boyd. Perhaps he had done business only with him. He may not have known Driggs, or perhaps if he did, he didn't like him. No one can say; Kennally's reasons for trying to spring Boyd, while leaving Driggs in prison, have not come down to us.

The larger question is, what inspired Big Jim Kennally the counterfeiter to branch out into body-napping? Grave robbing was an old, old crime. Since the eighteenth century at least, it had been an ongoing scandal that medical colleges paid "resurrectionists" (as some grave robbers preferred to be called) to furnish them with the bodies of the newly dead for anatomical study. In 1788, rioters in New York City rampaged through New York Hospital and the homes of the city's physicians, searching for bodies the mob believed had been stolen from city cemeteries.[60]

An especially notorious case in 1828 concerned two Edinburgh men, William Burke and William Hare, who supplied fresh bodies to a surgeon named Robert Knox. Technically, Burke and Hare were not grave robbers; they were murderers who sold the corpses of their victims to Dr. Knox.[61] When the pair was caught, Hare was let off because he gave evidence against his partner. Burke, however, was hanged, and, in a classic example of letting the punishment fit the crime, his body was handed over to the surgeons of Edinburgh's medical college for dissection.[62]

America suffered from grave robberies, too. In the mid-1870s southern Ohio experienced a rash of body snatching, culminating in the theft of John Scott Harrison's body in May 1878 from its grave in Congress Green Cemetery in North Bend, Ohio. The grave robbers sold it to the Medical College of Ohio in Cincinnati. This case attracted widespread attention because John Harrison was the son of William Henry Harrison, ninth president of the United States and the father of Benjamin Harrison, twenty-third president of the United States. In the uproar that followed, the dean of the medical college, Dr. Roberts Bartholomew, published an open letter in the Cincinnati newspapers explaining that grave robbing was a necessary evil, for it was nearly impossible for medical schools to obtain bodies for anatomical study any other way. Dr. Bartholomew misjudged his audience; his letter further enraged the already angry citizens of Cincinnati. Emotions ran so high that three years passed before the Ohio state legislature was prepared to address the grave-robbing situation by passing a law that would permit medical schools to acquire unclaimed bodies from city morgues.[63]

The Harrisons and the Lincolns were not the only presidential families troubled by "ghouls." In 1830 John Augustine

Washington II, a nephew and heir of George Washington, fired one of the gardeners (the man's name is unknown) who tended the grounds at Mount Vernon. Angry and vengeful, the unemployed gardener returned to the estate at night, entered the Washington family tomb, and stole what he believed to be the skull of America's first president.[64] In fact, he didn't disturb the bones of George Washington at all—the skull he ran off with belonged to one of the Blackburns, the in-laws of yet another of the president's nephews, Judge Bushrod Washington.[65]

How could the disgruntled gardener have made such a mistake? Blame it on the deplorable condition of the Washington family tomb and the indolence of Washington's executors. Around the year 1745, Lawrence Washington, an elder half-brother of George, from whom he inherited Mount Vernon, built a tomb overlooking the Potomac River. The site may have been picturesque, but it was ill chosen nonetheless: whenever the Potomac flooded, river water poured into the mausoleum. George Washington stipulated in his will that his executors were to construct a new family tomb and transfer all the remains from the old vault to the new one. After the general's death in December 1799, his executors put off constructing the new tomb because there was some discussion that George and eventually Martha Washington would be buried beneath the U.S. Capitol in Washington, D.C.[66]

By 1830, the year of the break-in, the old tomb held the remains of about twenty members of the extended Washington family. None of the coffins were buried; either they were placed on sawhorses, or they were just stacked up, one on top of another. The dampness inside the tomb was so pronounced that the wooden coffins rotted away, and the bones of the dead spilled out onto the floor. Only George and Martha Washington were spared this indignity: their remains were intact, sealed inside lead coffins that lay side by side on a large wooden table. Given the deplorable conditions inside the tomb, it is hardly surprising that the ex-gardener grabbed the wrong skull.[67]

The desecration did accomplish one thing—it motivated the Washington heirs to build a secure new tomb. As for the grave robber, he was discovered in Alexandria the next day, and the stolen skull was returned to Mount Vernon.[68] But tomb desecration and grave robbery are not the same as holding a body for ransom. Where could Kennally have gotten such an idea? The answer may lie in a story John Carroll Power, custodian of the Lincoln tomb, told in his 1890 book on the attempt to steal Lincoln's body.

According to Power, in 1867 a Springfield attorney concocted a half-baked scheme to steal Lincoln's body from its tomb, spirit it away to the Deep South, or perhaps even out of the country, and hold it for ransom. Power does not explain why the man wanted to steal Lincoln's body, but he does say that the lawyer asked two young men from Springfield, one a telegraph operator, the other a mechanic, to help him; and no doubt the attorney sweetened the offer by promising them a share of the ransom money. The two honest tradesmen turned him down; apparently, the lawyer could not find anyone else to help him, and so the plot fizzled out. The would-be body snatcher died a few years later; by the time Power was writing his book, the telegraph operator and the mechanic had moved away from Springfield.[69]

What the reader misses in this intriguing little story is names. Who was the scheming lawyer? Who were the telegraph operator and the mechanic? Certainly Power, a man who to this day in Springfield enjoys a reputation as a meticulous researcher, knew the identity of these men. But Power also had notions about privacy that seem bizarre when viewed from the perspective of the "tell-all" culture of our age. Often in his book Power will quote an informant but not mention his source's name; or he will reprint the text of an entire document but not say who wrote it. Even when he identifies a source by initials, he is purposely misleading his readers, for, as Power himself admits, those initials "do not give any clue to the real names of the parties" who supplied the information. To a historian, Power's extreme scrupulosity and sense of discretion are maddening.[70]

Kennally may have heard talk of the oddball lawyer's scheme during a visit to Springfield, which since 1865 had been a familiar stop on Kennally's counterfeiting circuit, along with Peoria and Chicago. If so, the 1867 plot that went nowhere could very well have been the inspiration for Kennally's scheme.

Sometime in late February or early March 1876, Kennally traveled to Lincoln, a town in Logan County thirty miles north of Springfield. Lincoln was the home base for more than a dozen of Kennally's shovers, the men who put counterfeit currency into circulation in central Illinois. The leader of the Logan County gang was Thomas J. Sharp, a newspaperman who at that time was editor of *Sharp's Daily Statesman*, a Democratic paper in the heart of Republican country. In addition to Sharp, the gang included Robert Splain, a saloonkeeper; James L. Fox, a down-and-out farmer with a weakness for betting on the ponies; his son, James L. Fox, Jr., who tended bar for Splain; Benjamin F. Sheridan, who lived outside the nearby town of Chestnut; and Vine G. Williams, a loafer who filled the hours by hanging out in barrooms.[71] Like everyone else in Kennally's ring of counterfeiters, the Logan County boys wanted Boyd back in circulation, so they were predisposed to listen to any plan that might get him out of jail. By the time Kennally arrived in Lincoln, he had revised his plan slightly: to secure the safe return of the body of Abraham Lincoln, the governor of Illinois would have to pardon Benjamin Boyd and hand over a large cash ransom, in an amount to be determined later.

The Logan County boys said they would be willing to take on the job and immediately adopted a businesslike approach to planning the safest method for stealing the body. The first issue was distance. At thirty miles' remove from Springfield, the town of Lincoln was not a suitable site for the gang's base of operations. So in March 1876 Sharp, Splain, the two Foxes, and Sheridan all moved to Springfield. They rented a building on the north side of Jefferson Street, between Fourth and Fifth Streets, where they opened a saloon on the first floor and a dance hall on the second. Splain worked the bar, while the others played the parts of regulars. The Logan County boys had been to Springfield often. In fact, they were notorious among the city's prostitutes for paying for their evenings of pleasure with counterfeit currency.[72]

Meanwhile, singly and in pairs, the Logan County boys made the trip out to Oak Ridge Cemetery to inspect the Lincoln tomb. Power himself showed them around, answering all their questions—just as he did for every other tourist.[73] What they saw and heard delighted them. The late president's coffin was encased aboveground in a marble sarcophagus; they would not have to dig for him. Only a single padlock secured the door that opened directly from the back of the tomb into the burial chamber. And no guard or night watchman was posted at the tomb. By early June they had worked out the details of the heist. They would break into the tomb on the night of July 3, 1876, transport the coffin two miles north to a bridge that spanned the Sangamon River, and bury the coffin in a gravel bar there, until Boyd was free and the cash had been delivered.

Sharp especially was euphoric. With Boyd loose again, their cash-flow problems would be over; and the obscure Logan County gang would be famous and respected among fellow criminals. To celebrate, Sharp treated himself to a night in a Springfield brothel. He was fairly well liquored up when he revealed, confidentially, to Belle Bruce, a Springfield prostitute who had serviced Sharp and his friends before, that he was about to strike it rich.[74] He and his friends had a foolproof scheme to "steal old Lincoln's bones," and after they received the ransom, they hoped Belle and her friends would help them spend it. Belle may or may not have had a heart of gold, but she did have a conscience. She passed the story along to a friend of hers—Abner Wilkinson, Springfield's chief of police.[75]

The next morning Wilkinson chanced to meet Power on the street. Drawing the custodian of the tomb aside for a private word, Wilkinson told him that "in the discharge of his official duties" he had learned of a plot to steal Lincoln's body. Power hurried off to find the three members of the Monument Association's executive committee: John Todd Stuart, Mary Lincoln's cousin; Jacob Bunn, the banker who managed Mary's finances; and Colonel John Williams, an old friend and staunch ally of the Lincoln family. The committeemen heard Power out but dismissed his fears as unfounded. Power recalled that the notion that anyone might be plotting to steal Lincoln's body "seemed to them so incredible that no attention was given to it."[76]

While Power was trying to alert the gentlemen of the Monument Association, Sharp was trying to sober up. Through an alcoholic haze, he remembered his drunken confession to Belle Bruce the night before and realized that he had ruined any chance he and his gang might have had of stealing Lincoln's body. The secret was out; at any moment the police might start pounding on their door. So in the middle of the night, Sharp and his friends packed up the contents of their temporary saloon and dance hall, loaded it all into wagons, and rolled out of Springfield—without paying their rent.[77]

3

The Boss Body Snatchers of Chicago

After the debacle with Thomas Sharp and the Logan County gang, Big Jim Kennally traveled to Chicago on a quest for more reliable accomplices. He was a silent partner in a saloon and billiard hall known as the Hub, located at 294 West Madison Street, a few doors down from Aberdeen Street, on Chicago's near West Side, about a mile from the Loop. Kennally's partner, the man who handled the day-to-day operation of the Hub, was Terence Mullen. Like Kennally, he was an immigrant from Ireland. He may have emigrated to America as a child—Mullen spoke with only a trace of a brogue. He was a bow-legged little man with glossy black hair, a thick black moustache, and large bright eyes. The rumor around the Secret Service office in Chicago was that Mullen had moved there from the East Coast, where he had a criminal record. The Hub was known to the Secret Service as a hangout for counterfeiters, yet Mullen stayed out of trouble.[1] At twenty-eight, Mullen was still a single man. He did not own a house or rent an apartment in Chicago; he boarded at 30 Aberdeen Street, just around the corner from his saloon.

Before the Great Chicago Fire of 1871, West Madison Street had been a posh area where well-to-do Chicagoans lived in handsome, marble-fronted homes. Carter H. Harrison, five-term mayor of Chicago, who had grown up in the neighborhood, recalled the mini-estates of his boyhood in the 1860s, when only six houses stood on Ashland Avenue between Madison and Congress Streets. After the fire, Chicago's wealthy families moved elsewhere, working-class Chicagoans moved in, and the neighborhood took a turn toward the ordinary.[2] West Madison wasn't fancy, but it wasn't dangerous, either. The Hub shared the street with three confectioners, three dressmakers, three milliners, two competing clairvoyants who had set up shop directly across the street from each other, two billiard halls, a druggist, a photographer, a bookseller, a florist, a restaurant, a purveyor of corsets and undergarments, and Drew's Business College, W. A. Drew proprietor.[3]

The Irish were among the first to enter the saloon business in Chicago. In 1880 nearly 15 percent of Chicago's saloons were owned by Irishmen. Many of these establishments, like the Hub, were rough, dimly lit places that catered to working-men and perhaps served as a hangout for crooks and felons. As an Irish-run, working-class saloon with underworld connections, the Hub would have been almost painfully plain—no marble counters, no stained glass windows, no gleaming carved woodwork, no plush velvet drapery. The Hub probably had few if any tables, because in the Irish saloons of Chicago men were expected to drink their whiskey standing up or leaning against the bar.[4] Curiously enough, the Hub's one attempt at ornamentation was a bust of Abraham Lincoln.[5]

It is not surprising that Kennally, a convicted counterfeiter, would have received a license to open a saloon. In Chicago, saloon licenses could be had for the asking, and background checks on prospective saloonkeepers were virtually unknown. In fact, it took a veto from the mayor of Chicago to derail an application for a saloon license—a rare occurrence.[6]

It was canny of Mullen and Kennally to offer billiards at the Hub. Of all the legal "extras" a saloon might install to attract customers, the billiard table was the most popular and the most lucrative. It kept men in the barroom during the slow hours of the day, and the fees for using the table generated additional income for the saloonkeepers. There was a law on the books in Chicago that required saloonkeepers to purchase a license for their billiard tables but, like the Sunday closing law, it was not enforced. Every time a reform-minded mayor or city councilman raised the subject, the saloonkeepers' lobby swore there would be hell to pay at the polls if the city made bars procure a billiards license.[7] And if any group of merchants had the muscle to back up such a threat, it was the saloonkeepers. In 1876, Chicago boasted 2,501 saloons. There were more of them than of any other type of business in the city, with retail grocery stores coming in a distant second at 1,425.[8]

Mullen's crony at the Hub was Jack Hughes, one of the most active shovers in Chicago. He had worked out his own method for passing the queer. Almost every day he went out shopping, taking a teenage boy along with him. The kid carried a large wad of counterfeit cash, but Hughes had only a single bad bill in a pocket full of good money. While the kid waited a short distance away, Hughes entered a store to make a purchase using his counterfeit bill. If the clerk accepted it, Hughes would meet his boodle carrier outside and get a fresh counterfeit from him. Then it was on to the next shop. If the clerk suspected Hughes's money was no good, Hughes would curse and fume and then, with profuse apologies, reach back into his pocket and pay the man with good money.[9] It was a clever scheme, but Tyrrell and the other Secret Service operatives of Chicago were onto Hughes.

Hughes's criminal record dated back at least to January 1870, when he was arrested in Philadelphia for manufacturing and passing counterfeit nickels. During a search of his room, the Secret Service men found a hoard of finished and unfinished five-cent pieces. Over the next four years Hughes was convicted of counterfeiting three times in Philadelphia.[10] Clearly, the old town had gotten too hot for him. By 1875 he had moved to Chicago, where he rented a room at 72 North Sangamon Street, just four blocks from Mullen's saloon and billiard hall.

Sometime in the summer of 1876, Big Jim strolled into the Hub. With Mullen and Hughes in the bar that day was Herbert Nelson, the owner of a successful freight-hauling business in the city. Like Kennally and Mullen, Nelson's honest job served as a front for his less savory activities. He was a middleman who received the counterfeit currency from Kennally, then wholesaled it to dealers in and around Chicago.[11]

At a quiet end of the bar, or perhaps at a table in the back room, Big Jim laid out his scheme for getting Benjamin Boyd out of prison and jump-starting their counterfeiting business again. He wanted Mullen, Hughes, and Nelson to break into the Lincoln Monument in Springfield, remove the coffin from its sarcophagus, and then transport it in one of Nelson's freight wagons to the dunes on the Indiana side of Lake Michigan and bury it in the sand. Once the body was safely concealed, Kennally would tip off Boyd in the Joliet penitentiary. Boyd himself would contact the governor of Illinois and make the offer he could not refuse: as soon as the governor released Boyd from prison and handed over two hundred thousand dollars in cash, the body of Abraham Lincoln would be returned, intact and unharmed.[12]

Clearly, Kennally had been giving some thought to the details of the heist. Having Boyd approach the governor was an inspired touch—it kept Kennally, Mullen, Hughes, and Nelson out of the picture. It is possible that Kennally had already visited Boyd in prison and told him the details of the plot; it is also possible that Boyd never learned about the plot until Mullen and Hughes arrived at the Joliet prison. The surviving documents make no mention of the subject, so this detail must remain one of the mysteries of our story.

Kennally's revised plan to cart the body all the way to the Indiana Dunes was folly. In the dark of night, Mullen, Hughes, and Nelson would have had a decent chance of burying the coffin in a gravel bar along some quiet stretch of the Sangamon River outside Springfield. But the Indiana Dunes were almost 220 miles from Oak Ridge Cemetery, a journey that could take ten days, depending on the weather and the condition of the roads. And during all that time they would be hauling Abraham Lincoln's coffin through open country. Even if they escaped detection on the road, at night when they stopped at some roadside inn or small-town hotel, the men who stabled the horses were bound to notice the coffin in the back of the strangers' wagon.

Such considerations did not trouble Mullen, Hughes, or Nelson. Like the Logan County gang, they were focused on the idea of divvying up two hundred thousand dollars. They accepted the job. Whether Kennally had more confidence in Mullen, Hughes, and Nelson than he had had in Thomas Sharp and his band of counterfeiters is not known. It does appear that after the three men signed on, Kennally left them on their own—and that was a mistake.

Kennally had barely left the saloon when the scheme started to fall apart. Nelson lost his nerve and dropped out.[13] Mullen and Hughes felt they couldn't pull off the job alone; they needed another man. They picked a regular at the Hub named Lewis C. Swegles.

Swegles had made his first appearance at the Hub in the summer of 1876. To establish his credentials, he liked to brag about his underworld connections, particularly a burglar pal of his named Billy Brown. According to Swegles, he and Billy had pulled off a lot of jobs together. The regulars at the Hub listened to Swegles's stories but did not accept him immediately as one of their own. He was a stranger, and experience had taught them to be wary of strangers. Mullen was especially close-mouthed when Swegles was in the bar. Then, one day in a saloon near the Central Station, Mullen and Hughes ran into an acquaintance, a police detective who claimed that he knew everything about everybody in Chicago. After a few beers Mullen and Hughes asked the detective if he had ever heard of a man named Swegles. "Why," the detective replied, "he is one of the biggest horse-thieves in the country."[14] The detective was right; Swegles had been picked up several times for horse stealing, although the charge had never stuck.[15] The detective's disclosure reassured Mullen and Hughes, but they weren't ready to lower their guard completely.

Mullen and Hughes should have had more confidence in their instincts, because Swegles the horse thief was also Swegles the Secret Service informant. Sometime in the middle of 1876 a Chicago attorney, Charles Werden Deane, introduced Swegles to Patrick Tyrrell and recommended him as "a youth of excellent ability as a 'roper,'" the slang term for an informant.[16] Deane himself had impeccable credentials. During the Revolution his grandfather, Job Deane, had fought with General Gates at Saratoga and shivered with George Washington at Valley Forge. His father, Peter Deane, was for fifty years a deacon of the Baptist Church, a county judge, a state legislator, and a successful entrepreneur who opened one of the first woolen mills in Vermont.[17] As a captain of the Sixth Regiment Michigan Cavalry, young Charles became a Civil War hero. In May 1863, while encamped near Seneca Locks, Maryland, Deane, with 39 men, was attacked by 250 Confederates under the command of General John Singleton Mosby. Yet in thirty minutes the outnumbered Union men, led by Deane, had fought their way through the enemy force and come out of it with only four dead. During General Philip Sheridan's devastating sweep through the Shenandoah Valley, Deane's regiment was assigned to act as Sheridan's bodyguard. By the end of the war Deane had fought in twenty-nine major battles, including the Wilderness and Gettysburg, and risen to the rank of major.

After the war he took up law, opening a private practice in Chicago in 1869. His business interests extended beyond the court, however: Deane owned a farm in Vermont and had invested in the quarries along Lake Superior and in several mines in the Rocky Mountains and in Arizona.[18] How a man like Deane, whose contemporaries praised him for his honesty, loyalty, and devotion to duty, met a man like Lewis Swegles is a puzzle.[19] What we do know is that on Deane's recommendation Tyrrell took Swegles on as an informant and paid him the standard rate of five dollars a day.[20] Swegles's job was to collect incriminating information about the activities of Jack Hughes and the other counterfeiters at the Hub.[21]

In the middle of October, Mullen and Hughes approached Swegles with an offer. A wealthy man named King had just died in Kenosha, Wisconsin. They planned to steal the body, "plant" it in Illinois, then demand a large ransom from the family. Did Swegles want in on the job? Swegles recognized the offer as a test, but he wanted to buy himself some time. He said that before he committed himself, he would look up the penalty for grave robbing in Wisconsin—just in case they got caught. Swegles went to see Deane, who agreed that the proposed grave robbery was just a "feeler." He looked up the minimum sentence for grave robbing in Wisconsin—two years—and suggested that Swegles tell Mullen and Hughes that the job was too risky and the outcome too uncertain. So Swegles begged off the King body-napping. A few days later Mullen and Hughes took Swegles aside to tell him about a much bigger job. They were going to steal the body of Abraham Lincoln, and the ransom would be two hundred thousand dollars, plus the release of Benjamin Boyd from the penitentiary at Joliet.[22]

Swegles was stunned, but he concealed it by bragging that he was "the boss body-snatcher of Chicago"; then he launched into a series of stories about his adventures digging up corpses and selling them to medical schools all around the city.[23] It must have been quite a performance, because Mullen and Hughes never suspected that all the while Swegles was spinning yarns about his exploits in Chicago cemeteries, he was desperate to get out of the Hub. Finally he thought of a plausible excuse to leave. Once outside the saloon, Swegles turned east toward Monroe Street and Patrick Tyrrell's office.

But Tyrrell was out of town. So Swegles went to see Deane. The attorney could scarcely believe what the young man was telling him. Swegles thought Mullen and Hughes ought to be arrested right away, because if the plot were permitted to go forward, "it would be the most damnable thing."[24] Deane was of the same mind, but although the situation was urgent, they did have a little time. Mullen and Hughes had not yet set a date for the crime, and Tyrrell would be back in a day or two. Deane advised that they wait until they could discuss the case with Tyrrell.

By the evening of October 26, 1876, Tyrrell had returned to Chicago and was finishing up his daily report to Chief James J. Brooks in Washington when Swegles knocked on his door. Like Deane, Tyrrell was horrified by the story his informant had to tell. Deeming the case to be "of National importance," Tyrrell would not wait for the U.S. mail to carry the news to Brooks; he sent his chief a telegram outlining the essential points of the plot. Then he arranged to meet with Deane at his law office the next morning.[25] But the man Tyrrell really wanted to see was another Chicago lawyer, Leonard Swett.

Abraham Lincoln's two closest friends and political advisers had been David Davis and Leonard Swett. As young attorneys riding Illinois's Eighth Circuit together, the three men had come to like and trust each other. Lincoln, the future president, and Davis, the future Supreme Court justice, longed for success; Swett, on the other hand, was not so enterprising. Unlike his unabashedly ambitious friends, Swett held back. He was a man who, as one biographer has put it, only "flirted with greatness."[26]

Leonard Swett had been born in 1825 in the little village of Turner, Maine. Since his elder brother was destined to inherit the family farm, the parents decided to compensate young Leonard by sending him to college. He studied for three years at what is now Colby College, pursued an interest in the law at a firm in Portland, and then, for some inexplicable reason, took a job as a traveling bookseller. He was a wretched salesman, but he escaped his failing business by enlisting in the army and going off to fight in Mexico. He marched into Mexico City with General Winfield Scott. Soon after, however, he was struck down, like so many of Scott's troops, by malaria. Along with dozens of other ailing soldiers, he was loaded aboard a ship bound for New Orleans; a third of the sick men died along the way. In New Orleans Swett recovered his strength; in St. Louis he was mustered out of the army. He was in Illinois, on his way home to Maine, when he suffered a second bout of malaria that almost killed him—this man more than six feet tall wasted away to only 126 pounds.[27]

After Swett recovered his health, he picked up where he had left off in his law studies. He was admitted to the Illinois bar and made the acquaintance of David Davis, the newly appointed judge of the Illinois Eighth Judicial Circuit. It was Judge Davis who introduced Swett to an ex-congressman and fellow attorney named Abraham Lincoln. In the years that followed, these three men became nearly inseparable on the circuit, even though they sometimes found themselves on opposite sides in the courtroom. A celebrated murder trial in 1857 pitted Swett, counsel for the defense, against Lincoln, who was serving as the prosecutor. In a bold move, Swett adopted the insanity defense, a new tactic at the time, but one that Swett argued convincingly, thanks to an interview he had conducted with the superintendent of a Boston asylum. Swett won the case.[28]

As Lincoln's interests evolved from practicing law to practicing politics, he turned to Swett and Davis for help and discovered that his friends were born political operators. In 1860, when Lincoln was actively seeking the Republican presidential nomination, Swett and Davis exerted themselves to deliver Illinois, Indiana, Pennsylvania, and Maine (Swett's home state) for Lincoln.[29] The convention met in Chicago in an immense barn of a building known as the Wigwam. It could accommodate twelve thousand delegates, conventioneers, and spectators; and when the Wigwam was full, the noise was awful. Swett recalled that the racket was so loud that "a thousand steam whistles, ten acres of hotel gongs, [and] a tribe of Comanches headed by a choice vanguard from pandemonium, might have mingled in the scene unnoticed."[30]

As president, Lincoln showed his gratitude by naming Davis a justice of the U.S. Supreme Court. He tried to appoint Swett to at least three different jobs, including one as commissioner of Peruvian claims, but Swett declined them all. Perhaps he felt unappreciated: certainly the title "commissioner of Peruvian claims" is not comparable to "justice of the Supreme Court." Whatever his reasons, after Swett's third refusal Lincoln made no more offers; in the end, Swett never did receive an impressive post in the Lincoln administration, but he never complained about it either. He remained part of Lincoln's trusted inner circle of advisers, and that may have been enough for him. Lincoln sent him to remove the maverick General John C. Fremont as commander of the Union troops in the West; he invited Swett to accompany him to Gettysburg for the dedication of the cemetery; and when Lincoln was debating with himself over the emancipation of the slaves, he spent an entire morning closeted alone with Swett, thrashing out the arguments pro and con.[31]

In later years Abraham Lincoln's friends became his son's friends. In May 1875, when Robert Lincoln swore out a warrant to have his mother taken into custody for lunacy, he asked Swett to serve it, escort Mary to the hulking Cook County courthouse, and act as the attorney for the prosecution in the trial. It was an unpleasant task, but Swett accepted it. He even dragooned fellow attorney and Lincoln friend Isaac N. Arnold to act as Mary's defense counsel. When Arnold balked, Swett lost his temper. "You will put into her head that she can get some mischievous lawyer to make us trouble and defend her," Swett said. "Do your duty." Conscience-stricken but compliant, Arnold, acting exactly as Robert Lincoln and Swett wished, put up virtually no defense at all. The jury found Mary mentally ill; the judge sentenced her to confinement in the Bellevue Place sanatorium in Batavia, Illinois.[32]

Tyrrell's plan was to hear Swegles out at Deane's office, then discuss the matter with Leonard Swett. The morning of October 27 Swegles told Tyrrell and Deane everything he knew about the plot, but one piece of information was missing—the name of the mastermind. From his conversation with Mullen and Hughes, Swegles knew that it was someone from St. Louis, but he knew no more than that. Even at this early stage, Big Jim Kennally had managed to keep his name out of the affair.

From Deane's office Tyrrell called on Leonard Swett. He was occupied defending a client on a charge of murder, but he broke away from court long enough to hear about the plot to steal his old friend's body. Later in the day Tyrrell sat down with Robert Lincoln for a long conversation about the case. Then, while Robert and Swett sent a joint telegram to John Todd Stuart warning him that the tomb was in danger of desecration, Tyrrell wrote to the chief of the Secret Service, James Brooks, asking for further instructions.

"*Chief,* I do not know your views of what my actions should be in a matter," he wrote, "not exactly a counterfeiting case, yet they are well represented in this matter. But *Sir,* I consider it of *National importance,* should such an attempt be made and there should be a National Hanging Bee for those who make the attempt. I shall await your instructions and be governed thereby."[33]

While Tyrrell waited for instructions, Mullen and Hughes tinkered with some of the details of the scheme. In the belief that Kennally ought to be their negotiator, they questioned the wisdom of letting Benjamin Boyd cut a deal with the governor. Another option was to approach the members of the National Lincoln Monument Association to see what they would be willing to pay to get Lincoln's body back. And perhaps the best plan would be to go directly to the federal government, which certainly had the means to pay more than two hundred thousand dollars for the return of Lincoln's remains.

In Mullen and Hughes's revised plan, while Kennally was cutting a deal, Mullen would remain in Chicago with an attorney available to "see he was treated squarely" and not pressured by the police or the Secret Service to disclose the place where they had concealed the body. As for Swegles and Hughes, they would decamp to Canada and lie low for a time.[34] Booze and a brothel had undone the Logan County gang; now stupid, needless complications were undermining Mullen and Hughes's chances of successfully pulling off the job. Then there was the matter of expenses—train fare to Springfield, room and board at a Springfield hotel, plus any incidental, out-of-pocket costs. Since the gang was taking all the risks and going to all this trouble primarily to spring Benjamin Boyd from the Joliet penitentiary, they concluded that they ought to be bankrolled by Almiranda Boyd. They paid a call on the lady to tell her of their plan and their desire that she should foot the bill for all expenses.[35]

Tyrrell and Swegles were on edge, waiting for Mullen and Hughes to set a date for the break-in. Hughes wanted to act fast; he reminded Mullen and Swegles that winter would arrive soon and while he had no objection to digging in an Indiana sand dune to conceal Lincoln's body, "he did not like to dig snow." Grave robbing did not trouble the man, but he drew the line at shoveling snow.[36]

On Sunday night, November 5, Mullen and Hughes met in Swegles's rooms at 140 South Halsted Street to name the day of the grave robbery.[37] Mullen insisted that election night, November 7, was "a damned elegant time to do it." There would certainly be very few visitors to the cemetery during the day—the election would keep everyone in town; the streets of Springfield would be full of people, and a wagon going along the road at night would not be noticed, since those who saw it would think that it was carrying farmers home from the polls.[38]

At eight o'clock on Monday morning, November 6, Swegles and Tyrrell met again in Deane's office; this time the informant had solid information. He, Mullen, and Hughes would travel down to Springfield that night on the nine o'clock Chicago and Alton train. Four days earlier Chief Brooks had authorized

Tyrrell to take charge of the grave-robbing case; now that he had specific information, Tyrrell acted quickly. Elmer Washburn was in town, staying at the Palmer House. From Deane's office Tyrrell hurried to the hotel, where he told his former chief about the plot and asked for his help. Washburn agreed and suggested that they recruit John McDonald too. McDonald had been one of the Secret Service operatives who had helped Tyrrell nab the Boyds in Fulton; currently he was stationed at the Secret Service office in Joliet. Washburn sent him a telegram ordering him to be ready to travel to Springfield the next day; they would meet aboard the train to Springfield. But Tyrrell and Washburn needed still more assistance. They called on Allan Pinkerton and arranged to borrow two of his private detectives—John McGinn and George Hay. Tyrrell accomplished all this before three in the afternoon, when he had his last formal appointment of the day, with Robert Lincoln.[39]

Deane joined Tyrrell and Washburn at Lincoln's law office at the corner of Washington and Dearborn Streets. Tyrrell did all the talking, laying out what he had learned from Swegles about the plot and naming the Secret Service operatives and private detectives who would seize Mullen and Hughes in the act. It is unfortunate that no one thought to make a transcript of the proceedings; the closest thing to an account of the meeting is Tyrrell's daily report to Brooks. Tyrrell was clearly worked up by the scheme, marveling that there could be a "human being so foul as to conceive such a horrible and Damnable an act." Robert Lincoln, on the other hand, appears to have remained exquisitely detached, expressing nothing more than an assurance that Tyrrell could count on him for any assistance he required. Incredibly, he did not insist that Tyrrell arrest

Mullen and Hughes right then, on a charge of conspiracy to commit a crime, before they had a chance to vandalize the tomb where his father and his three brothers lay buried.[40] How could a man be indifferent while the desecration of his family tomb was under discussion? But the personality of Abraham Lincoln's sole surviving son has always puzzled historians. Lincoln biographer Carl Sandburg summed up Robert as "distinguished, troubled, peculiar." Even the charitable Ruth Painter Randall, biographer of the four Lincoln children, conceded that it was impossible to unravel "the enigma of Robert Lincoln."[41] Perhaps it is not so strange that Robert was emotionally aloof as he discussed the planned theft of his father's body. After all, just a year earlier, he had rigged his mother's insanity trial.[42]

At eight that night Tyrrell, McGinn, and Hay arrived at Chicago's Central Station. There they ran into Robert Lincoln; he had just sent a telegram to his cousin, John Todd Stuart, president of the Monument Association, instructing him to call on Tyrrell at the St. Nicholas Hotel in Springfield very early the next morning. At 8:27, Swegles sidled up to Tyrrell. Everything was set. Mullen and Hughes were collecting money for the journey; the plan was to board the first car of the train at the last possible moment.

On the platform Tyrrell, McGinn, and Hay positioned themselves beside the last car of the Springfield train and watched for the gang. At nine o'clock the conspirators still had not arrived. Then, just as the train began moving out of the station, Mullen, Hughes, Swegles, and a fourth man appeared and jumped into the front passenger car. Relieved, the detectives leaped into the last sleeping car and settled in for the overnight journey to Springfield.[43]

4

"The Devils Are Up Here"

When the train pulled into the Springfield station at six the next morning, Tyrrell and the Pinkertons headed for the St. Nicholas Hotel, which occupied the house numbers 400 through 412 on East Jefferson Street in the heart of the city. (The structure is still there, although the hotel has been converted to an apartment building.) Mullen, Hughes, Swegles, and the mysterious fourth man took rooms at the St. Charles House hotel, also located on East Jefferson Street.[1] The detectives and the grave robbers were staying only two blocks away from each other. That their paths never crossed is close to miraculous.

Just about all the main players were traveling under aliases—Tyrrell as C. A. Demerost, Mullen as T. Durnan, Hughes as James Smith.[2] The fourth man Swegles had introduced to Mullen and Hughes as Billy Brown, his burglar pal. Brown would take over Herbert Nelson's job, getting a wagon and a team of horses to transport the body up to the Indiana Dunes. But the man Swegles called Billy Brown was not a burglar; he was another informant, named William Nealy. "He is straight," Swegles said in an interview with the *Chicago Tribune*, "[but] he can talk crooked; he had driven a hack and learned all the slang."[3]

While McGinn and Hay went up to their rooms to get some rest, Tyrrell waited in the lobby for John Todd Stuart. It was a long wait—Stuart did not get to the St. Nicholas until nine. But if Stuart was late, at least he was well organized. He escorted Tyrrell out to Oak Ridge Cemetery to look over the Lincoln Monument and the terrain and to introduce him to John Carroll Power, the monument's custodian.[4] Power had been born in rural Fleming County, Kentucky, in 1819, into a struggling farm family. It was his intention to follow his family's tradition of working the land, and he dreamed of finding fertile acres that would make his fortune. He bought land in Kansas and took up the life of a sodbuster. It was backbreaking work, and in the end, his only reward was three years of poor crops. Discouraged and disgusted, Power gave up farming. He had always been bookish, and he had always been an ardent Lincoln supporter; so he moved to Illinois, choosing Springfield as his new home. In Lincoln's hometown he began writing a biography of his hero. The resulting book, one reader recalled, had "the spice and charm of a novel." Power's biography of Lincoln has been forgotten, but his next book, *The Early Settlers of Sangamon County*, is still regarded by historians as a meticulously researched guide to the region's founding families. Power's books made his reputation in Springfield. Soon after the dedication of the Lincoln Monument in 1874, the Monument Association hired him as custodian of tomb.[5] The pay was fifty dollars a month.

The members of the Monument Association could not have selected a more dedicated man for the job. Power never tired of showing visitors around the tomb. He collected Lincoln relics, which he displayed in Memorial Hall, the entrance chamber to the monument. It was Powers's unshakable conviction that the Lincoln Monument should be accessible to everyone free of charge, so when the Monument Association decided to charge twenty-five cents for admission and hired a man to collect the fee at the cemetery gate, Power was genuinely distressed. He wrote a formal complaint to the Monument Association, filling page after page of legal-size paper with reasons and arguments backing up his basic assertion that nothing should obstruct the public's access to Lincoln's tomb. He argued that it offended distinguished visitors when they were asked to surrender a quarter before being admitted to the Lincoln gravesite and that families of limited means were barred from paying their respects to the Great Emancipator because they could not afford the price of admission. Besides, Power complained, the man selling tickets at the cemetery gate was ill-mannered. To prove his point, Power included a deposition from a cab driver who had overheard the gatekeeper speak rudely to a gentleman who had come to see the tomb.[6]

The biggest problem at the Lincoln Monument was not accessibility, but security. No sexton lived by the cemetery. No night watchman guarded the monument. And the only thing standing between a grave robber and the Lincoln tomb was a single padlock. Tyrrell took it all in during his morning visit to the monument. At the end of the tour, Tyrrell asked Power to join him and the other detectives at the tomb that night, for they "might need [Power's] counsel and advice" in arranging the stakeout. Without hesitation, Power agreed.

That afternoon Power had two more visitors. Swegles and Hughes, acting like ordinary tourists, called at the tomb. As Power guided them through the monument, Hughes asked a lot of questions. It could not have been easy for the custodian to pretend to be at ease as he explained the layout of the tomb to a man he knew planned to break into it within a few hours, yet Power carried it off. As they left the cemetery, Hughes was very pleased with himself for learning so many useful details that would help him plan the night's work. He never suspected that Power was onto him. Nor did he notice that all the way to the cemetery he and Swegles had been tailed by the Pinkertons, McGinn and Hay.[7]

Back at the St. Charles House, Swegles and Hughes met Mullen, who was also mighty pleased with himself. He had dropped by the Germania House near the depot for a few beers.[8] On his way out of the tavern, he noticed a good ax leaning against the woodpile, so he stole it. He was sure it would come in handy that night.[9]

It had been gray and overcast all day; not once did the sun break through the thick pall of clouds.[10] But the weather had no effect on the crowds that had gathered in downtown Springfield for Election Day. Rutherford B. Hayes, the Republican governor of Ohio, was running against Samuel Tilden, the Democratic governor of New York. As Mullen had predicted, in the commotion surrounding the presidential election, no one paid any attention to them.

At five o'clock, Elmer Washburn and the operative John McDonald arrived at the Springfield depot from Joliet. Tyrrell,

McGinn, Hay, and Swegles had come to meet them in a hired hack. As they pulled up to the station, Tyrrell saw a stranger standing with Washburn and McDonald, clearly not an idler or a fellow passenger, but a member of the party.[11] Washburn introduced the man as Percy English, a reporter for the *Chicago Tribune*.[12] During Washburn's term as Chicago chief of police, English had served as his confidential secretary.[13] When Washburn strolled into Chicago's Central Station that morning, English had been waiting for him. Someone had given the newspaperman a tip that something big was about happen in Springfield, something that involved the Secret Service and Washburn. It is probable that Washburn himself was the source of the leak, that he invited English along to document the entire affair. The result would prove to be the scoop of English's career, as well as an invaluable record of what happened that night in Oak Ridge Cemetery.

At the depot, Washburn grilled Swegles, asking "a great many questions touching his honesty and sincerity in this important matter." Swegles answered to Washburn's satisfaction, and Tyrrell chimed in, vouching for his informant's integrity. It was six o'clock and probably already dark when Swegles set off on foot to meet Mullen and Hughes, while Tyrrell, Washburn, McDonald, McGinn, Hay, and English climbed into the hack and directed the driver to take them to Oak Ridge Cemetery.[14]

Forty minutes later they pulled up before the cemetery gates. The detectives told the driver to go back to town—a hack waiting for a fare outside the cemetery would only make Mullen and Hughes suspicious.[15] Then the detectives walked the short distance to the Lincoln Monument. Power was waiting for them at the door that led into the Memorial Hall, an oval chamber that served as the reception area for the monument.

To visit the tomb chamber, one walked outside and around to the opposite end of the building, about 120 feet away, where a heavy steel door led directly into the little room where the coffin of Abraham Lincoln lay within a white marble sarcophagus.[16]

Because the night was very chilly, Washburn and Power agreed that the men should wait inside the steam-heated Memorial Hall. Fearful that the sound of footsteps on the marble floor might carry to the catacomb, Washburn ordered his men, "Take off your boots."[17] Then Power locked the door to Memorial Hall, and the men extinguished their lamps. For two hours or more they stood in the dark, in their stocking feet, silent and as motionless as possible, waiting for the tomb robbers.[18]

Mullen, Hughes, and Swegles walked the two miles out to Oak Ridge. They had arranged with Nealy to meet them later with the wagon for the journey to the Indiana Dunes. Rather than enter boldly through the main gate, the three grave robbers jumped the fence and made a beeline for the rear of the monument and the catacomb door. There they unpacked their tools and prepared the lantern. Then Swegles, unable to resist having a bit of fun at the expense of the unsuspecting Mullen and Hughes, suggested that they ought to have a look around, to make certain no one was in the cemetery, and especially to check whether the custodian might be inside the monument. That spooked Mullen. He wondered if there might be a bed some place inside where Power spent the night. With Hughes in tow, Swegles went on a quick scouting mission of the area, ending at the Memorial Hall door. By now Hughes was nervous, too, and he stood a ways off, as Swegles walked up to the door, grabbed the handle and rattled it a little. Turning to

Hughes, Swegles said, "This is all right." Then they returned to the back of the tomb, where Mullen was waiting.[19]

Mullen had brought along a steel hacksaw to cut through the staple of the padlock, but as he went to work, he found that the staple was stronger than he had expected and the hacksaw's blade more brittle than he might have wished. He had cut only a third of the way through when the saw blade snapped into pieces. Angry and frustrated, Mullen and Hughes set to work with a three-cornered file. It was hard going, and they took turns, one holding the padlock steady while the other filed. It took half an hour before they succeeded. Then they pulled open the heavy door, lit their lantern, and stepped into Abraham Lincoln's tomb.[20]

At first Mullen and Hughes seemed transfixed by the sight of the white marble sarcophagus. But Mullen came out of the reverie first; he took the ax he had stolen that day from the German tavern and swung it over his head to smash the sarcophagus lid. Before he could start the downswing, Swegles stopped him. "Hold on!" he said. "If we can get the lid off we can put it on again and it won't be known that the coffin is gone." Mullen scoffed at the idea, saying the lid must be cemented in place, but Swegles ignored him, jammed a crowbar beneath the lid and found the sealant was only plaster of Paris. With the seal broken, the three men lifted the lid and leaned it against a wall. Then they went to work removing the marble panel at the foot of the sarcophagus. It was a beautiful piece of sculpture—a carved garland of oak leaves surrounded the name LINCOLN, and the epitaph, "With Malice toward None, with Charity for All," had been taken from the president's second inaugural address. With a second, larger saw they cut through the marble, shoved the carved slab aside and tried to drag the coffin out.

But the double-layered lead and cedar coffin was too heavy for the three men. Mullen ordered Swegles to walk down to the road and look for Nealy and his wagon; with a fourth man they should be able to carry the coffin out of the tomb.[21]

Of course, Swegles did not head for the road; he walked directly to the Memorial Hall door, where he gave the password he and Tyrrell had agreed on—"wash." Swegles whispered that Mullen and Hughes were inside the catacomb, that they had removed the sarcophagus lid and tried to haul out the coffin but it was too heavy. This was the moment to move in on the grave robbers. Tyrrell beckoned to Washburn, McDonald, McGinn, and Hay, and together they headed for the back of the monument; presumably, English, the *Chicago Tribune* reporter, and Power, the tomb custodian, followed. Eager to catch Mullen and Hughes in the act, Tyrrell had not even waited to put his boots back on. In his stocking feet he hurried down the path to the rear of the monument, while the other men fanned out across the grass.[22]

As George Hay stepped outside, the nervous and overeager detective cocked his pistol. It was a mistake. The detectives were only a few steps from the front door of the tomb when the hammer on Hay's pistol accidentally slipped and struck the cap. In the silence of the cemetery, that single gunshot sounded like the roar of a cannon. There was no hope now of taking the grave robbers by surprise, yet Tyrrell still ran ahead, yanked opened the door to the tomb chamber, and commanded Mullen and Hughes to surrender. No one answered. Striking a match, he stepped inside the burial chamber. It was empty. "The marks of their Devilish work [were] plainly visible," he reported to Chief Brooks. Scattered across the floor were the stolen ax, the broken hacksaw, the now-useless padlock, the lantern, and other tools; the carved marble slab had been shoved to one side; and most horrible of all, the coffin containing the body of Abraham Lincoln had been pulled about fifteen inches out of its sarcophagus. But Mullen and Hughes were gone.

Tyrrell ordered his men to search the grounds, while he and Washburn went back to the Memorial Hall, where Tyrrell pulled on his boots. Then they climbed the exterior stairs to the terrace of the monument, half-expecting to find Mullen and Hughes hiding up there, waiting for Swegles and Nealy to appear with the wagon. Carefully, Tyrrell, with Washburn behind him, searched the terrace. In the dark Tyrrell saw the shape of a man standing beside a column. "I fired my revolver at him," Tyrrell recalled; "he retreated behind the column, firing one shot at me." Guessing that his assailant was heading for the stairs, Tyrrell tried to intercept him and fired again. The man fired two more shots at Tyrrell. By now Tyrrell and Washburn were at the top of the stairs; they had their man trapped. Tyrrell shouted to McDonald, McGinn, and Hay, "The Devils [are] up here," and ordered the detectives to surround the monument. Suddenly the man on the terrace called out, "Tyrrell, is that you?" Thinking it was Hughes, who knew him on sight, Tyrrell did not answer. The man came out from his cover behind the column and called again, "Tyrrell, for God's sake, is that you?" It was McGinn.[23]

The night had been an utter fiasco. The Lincoln sarcophagus had been vandalized. Mullen and Hughes had escaped. Tyrrell and McGinn had almost gunned each other down. But at least the body of Abraham Lincoln was still inside the monument—that was the only saving grace in a night of botched detective work. It was, Tyrrell conceded, "one of the most unfortunate nights I have ever experienced." Yet he felt blessed, too, declaring his "escape from Death most miraculous . . . [for which I] thank God from the bottom of my heart."[24]

In the warmth and light of Memorial Hall, the detectives discussed what to do next. Tyrrell said he, McDonald, and Hay would catch the next train to Chicago, on the off chance that Mullen and Hughes were on board. McGinn and Washburn would remain in Springfield for at least one more day, to make inquiries around town. On the train Tyrrell did not find Mullen and Hughes, but he did meet Swegles, who, because he did not have enough money on him for train fare all the way back to Chicago, was especially glad to see the detective. Tyrrell gave Swegles ten dollars, which would cover the price of his ticket and serve as an advance for helping Tyrrell track down Mullen and Hughes once they got back to Chicago.[25]

As for Mullen and Hughes, when they had heard Hay's pistol go off, they had dropped their tools and bolted out of the tomb. Sprinting across the cemetery grounds, they found the eastern gate, which stood close to the terminus of the Fifth Street line of the Springfield streetcars. The streetcar conductor had just brought his car to the end of the track when he heard the sound of a gunshot coming from the cemetery. A moment later he heard a man shout, "Damn you, you cannot shoot us, you are not smart enough for that!"[26]

The conductor was the last man in Springfield to see, or at least hear, Mullen and Hughes that night. After escaping the detectives in the cemetery, Mullen and Hughes headed north, walking all night without ever encountering a soul. Then, about eight in the morning, they stumbled upon the Dixon farm near the town of Sherman, about eight miles from Springfield. John Dixon and his neighbor Thomas Keagle were bringing in a load of potatoes when they spotted the two strangers. Realizing that they had been sighted, the fugitives tried to pass themselves off as law enforcement officers. There had been a riot in Springfield the night before, they told Dixon and Keagle, during which a white man "had been killed by some negro." Had a strange black man passed that way? Mullen and Hughes asked. Dixon and Keagle replied that they hadn't seen anyone. Then Dixon asked why they were hunting for a killer on foot. The strangers said they had come out in a buggy as far as the river but had gotten out there and sent it back to town. Then they asked for something to eat and made inquiries about local depots and train schedules. Finally, Mullen and Hughes set off in the direction of the Buckley train station.

Dixon and Keagle were not fooled by the story the strangers told. Bedraggled and travel-stained, they looked more like tramps than like cops. Keagle remarked to Dixon that he had a hunch the two men were criminals. Keagle's instincts, of course, were correct. Ten days later, when he read in the *Chicago Tribune* of the arrest of two men charged with violating the tomb of Abraham Lincoln, Keagle made a visit to the jail in Springfield, to see whether the suspects were the strangers he had encountered on Dixon's farm. There were thirty-six men in jail that day, and the guards did not point out the tomb robbers to Keagle. When he came to the cell that held Mullen and Hughes, he recognized them at once. "Hello!" Keagle said. "Have you fellows got here already?" Mullen smiled back in recognition, but neither he nor Hughes said a word.[27]

From Dixon's farm it is easy to trace Mullen and Hughes's route, thanks to the station agents, train conductors, farmers, and others who had seen them as they made their way home to Chicago. On Thursday morning, November 9, they had boarded a train in Chestnut, about thirty-two miles northeast of Sherman. The conductor later recalled that they looked exhausted. They wanted to go to Melvin, a journey of about fifty-six miles, but had no money for the train fare, so they struck a deal—Hughes pulled a revolver out of his pocket and gave it to the conductor as security. The conductor would hand over the gun to the station agent in Melvin for safekeeping until Mullen and Hughes returned with the money to pay for their train tickets and redeem the pistol.

At Melvin, Mullen and Hughes walked to the Owen McMahon farm, about two miles northeast of town. McMahon was an old friend of Hughes's, and he gave the travelers dinner. They told McMahon that they were going home to Chicago but had gotten lost. They told a different story to other people they met on the McMahon farm: the two travelers had just come from Texas, where they had been buying cattle. Neither McMahon nor any of his friends believed any version of any story Mullen and Hughes told them. Everyone who ran into the two men that week thought they were fugitives.

From McMahon's farm, Mullen and Hughes traveled the ten miles or so to Buckley, where Hughes's father lived. They must have borrowed money from him, because the next day, Friday, they were back in Melvin, paying their debt to the railroad and recovering Hughes's revolver.[28]

At 10:30 the morning of November 8, 1876, as Mullen and Hughes were slogging across the farm country of Sangamon County, Patrick Tyrrell was delivering his report of the break-in to Robert Lincoln. "Mr. Lincoln expressed satisfaction" that his father's body had not been stolen, but wondered whether there was any chance now of capturing Mullen and Hughes. Tyrrell promised him that "it was only a question of time, that in a few days they would both show up." And indeed they did.

On Friday, November 10, Swegles reported to Tyrrell that Mullen and Hughes were back in town.[29]

Now a new problem arose. Grave robbing was a state offense. If he had caught Mullen and Hughes in the act of attempting to steal Lincoln's body, Tyrrell, as an officer of the law, could have arrested them. But that is not how the game had played out. Mullen and Hughes were now suspects in a state criminal case, and Tyrrell, as a federal officer, could not serve the warrant on them. In a hastily arranged conference with Leonard Swett and prosecutor Charles H. Reed, Tyrrell suggested that a detective from the Chicago police force named Dennis Simmons serve the warrant and make the arrest. Reed replied, "Do not trust an Irishman." It was a tactless remark, given Tyrrell's name and unmistakable brogue, and the Secret Service agent complained about it bitterly in his report to Chief Brooks, reminding him of "the active part I have taken in this matter, running the risk of my Life, being the first to enter the Catacomb on that eventful night, together with the shots exchanged with McGinn on the Terrace of the Monument."[30]

Tyrrell does not say whether Reed apologized. It does not appear likely. If Reed had made amends, Tyrrell, a man who never let a detail escape him, would have recorded it in his report. In any case, with Mullen and Hughes in Chicago Tyrrell did not have the leisure to nurse a grudge. With Simmons the Chicago cop and McGinn the Pinkerton detective, Tyrrell and Washburn trailed the suspects, waiting until they were both in the same place and could be arrested simultaneously. Canny criminals would never have returned to their hometown at all, so it says a lot about Mullen and Hughes that after escaping from Oak Ridge Cemetery, they went directly to the Hub.

The arrest could not have been easier. At 10:30 at night McGinn and Simmons, both of whom were unknown to Mullen and Hughes, sauntered into the saloon. Outside, Tyrrell and Washburn tried to keep out of sight, but neither man could resist peeking through the window to see what was happening. The common rumor around the West Madison neighborhood was that Mullen went about with a pistol in his pocket and that he kept one within reach at the Hub. McGinn and Simmons were armed, but no one wanted the arrest to degenerate into a gunfight. As a precaution, McGinn and Simmons had worked out a signal.

Hughes was asleep in a chair near the stove; from his place behind the bar Mullen smiled at the two strangers who had come in for a late-night drink. Going up to the bar, the men called for glasses of beer. Grabbing two beer mugs, Mullen walked around to the end of the bar where the icebox that held the beer keg stood. He stooped down, holding the mugs in one hand while operating the tap with the other. That was the prearranged moment for the arrest. Pulling out his revolver, McGinn held it against the saloonkeeper's head and said, "Mullen, you are my man." Simultaneously, Simmons pulled out his revolver and hurried over to the stove where Hughes was half-asleep. Pointing the pistol just inches from Hughes's face, Simmons said, "Come along with me, my boy." Now fully awake, Hughes stood up, asking, "Who are you?" Hughes got his answer a moment later when Tyrrell and Washburn entered the saloon.

The detectives permitted Mullen and Hughes to put on their coats and overcoats; then they handcuffed them and led them to a carriage waiting in the street to take them to the city jail. Tyrrell and Washburn climbed in and took their seats opposite the culprits. McGinn and Simmons rode on top of the carriage.[31]

The arrest went so smoothly that it made up, in its way, for the fiasco at the cemetery, and Tyrrell telegraphed the good news to Brooks in Washington. By the time Mullen and Hughes were booked and locked up securely in their cells, it was one in the morning. Tyrrell headed for home, "tired but pleased by the results of the day."[32]

The next morning Tyrrell returned to the city jail, eager to escort his prisoners to Springfield for indictment. Swett and Washburn showed up at the jail, too, and when Mullen and Hughes laid eyes on Swett, they began to make noises about seeing an attorney. Swett assured them that they could remain in Chicago for the time being and see any lawyer they wished. Tyrrell objected. They could find legal representation in Springfield, he said. Privately, he was afraid his prisoners would ask for some shifty Chicago lawyer, who would file a writ of habeas corpus and then demand, on the basis of some technicality, that the court release Mullen and Hughes from police custody. Once they were free, Mullen and Hughes would certainly skip town, thus making it difficult if not impossible for Tyrrell to find and arrest them again. Nonetheless, Swett insisted that the prisoners' rights must be respected. Mullen and Hughes asked for William O'Brien, of O'Brien and Kettelle, a new law firm that had opened in Chicago only a few months earlier.[33]

The firm may have been new, but its senior partner was famous. William O'Brien, forty-two years old, was one of the most successful criminal defense attorneys in the state. He had been born into a Protestant family in County Leitrim, Ireland, in 1834. Twenty years later, he came to America and settled in

Peoria, Illinois, where he took a job as a porter at the Peoria House hotel. An attorney who boarded at the hotel, having noticed that O'Brien was an especially intelligent young man, suggested that the porter study law. O'Brien took the boarder's advice, and two years later he was admitted to the Illinois bar. In his first case he defended a man charged with larceny. O'Brien's argument was so learned, so convincing, that he got his client off. Impressed by this debut performance, the presiding judge publicly congratulated O'Brien from the bench. Soon O'Brien had a reputation throughout the Midwest as a skillful defense attorney who did not shy away from difficult cases or notorious clients.[34]

Just as Tyrrell feared, O'Brien took Mullen and Hughes's case, then went immediately to the courthouse to file a writ of habeas corpus. Unfortunately for Mullen and Hughes, however, the court was so busy that day that O'Brien was refused a hearing. To Tyrrell's mind, the entire day had been wasted, thanks to Swett's hypersensitive notions of prisoners' rights. It was early evening before Tyrrell, fully "indignant at the conduct of Mr. Swett," along with Washburn, McGinn, and Simmons, finally set out with Mullen and Hughes for Chicago's Central Station and the overnight train to Springfield.[35] As they waited at the depot, a reporter from Chicago's *Inter-Ocean* approached the group, hoping for an interview with Mullen and Hughes. The detectives did not object, and although Mullen kept his mouth shut, the reporter found Hughes eager to "statementize."[36]

They had been the dupes of Swegles, Hughes said, "and to commence with him I must go a long way back." And so he did, starting on a day in September 1875, when he had $140 in his pocket and too much liquor in his system. He was buying a round for the house at Gavin's, a saloon on West Randolph Street, when he met Swegles (whom he also called by his alias, Jim Morrissey) for the first time. In a long-winded and round-about way, Hughes portrayed himself as a hapless victim, falsely accused and taken advantage of at every turn. He had even lost his $140 because he had trusted Gavin the saloonkeeper to keep the money safe for him while he was drunk. But when Hughes had sobered up and gone back to Gavin to collect his bankroll, the dishonest barkeep had returned only $70.

A few days later Hughes was having a quiet drink at Mullen's saloon, the Hub, when out of the blue Patrick Tyrrell with two other Secret Service operatives walked into the place and started insinuating that Hughes passed counterfeit money. Hughes denied it, but Tyrrell arrested him on the false charge anyway. He made bail, thanks to a kind friend who came forward with a certified check. Hughes hadn't been out long when he received an anonymous tip that he had become the target of a put-up job planned by Tyrrell.

Meanwhile, Hughes ran into Swegles often at the Hub. One day Swegles told Hughes how he and two men he had met in prison in Michigan City—Bill Wray and another known only as Frenchy—had stolen seven thousand dollars' worth of dry goods from a freight train and hidden the lot in a barn in Valparaiso, Indiana. Swegles and his friends were going to bring the merchandise up to Chicago to sell, and he asked Hughes if he wanted a piece of the action. Adopting the tone of an honest man whose honor had been offended, Hughes said to the *Inter-Ocean* reporter, "I told him I wasn't that kind of a man and I wouldn't go into the thing. I thought I saw some catch about it and I didn't want any truck with the fellow."

Some time passed before Hughes ran into Swegles again. This time Swegles bragged of going up to Wisconsin with his friend Bill Nealy to rob a tannery outside Kenosha. Convinced that Swegles was a bad lot, Hughes tried to keep his distance from Swegles. "When I met him afterward," Hughes said, "I did not speak to him."

By now it was November 1876, more than a year since Hughes had first met Swegles at Gavin's saloon. Hughes confessed to the reporter that he owed Mullen some money and it weighed on his conscience. He thought he would visit his father in Buckley, Illinois, and borrow enough to pay back what he owed Mullen. When Mullen heard of Hughes's trip to central Illinois, he said he would come along. Word had reached him that his brother, whom he had not seen in years, lived in Springfield; Mullen decided "he would go down and try to find him." They caught the train to Springfield on the night before Election Day, and by chance Swegles was on the same train. He came into their car with a small bottle of whiskey, which he offered to share, but Mullen and Hughes would not take a drink. So Swegles stretched out on the seat opposite and fell asleep.

In Springfield Mullen went off to search for his brother, while Hughes accepted Swegles's invitation to join him at a saloon for a drink. In the course of conversation, Hughes mentioned that he was going to see his father, to get some money. Swegles "made the remark that there was money to be made in Springfield." When Hughes asked what he meant, Swegles revealed his plan to steal Abraham Lincoln's body and hold it for ransom. He asked if Hughes "wanted to go into it."

"What did you say to that?" the reporter asked.

"I never was so astonished in my life," Hughes replied. "I told him it was out of my line of business and I wouldn't have anything to do with it."

It took some doing, but eventually Hughes got away from Swegles, met Mullen for dinner, then boarded the 5:30 afternoon train from Springfield to Gilman to see his father. Assuring the *Inter-Ocean* reporter that the conversation in the Springfield barroom was the only time he had heard of the grave robbery from Swegles, Hughes concluded, "I have told you all I know."

But the reporter had a few more questions. Asked why Swegles would try to set him up, Hughes replied that Swegles's landlady had warned him, Hughes, that Swegles would be paid a thousand dollars if he could get Hughes into some kind of "scrape." The reporter asked who was behind this scam; Hughes replied, "Tyrrell and Washburn. . . . I think it's been done to give Washburn notoriety and Tyrrell has a grudge against me and my friend [Mullen]."[37]

The *Inter-Ocean* editors were inclined to believe that the Lincoln tomb case was indeed a hoax concocted by Elmer Washburn. "Knowing that certain newspapermen had Washburn's confidence and were ready to serve him in almost any way," the paper said, "knowing the prestige which would follow the prevention of such an awful outrage must greatly cling to Washburn; knowing further that he was at that time prominently mentioned as a candidate for the position of chief of police of Chicago, the public received the story with doubting shrugs . . . many went so far as to doubt whether there was anybody in the Lincoln mausoleum on the night of the 7th Inst[ant] except Elmer Washburn, his man Tyrrell and his ever-obedient reportorial adjunct."

The editors' suspicions extended to John Hughes, as well; they were not so gullible as to swallow his story. In the lead-up to the interview, the reporter characterized Hughes's version as "a full statement of what—by a slight stretch of the imagination—may be termed the facts of the case."[38]

Three days after the *Inter-Ocean* ran Hughes's rambling account of his and Mullen's innocence, the newspaper published another article, which conceded, "That Hughes and Mullins [*sic*] took part in the Lincoln monument business is pretty conclusively proven . . . and their story is doubtless a lie."[39] The *Inter-Ocean*'s editors had no choice; every day new witnesses, new details, and a host of hitherto unknown facts about the case and the accused were emerging. In one respect, however, the editors of the *Inter-Ocean* would not back down—Mullen and Hughes "were at best the accessories and the pliant tools in the hands of Swigel [*sic*]."[40] Whether they harbored some animus against Elmer Washburn or had a weakness for conspiracy theories, the editors of the *Inter-Ocean* persisted in their misguided belief that Lewis Swegles was the link between Washburn's ambition to return to power in Chicago and Mullen and Hughes's hunger for a share of the two-hundred-thousand-dollar ransom.

5

The Body in the Basement

Percy English must have dashed from Oak Ridge Cemetery to the nearest telegraph office to file his story with his editor, because the next day, November 8, 1876, his newspaper, the *Chicago Tribune*, carried a longish article on the attempted tomb robbery. The day after that, November 9, the *Tribune* ran a second, more detailed account of the "Desecrators of Lincoln's Remains" and the "Damage Done to the Sarcophagus by the Miscreants." Finally, on November 18, the *Chicago Tribune* devoted its entire front page to the in-depth story of the plot, the break-in, Mullen and Hughes's escape, and their capture in Chicago. Centered prominently beneath the newspaper's banner was a large engraving that showed the floor plan of the Lincoln Monument and the grounds surrounding it. As was the case with most American newspapers in the nineteenth century, the *Tribune*'s articles did not carry bylines, yet it is likely that Percy English wrote most if not all of these articles.

If not, he must have been the primary source for them, because the stories in the *Tribune* are substantially the same as the two other eyewitness accounts of that night at Abraham Lincoln's tomb: the reports Patrick Tyrrell sent to his superior, Chief James Brooks of the Secret Service, and John Carroll Power's narrative of the events as recorded in his 1890 book, *History of the Attempt to Steal the Body of Abraham Lincoln.*

Outside Illinois, however, almost two weeks would pass before many of the nation's newspapers reported that a gang of counterfeiters had broken into the tomb of Abraham Lincoln and tried to steal his body. Newspaper editors were not indifferent to the story; they were distracted by a bigger one. On the morning after Election Day in 1876, most newspapers reported that the Democratic candidate, Samuel Tilden, had been elected president of the United States. Kentucky's Democratic *Louisville Courier-Journal* exulted, "Thank the Lord! Boys, We Got Em." A northern Democratic paper, the *New York Sun*, opted for a simple assertion, "Tilden Is Elected." Meanwhile, in the Midwest the Republican *Chicago Tribune* mourned, "Lost. The Country Given Over to Democratic Greed and Plunder."[1] In Nashville, Tennessee, the *Daily American* cheered "Our Gallant Little Democratic Bird Still Crowing for Victory."[2]

Chicago Republicans had reason to lament. As things stood (or appeared to stand) on November 8, Tilden, the Democrat, had 184 electoral votes; Hayes, the Republican, was trailing with 166 electoral votes. Everyone was waiting for the returns from Florida, South Carolina, and Louisiana; but it was hardly a cliff-hanger. To win, Hayes needed all 19 electoral votes from those three states; Tilden needed only 1 electoral vote. Since secession in 1861, the Southern states had been solidly Democratic, a loyalty now set in stone, thanks to the excesses and abuses of Reconstruction, as masterminded by the Republicans. Only a fool would suggest that three Deep South states—and one of them South Carolina, the cradle of the Confederacy—would put another Republican in the White House. Even Zachariah Chandler, national chairman of the Republican Party, despaired. He dismissed the workers at his party's New York campaign headquarters, locked up, then headed for home, where he climbed into bed.[3]

Chairman Chandler had not been asleep long when there came a pounding on his door. Half-asleep, not bothering even to pull on a dressing gown, he stumbled to answer it. His early-morning callers were a Republican Party powerbroker, William E. Chandler (no relation), and John C. Reid, managing editor of New York City's stalwartly Republican newspaper, the *New York Times*. Reid had figured out a way to ensure that Hayes would become president.[4] Florida, South Carolina, and Louisiana all had Republican governors. Furthermore, Republicans controlled the election boards in the three states. Reid's idea was to order Republican Party loyalists on these boards to scrutinize the returns, then announce that all the electoral ballots in Florida, South Carolina, and Louisiana had gone to Hayes.[5]

The scheme hatched by Reid and the two Chandlers that morning was one of the most shameless acts of election fraud in American history, but the Democrats were prepared to meet the challenge. Abram S. Hewitt, national chairman of the Democratic Party, wired the governor of Oregon. Although the governor was a Democrat, his state had voted solidly for Hayes, and the three electors for Oregon were all Republicans. Hewitt reminded the governor that one of the electors, John W. Watts, was a postmaster; and by law, federal employees were ineligible to serve as electors. Oregon's governor corrected the oversight at once, dismissing Watts and appointing a new elector, a Democrat named E. A. Cronin.

To no one's surprise, Oregon's two remaining Republican electors refused to play ball. They convened to review and certify the election returns, found they were short one elector, and promptly reappointed the recently disqualified John W. Watts to fill the vacancy. Predictably, all three men cast their electoral votes for Hayes. In the next act of this farce, Cronin summoned two fellow Democrats to act as witnesses as he recorded that two of Oregon's electoral votes had been cast for Hayes and one electoral vote—Cronin's own—had been cast for Tilden. Then the two conflicting certifications of Oregon's election returns were sent off to Washington.[6]

Meanwhile, observers from both political parties were scurrying south. The evidence of political corruption, fraud, and even intimidation on both sides is overwhelming. In Louisiana, for example, members of the all-Republican election returns board locked themselves away in an illegal secret session, during which they invalidated thirteen thousand votes for Tilden. By the time the gentlemen emerged from their conference, Hayes was the victor in the solidly Democratic state of Louisiana.[7]

In the North and the South, outraged Democrats were chanting "Tilden or Blood!" There were rumors that well-armed Tilden men were ready to march on Washington, D.C., and install their candidate in the White House by force. The *Argus* newspaper of Albany, New York, warned its readers to brace themselves for "war in every street and on every highway of the land." Tilden's friends, meanwhile, were urging him to take any measure to ensure his victory. From Memphis the ex-

Confederate general Gideon J. Pillow pleaded with Tilden to act: "You are the only man who can save the government, preserve the Constitution and the liberties of the people."[8]

At a time when the American public was enraged, or at least preoccupied, by the election crisis and anxiety was widespread that the country might be plunged into another civil war, it is understandable that the news from Springfield might have passed unnoticed. Even those who did hear about the break-in at the Lincoln tomb were not entirely sure what to make of the story—it struck them as grotesque, even unbelievable. The editors of the *Inter-Ocean* in Chicago dismissed the story as "a stupid affair," then went on to tell their readers that Mullen and Hughes were dupes who had been lured into the scheme by the prospect of divvying up two hundred thousand dollars in ransom money.[9] The tomb robbery was all a setup to make the unemployed Elmer Washburn look like a hero, so that he would be reappointed chief of police in Chicago, and to boost Patrick Tyrrell's reputation in the Secret Service. The real villain in the *Inter-Ocean*'s version of the story was Lewis Swegles. The paper quoted an anonymous source identified only as a private detective, "second to none in his profession," who claimed to have all the facts regarding Swegles's criminal past and sordid character. "Knowing the man as I do," the paper's informant said, "I would not hang a dog on his testimony."[10]

The *News and Courier* of Charleston, South Carolina, dismissed the report of the attempted body-napping as "altogether apocryphal, especially as it is based wholly on the words of 'secret service' agents, which people may well be pardoned for receiving with incredulity."[11] The *Daily Picayune* of New Orleans had no faith in the story either. The paper ran this bit of news from the North as "another fraud—the story of an attempt to steal the bones of Abraham Lincoln." That is all the attention the crime received in the *Picayune*—just fourteen words in a column of news trivia, sandwiched between the size and value of the tea crop produced in India that year and the yield, in bushels, of the Maine potato harvest.[12] As a point of comparison, two days earlier, the *Picayune* had devoted thirty-four lines to the story of a mother who had found "a bright red worm" in her five-year-old daughter's ear.[13] A newspaper reporter in Memphis admitted, "The crime is so incredible that there has been some difficulty in making the public understand that the atrocious attempt [to steal Lincoln's body] was really made."[14]

There were some, however, who saw a connection between the scandal at the polls and the outrage at the Lincoln Monument. The Democratic newspaper of Springfield, the *Illinois State Register*, denounced the "ineffable meanness" of its rival, the Republican *Daily Journal*, for suggesting that Democrats had desecrated Lincoln's grave as part of their election night victory celebration.[15] And the rumor making the rounds in black communities was that the break-in was the work of "ex-Rebels" whose bitter hatred for Abraham Lincoln extended even to his remains. In a lengthy front-page story on the crime, the *Chicago Tribune* reported that even "expert detectives (honest ones),—men having knowledge of the habits and actions of scoundrels,—they were inclined to laugh at it. Never having met in their experience any one whom they thought low and mean and devilish enough to imagine such a thing, they could not conceive of a mind so debased as to propose the robbery, let alone execute it."[16]

Certainly, in nineteenth-century America everyone knew

that bodies disappeared from their graves all the time, but in such cases, the bodies were stolen by grave robbers who had dug up the newly dead to sell the cadavers to medical schools. Who had ever heard of hauling a corpse from its tomb and holding it for ransom? "This species of robbery is entirely new," lamented the *Chicago Tribune*, "and it will probably spread all over the country, as do new devices for picking pockets and burglarizing houses and similar occurrences will undoubtedly take place and attempts be made to blackmail the friends of the dead."[17]

As Democrats and Republicans howled over who was president and Mullen and Hughes scurried from farmhouse to farmouse trying to get home, while newspapermen debated whether Lewis Swegles was a manipulative scoundrel and Elmer Washburn and Patrick Tyrrell were publicity hounds and crass opportunists, one figure was forgotten. The body of Abraham Lincoln lay where Mullen and Hughes had left it— partway out of its vandalized sarcophagus. The night of the crime, after the robbers and the detectives had dispersed, John Carroll Power put a fresh padlock on the tomb chamber door, but that was as far as the restoration went. It was not until Thursday afternoon, November 9, that Power called on John Todd Stuart, chairman of the Monument Association, to ask what should be done about the damage to the tomb. Stuart promised to send out men to repair the sarcophagus, and late that same afternoon, Adam Johnston, a marble dealer whose business had been in Springfield for thirty-five years, arrived at the tomb with two assistants. Power led them to the catacomb, where first they inspected the red cedar outer coffin. It was undamaged, the rust on the brass screws proving that the thieves had not gotten to the inner lead coffin that held Lincoln's body.

Relieved that the martyr-president's remains had never been touched by the grave robbers, the men shifted the coffin back into place inside the sarcophagus; then Johnston and his crew went to work patching up the broken marble and replacing and resealing the lid.[18] Abraham Lincoln was resting in peace once again.

Six days later, however, Stuart traveled out to the monument, where he confessed to Power that he was having great trouble sleeping. The break-in had proved just how vulnerable the tomb was to vandals and thieves. More to the point, eleven years after his assassination, Abraham Lincoln was still a target. Stuart was convinced the sarcophagus and the tomb were not sufficiently secure, but he had no idea how to protect Abraham Lincoln's body from possible assaults in the future. After hashing out the matter for a time, Power and Stuart came to a drastic conclusion. To ensure both the safety of the president's body and their own peace of mind, they would remove the coffin from the sarcophagus, carry it down to the basement of the monument, and bury it there in an unmarked grave.

By the standards of their time, Stuart and Power's decision was shocking. Most Americans and Europeans would have been scandalized to learn that the remains of the martyr-president had been moved from his gleaming white marble sarcophagus and stuck in a shallow grave in a dank, filthy basement. Funeral and mourning traditions in the 1870s were elaborate and widely regarded as non-negotiable. Widows, for example, were expected to publicize their grief for two and a half years by wearing suitable clothing, which occupied a narrow color spectrum running from darkest, dullest black during the first year, known as deep mourning, to shades of violet, gray, and lavender during the final six months, known as half mourning. Some widows, however, chose to mourn for the rest of their lives. Queen Victoria wore black for her husband, Prince Albert, from the day he died in 1861 until her own death in 1901.[19] Mary Lincoln, too, "made mourning a permanent condition." For the last seventeen years of her life, she wore the clothes appropriate to deep mourning.[20]

The Victorians had definite ideas about the treatment of the dead, too. Formerly, a corpse had been washed and wrapped in a shroud, little effort being made to masque the signs of death. Since the Civil War, however, embalming had become popular in the United States. The body was dressed in its best clothes, and undertakers strove to make the dead appear natural, as if asleep. This care and reverence for the body extended to the box that would hold it, as well. It was during the 1870s that people began to speak of caskets rather than coffins. The word choice was a conscious one—in the Victorian era, a casket was a chest in which one kept objects that were extremely precious.[21] In this context, Power and Stuart's decision to move Abraham Lincoln's body to a sodden, dirty hole would have been regarded as a violation nearly as bad as that which the grave robbers had attempted.

It was late in the day of November 15 when Adam Johnston returned to the Lincoln tomb with three workmen. They broke the seal on the sarcophagus and lifted out the coffin. Then they cemented the lid in place once again and went away. But at nightfall Johnston came back with Stuart, Colonel John Williams—one of Abraham Lincoln's staunchest political allies—and Jacob Bunn, Mary Lincoln's banker. Power was waiting for them. He led them to the catacomb, where they took up positions around the double coffin, which weighed between four hundred and five hundred pounds.[22] Together, the five men lugged it out of the tomb chamber, around the exterior of the monument, through the Memorial Hall entrance, and down to the basement, where they deposited it near the foundation of the obelisk that rises over the tomb. It must have been brutal work for men who were no longer young—Stuart was sixty-nine years old, Williams sixty-eight, Bunn sixty-two, Johnston sixty, and Power, the "youngster," fifty-six. Once the heavy lifting was concluded, Stuart, Williams, and Bunn headed home, but Johnston stayed. He had constructed a large wooden crate for the coffin, after bringing it out to the cemetery in pieces, in order not to arouse the suspicions of any casual observers. Now, in the basement, he assembled the box, slid the coffin inside, and nailed the last section in place. By then it must have been late, and perhaps Power used that as a pretext to urge Johnston to go home and leave Power to bury the box alone.[23] It is likely, however, that Power did not in fact want Johnston to see where Lincoln's body would be hidden. Already too many people in and around Springfield guessed that something was up at the tomb. Johnston's three workmen must have wondered why they were asked to lift Lincoln's coffin from the security of its sarcophagus and leave it exposed in the catacomb. No doubt they would talk about it with their families and friends. Power and Stuart must have regarded Johnston as trustworthy, or they would never have let him in on their secret. Nonetheless, the marble dealer was not part of the Lincoln Monument Association's inner circle. From Power's perspective, the fewer people knew the actual location of Lincoln's body, the safer the body would be.

The next morning Power started digging a shallow grave in the basement. He recalled that the air beneath the obelisk "was most villainous . . . to breathe, for in the original construction there was no provision made for ventilation." Over the next few days he stole "hours and half hours" from his duties at the monument to dig down in the cellar. Whenever he heard footsteps above, however, he would extinguish his lantern and rush up to the Memorial Hall to greet visitors. What must they have thought of the flushed and sweaty custodian? But Power had a more serious problem than interruptions from tourists. He had not dug down very far when he struck water. Abraham Lincoln's body could not be lowered into a muddy puddle, so Power went back to Stuart, to ask what should be done next. Unfortunately, Stuart was out of ideas. To return the coffin to the sarcophagus would be to invite trouble. To sink it in some underground pool was out of the question. Finally, Stuart told Power to place the box atop some wooden planks, to keep it off the damp ground, then hide it beneath a pile of old lumber until they thought of a better solution. Power went back to the monument and did exactly as Stuart instructed him to do. For the next year the body of Abraham Lincoln remained in the dank basement, under a pile of mildewed wood.[24]

Meanwhile, the preparations for the trial of Terence Mullen and John Hughes were moving forward. A grand jury in Springfield indicted Mullen and Hughes for "Conspiracy to steal the remains of Abraham Lincoln from the Lincoln Monument in Springfield, Illinois and . . . attempted Larceny in trying to steal the casket or coffin . . ., being the property of the Lincoln Monument Association."[25] The charge is perplexing; why didn't the grand jury indict Mullen and Hughes for robbing a grave and vandalizing a tomb? Historians have asserted that Mullen and Hughes were charged with conspiracy and larceny because there was no statute in Illinois that outlawed grave robbery.[26] Yet that is not true. Under the heading "Robbing

Graves," a statute dated 1845 states, "Whoever willfully and without authority, digs up, disinters, removes or conveys away from the place of sepulture or interment thereof any human body or the remains thereof, or knowingly aids in such disinterment, removal or conveying away, and whoever is accessory thereto, either before or after the fact, shall be fined not less than $100 nor more than $1,000, or be confined in the county jail not exceeding one year, or both."[27] If this law applied to anyone, it was Mullen and Hughes. For that matter, the state could have indicted Big Jim Kennally and even the onetime "third man," Herbert Nelson, if Mullen and Hughes had tried to save their own necks by fingering them.

Furthermore, the 1845 statute book gave prosecutors another way to get at Mullen and Hughes. A law entitled "Injuring Monuments" reads, "Whoever willfully and maliciously injures, defaces, removes or destroys any vault, tomb, monument, gravestone or other memorial of the dead . . . or wantonly or maliciously disturbs the contents of any vault, tomb, or grave, shall be fined not exceeding $500, or confined in the county jail not exceeding one year, or both."[28] Clearly the prosecutors could have made their case that sawing through Lincoln's marble sarcophagus and hauling out his coffin constituted malicious mutilation of a tomb.

Why, then, did the prosecutors opt for charges of conspiracy and larceny, rather than the more obvious ones of robbing a grave and defacing a tomb? No record of the prosecutors' rationale survives, so all one can do is speculate. Such crimes might be expected to provoke a strong negative response from a jury; but according to the 1845 Illinois statutes, grave robbers and tomb vandals could be sentenced to no more than one year in the county jail. If Mullen and Hughes were convicted of conspiracy and larceny, however, they would be sent to the state penitentiary at Joliet—a much harsher penalty. As a rule, prosecutors would shy away from a charge of conspiracy because they reasoned that it "requires proof of agreement to commit a criminal act and an overt act in furtherance of the agreement"—and often it is difficult to meet that standard of evidence.[29] In the case of Mullen and Hughes, however, the prosecutors must have felt confident that they could make the charge of conspiracy stick—the informants, Swegles and Nealy, were ready to swear that Mullen and Hughes had conspired to break into Abraham Lincoln's tomb, steal his body, and hold it for ransom; and a crowd of witnesses, ranging from John Carroll Power, the tomb custodian, to Elmer Washburn, the former chief of the Secret Service, could give eyewitness testimony that Mullen and Hughes had put their nefarious plot into action.

For a time it appeared that William O'Brien would be defending Mullen and Hughes. If any attorney had a chance of winning an acquittal for Mullen and Hughes, it was O'Brien. His fellow lawyers claimed that he "appeared in more serious criminal cases and defended more men charged with murder than any other member of his profession in Illinois."[30] But O'Brien had a standard: as Mullen himself recalled, O'Brien issued a warning to his new clients: "he will not try the case at all if cant beat thim [*sic*]."[31] As the weeks rolled by and O'Brien became better acquainted with the case, he changed his mind about it. On March 13, 1877, the Springfield newspapers reported that William O'Brien had "withdrawn from the defense."[32] His instinct told that him the Lincoln tomb robbery case was a losing proposition, so he had abandoned Mullen and

Hughes. Their new attorneys were two Springfield men, Alfred Orendorff and Lloyd F. Hamilton.

Alfred Orendorff came from pioneer stock—his grandfather, Christopher Orendorff, had been one of the first settlers in the Springfield area. In 1819 he had erected a cabin on Sugar Creek, north of the city, and built the first water-powered gristmill in the country. Alfred was born in the same neighborhood in 1845. His father, Joseph, died when Alfred was ten years old, yet somehow his mother, Elizabeth, managed to put her son through a succession of schools—Wesleyan University in Bloomington, Illinois, the military school in Fulton, and finally a law school in Albany, New York. At the age of twenty-two Alfred Orendorff began practicing law in Springfield.[33] In 1873 Abraham Lincoln's old law partner, William Herndon, invited the promising young attorney to join him as the junior partner in a firm they called Herndon & Orendorff.[34]

Orendorff's co-counsel was Lloyd F. Hamilton. He had been born on a farm in Kentucky in 1844 and was only a few months old when his father died. All alone, with a farm to run and an infant to raise, Jane Hamilton packed up and moved to Tazewell County, Illinois, near the home of her father and brothers. She did not come as a distraught and penniless widow, however; Jane Hamilton held on to her land in Kentucky and for the rest of her life spent part of every year down South, managing her property.

Lloyd Hamilton inherited his mother's ambition. Throughout his adolescence he demonstrated a keen interest in the law, and by the time he turned twenty-two, Hamilton had graduated from the Union College of Law in Chicago, passed the bar exam before the justices of the Illinois Supreme Court, and opened his own practice in Springfield. If Mullen and Hughes could not have O'Brien, then Hamilton was a good second choice—he had a reputation as an able defense attorney, especially in sensational murder trials.[35]

To prosecute the case, the state sent Chicago attorney Charles H. Reed down to Springfield. At forty-two, Reed was a tall, broad-shouldered man with large blue eyes and a receding hairline. His most distinguishing feature was the bushy mustache and goatee he wore in the style of the French emperor Louis Napoleon. Sixteen years earlier, Reed had been a founding partner in the Chicago firm of Knox, Eustace and Reed. He was a popular man in Chicago; time and again, the voters had elected Reed state's attorney, the title for prosecutors in Illinois at that time.

Charles Reed had been born on a farm near the village of Strykersville in western New York in 1834. Even as a boy, Reed showed an interest in the law. He studied first in the law office of Johnson Parsons in Lancaster, New York, then moved to Illinois, where he completed his legal education under Judge John H. Howe of Kewanee. The law, however, was not Reed's only interest. He was fluent in Greek, the language of the original texts of the New Testament. In his spare time, he studied the Greek versions of the Gospels and epistles and published his findings in a variety of scholarly journals.[36]

Reed's co-counsel was Robert H. Hazlett, the twenty-nine-year-old partner from the Springfield firm of Hazlett & Kane.[37] Like so many of the attorneys involved in this case, Hazlett had ties to Abraham Lincoln's former law partner, William Herndon. Fresh out of the University of Michigan law school, Hazlett had continued his studies at the firm that would shortly become Herndon & Orendorff. In 1873, only a year after he had been admitted to the Illinois bar, Hazlett struck out on his own, opening a law office with one of the youngest attorneys in the state, twenty-three-year-old Charles P. Kane.[38]

The judge who would preside over the trial was forty-six-year-old Charles S. Zane. On his mother's side Zane was related to Benjamin Franklin; and like the Founding Father, Zane followed an eclectic career path to become a self-made man. At age nineteen he left his parents' farm in Cumberland County, New Jersey, for the prairies of Illinois, where he found a job making bricks and doing farmwork for Rev. Peter Cartwright, for the wages of thirteen dollars a month. Two years later, Zane had saved up enough to enter McKendree College. After college he studied law, passed the bar exam in 1857, and immediately opened his own office. The next year the voters of Springfield elected him city attorney. In 1861 William Herndon asked Zane to fill the void left by the departure of his former law partner Abraham Lincoln. The firm of Herndon & Zane remained in business for eight years. In 1873 the former brick maker and sodbuster was elected judge of the Nineteenth Judicial Circuit of Illinois.[39]

Nearly eighty attorneys were listed in the *Springfield City Directory* for 1877, but by far the most famous law firm in town was headed by William Herndon, Abraham Lincoln's former law partner. It is curious that three of the most prominent players in the Mullen-Hughes trial—Judge Zane, the prosecutor Hazlett, and counsel for the defense Orendorff—were old associates of Herndon and thus, in a sense, Lincoln's heirs.

6

"The Tools of Smarter Men"

If Mary Lincoln ever wrote to a relative or friend about the outrage committed at her husband's tomb, the letter has not survived. Operating on the premise that his mother's private letters were embarrassing "relics of the long years of [her] distressing mental disorder," Robert Lincoln had put out the word among Mary's correspondents that he would like her letters back. In 1913 he wrote to a friend, "Hundreds of them have been kindly sent me for destruction." And it was not just Mary's "mad" letters that Robert burned; Lincoln biographers have lamented for years the loss of almost all of the letters that passed between Abraham and Mary Lincoln.[1] We know that such letters existed. In a letter to Mary Jane Welles dated July 11, 1865, Mary Lincoln referred to "a large package of *his* dear, loving letters to me, many of them written to me, in the 'long ago,' and quite yellow with age, others, more recent & *one* written from his office, *only* the *Wednesday* before [his assassination], a few lines, playfully & tenderly worded."[2] Yet not long after Mary's death in 1882, Robert wrote to a friend, "I have not examined any of my mother's papers and do not believe that anything will be found among them of sufficient importance for preservation." And in fact Robert did not preserve them; he destroyed them all.[3]

At one point, Robert had even considered destroying his father's papers. At the time that he donated the Abraham Lincoln Papers to the Library of Congress, Robert made a stipulation that they were not to be made available to the public until twenty-one years after his own death. In the deed of gift Robert explained, "This condition is imposed by me because some papers contain many references of a private nature to the immediate ancestors of persons now living, which, in my judgment, should not be made public." In a conversation with the renowned muckraking journalist Ida Tarbell, Robert admitted that the idea of the general public reading intimate details of the lives of the men and women of the Civil War generation had troubled him so deeply that he almost burned his father's papers too.[4]

Paradoxically, Robert's passion for privacy and for protecting the reputation of others did almost irreparable damage to the reputation of his own parents. In 1866, William Herndon—Lincoln's law partner and Mary's nemesis—published a biography of Abraham Lincoln that attracted enormous attention. Herndon and Mary had loathed each other almost from the moment they met at a party in Springfield in 1837. On that occasion, Herndon asked Mary to dance; and as he led her around the floor, he said she "seemed to glide through the waltz with the ease of a serpent." Mary Todd did not like the comparison and told Herndon so, then walked off, leaving him alone and embarrassed on the dance floor.[5] For the next twenty-five years, Mary snubbed Herndon, while Herndon sniped at Mary. Herndon got his revenge in his book, where he asserted that Abraham Lincoln had never loved his wife, that his home life with Mary had been "a domestic hell." Although many biographers and students of Abraham and Mary Lincoln have exposed Herndon's allegation as a lie, his version of the Lincoln marriage is the one that has passed into American popular culture. The Lincoln love letters would have gone a long way to refute Herndon's mean-spirited view—if Robert had not tossed them into the fire.[6]

Almost all of the Mary Lincoln letters that have survived from the period of the grave robbery are addressed to Jacob Bunn, her banker in Springfield, and are dated from Pau, a town in the French Pyrenees favored by British and American travelers in the nineteenth century for its mild winter climate. For the period November 28, 1876, to December 19, 1877, we have thirty-eight letters from Mary to Bunn, and almost without exception, they are all business—acknowledging the receipt of her pension check or the rent from the tenants who were leasing her house in Chicago, chiding him when payments were late, inquiring when she could expect the next check. From time to time Mary mentions the high cost of living in France or asks after the health of Bunn's family, but not one of these surviving letters even hints at the assault on the Lincoln tomb.[7]

Robert Lincoln, on the other hand, did write about the attempt to steal his father's body, and several of those letters have survived. Incredibly, Robert's extant correspondence on the subject is also all business. As an attorney, Robert understood that if Mullen and Hughes were to be convicted, the prosecution would need reliable witnesses. Although he refers to Lewis Swegles and William Nealy as detectives, Robert's instincts must have told him that these men were not the sort to hang around Chicago or Springfield for several months waiting for a trial to begin. As Robert explained to Judge David Davis, the Lincoln family's closest confidant, "it was absolutely necessary to promise a per diem of $2.50 each, in order to keep them under our eyes until the trial comes off."[8]

David Davis had been one of Abraham Lincoln's most trusted friends. As fellow attorneys, they had spent years riding the Eighth Judicial Circuit together, slogging along muddy trails that passed for roads, idling away the hours in county courthouses, and bunking together in shabby roadside inns. Private accommodations were virtually unknown in the rural America of the 1840s, where it was routine for travelers to share not only a room but even a bed. The rail-thin Lincoln almost always found another man—and sometimes two—in his bed. Davis, however, always had a bed to himself—at three hundred pounds, he took up all the available mattress space. But shared experiences were not the only tie that bound Lincoln and Davis together. They had similar ideas about slavery and the law. Although they both hated slavery, they also abhorred what they regarded as the extremism of the abolitionists. When it came to the law, neither Lincoln nor Davis was a profound legal scholar, but they shared a commonsense approach to jurisprudence, based more on what was right and just than on precedents handed down from the bench. Lincoln liked and respected Davis, yet he never opened his heart to him. Years later Davis admitted flat out, "Lincoln never confided to me anything."[9] Nonetheless, the Lincoln family knew Davis as a reliable, trusted friend; and they remained in close touch with him even after the assassination.

On Saturday April 15, 1865, the day Abraham Lincoln died, Robert Lincoln sent a telegram to Davis in Chicago, pleading, "Please come at once to Washington & take charge of my father's affairs."[10] In this crisis, the Lincolns needed not only a family friend, but also a man who knew the law and had a head for business. At his death Abraham Lincoln had left an estate worth approximately eighty-five thousand dollars, but he had died intestate.[11]

Through prudent investments, Davis had made a fortune for himself. Now he put those skills to work for his friend's widow and two surviving sons. By careful management of Lincoln's assets, as well as the timely purchase of bonds, Davis actually increased the value of Abraham Lincoln's estate. At the settlement in November 1867, Davis reported that the estate was now worth almost $111,000. Good friend that he was, Davis had not hired an attorney but had handled all the legal issues personally; he did not charge the estate for his work, nor did he ask to be reimbursed for any personal expenses; and he refused to accept the customary 6 percent fee that was owing by right to him as administrator.[12] The final accounting delighted Mary Lincoln. "Permit me to say," she wrote the judge, "that in no hands save your own, could our interests have been so advantageously placed—please accept my grateful thanks for all your kindness to myself & family."[13] As for Robert Lincoln, he regarded Davis as his "second father."[14]

Robert's letter to Davis during the grave-robbery crisis, then, was not a casual, newsy note to an old friend; he wanted to make use of that almost familial tie, as well as Davis's personal prestige in Washington, to collect some money he felt was owed to him. He hoped that Davis, as a justice of the United States Supreme Court, would be able to persuade Charles F. Conant, acting secretary of the treasury, that the government should reimburse Robert Lincoln for the per diem he had been paying Swegles and Nealy. We do not know whether Judge Davis, as Robert's intermediary, ever called on Conant. If he did try to persuade Conant that the U.S. treasury should foot the bill for keeping Swegles and Nealy "on retainer," he failed. In March, in April, and again in May, Robert wrote to Conant and to James Brooks, chief of the Secret Service, asking for the $628 he had paid out to Swegles and Nealy. All these letters are calm, polite, professional; although he mentions Mullen and Hughes by name and refers to their attempt "to break open my father's monument," he reveals no hint of pain, grief, outrage, or even resentment.[15] But then, Robert Lincoln was not a man to offer anyone "a glimpse into his own heart."[16]

While Mary Lincoln in Pau watched the mail for her pension checks and Robert Lincoln in Chicago watched the mail for a reimbursement check from Washington, defense attorneys Alfred Orendorff and Lloyd Hamilton were drawing up twenty-three subpoenas for witnesses who would testify on behalf of Mullen and Hughes. As all their witnesses lived in Chicago, Orendorff and Hamilton entrusted the subpoenas to Hughes's sister, Bridget Lewis, and instructed her to take them to Charles Kern, the sheriff of Cook County. It would be Kern's responsibility to round up the witnesses and ensure that they were in Springfield in time for the trial.

On May 17 Bridget Lewis was back in Springfield, but on a different errand. Along with Austin S. Field and Richard B. Fuller, Lewis offered to make bail for Mullen and Hughes. The three informed the court that they could put up as security a considerable amount of real estate. Field said he owned $157,300 worth of land in Hyde Park on Chicago's South Side, as well as property elsewhere in Cook County. Fuller swore that he owned property in Chicago valued at $13,500. Lewis said she owned lots and other land in Chicago and Iroquois County worth $7,700, minus a $500 mortgage on the Iroquois property. It sounded impressive, but prosecutor Robert Hazlett did not accept such claims at face value. He requested and received permission from the court to telegraph his fellow prosecutor, Charles Reed, in Chicago about Field's, Fuller's, and Lewis's claims.[17] Around six o'clock that evening came a telegram from Reed saying that from what he had been able to discover about the value of those properties, Field, Fuller, and Lewis were trying to bamboozle the court with a "straw bail." In other words, Bridget Lewis and her friends were trying to pledge property that either did not exist or was not nearly as valuable as they claimed.[18]

A reporter for the *Chicago Tribune* did a little investigating and found that Field was no real estate baron, but a "dead beat" who "didn't have a dollar in his pocket and for over a year has been . . . sleeping in a barn at the corner of State and Twelfth streets." As for Fuller, he ran "a one-horse shooting gallery . . . not worth $500." Meanwhile, Tyrrell, "his pockets crammed full of information concerning the straw bail and the job [Field, Fuller, and Lewis] were putting up on the authorities," caught a train to Springfield and laid all the evidence before a grand jury. Field and Fuller were arrested immediately, but Bridget Lewis had skipped town. Tyrrell, along with Springfield's sheriff, Temple Elliott, and his deputy, a man named Gibson, went after her, nabbing her on the train to Chicago.[19]

With Lewis in custody, Tyrrell led Elliott and Gibson on a sweep through Chicago that caught Big Jim Kennally, Herbert Nelson, and Eugene Hartman, an associate of Fuller and Milton S. Forbes, an ex-jailbird and onetime Secret Service agent. Hartman had come with Lewis, Field, and Fuller to Springfield, where his role, apparently, was to pay the hotel bills.

Tyrrell's arrest of Kennally was a gamble. Big Jim had been careful to keep his distance from the final planning and execution of the grave-robbery plot, so Tyrrell could not proffer any charges against him on that count. The surviving record does not suggest any reasons Tyrrell might have had for seizing Kennally in connection with the straw bail scam, but we can try to piece together the detective's train of thought. As co-owner of the Hub, Kennally might have had some interest in getting his business partner, Mullen, out of jail. From Tyrrell's perspective, it was worth the trouble of escorting Big Jim down to Springfield, where a judge could determine whether the wily crime boss was in any way complicit in the straw bail scheme.

On Tuesday, May 22, all seven members of the "straw bail gang" were brought before the circuit court. Kennally assured the court that he had had nothing to do with the straw bail conspiracy, that Mullen had indeed asked him for help in securing bail, but that Kennally could do nothing for his business partner—the Hub with all its fixtures was worth no more than $1,500. Nelson also denied that he was connected with the straw bailers. In fact, Nelson said, he was already $2,000 in the hole, having put up bail for Hughes on an old charge. When Eugene Hartman claimed that he was a poor man who owned only a few sticks of furniture, prosecutor Hazlett reminded him that just days earlier Fuller had sworn in court to having purchased nearly $40,000 worth of merchandise from Hartman. "What have you done with the proceeds of that sale?" Hazlett asked. Hartman did not answer. As for Milton Forbes, he claimed his personal property was worth no more than $1,000. Yet he could not explain why he had made the long journey to Springfield for Mullen and Hughes's sake, nor how a man as strapped for cash as he could afford to foot the hotel bills for Lewis, Fuller, and Field. The judge sent all seven to jail. As they were being led away, the straw bail gang protested—predictably—that they were the guileless victims of "a put-up job" devised by the Secret Service. Hamilton and Orendorff, arguing that they needed Bridget Lewis "to hunt up evidence" for their clients, managed to persuade the judge to release her on her own recognizance.[20]

Six days after the straw bail scheme collapsed, on May 28, 1877, Mullen and Hughes's trial began. That Monday morning, they walked into a courtroom packed with spectators but devoid of any witnesses for the defense. The twenty-three subpoenas that defense attorneys Lloyd Hamilton and Alfred Orendorff had prepared and that Hughes's sister, Bridget Lewis, had hand-delivered to Sheriff Charles Kern in Chicago had resulted in nothing.

As soon as the case was called, Hamilton was on his feet protesting that the trial could not proceed because none of the defense's witnesses had arrived. He asked for a delay of at least a day or two, so that witnesses could be collected in Chicago and brought to Springfield. Prosecutor Charles Reed objected. He reminded the court that the defense had had ample time to assemble its witnesses. If the attorneys had been the least bit diligent in this regard, Reed argued, the witnesses would be sitting in the courtroom now. Reed observed that the prosecution's witnesses were in court and insisted that the case proceed to trial. Now defense attorney Orendorff chimed in. The defense had been diligent about issuing the subpoenas, he said. Furthermore Bridget Lewis had done her work faithfully, turning over the subpoenas to Sheriff Kern in Chicago. If anyone had been negligent, Orendorff said, it was the sheriff.[21]

After permitting a little more debate, Judge Charles Zane reined in the attorneys by ruling that he would delay opening the case until two o'clock, at which time the trial would proceed, unless the counsel for the defense could show good reason for a continuance. But when two o'clock rolled around, Hamilton and Orendorff still had no witnesses. In a last-ditch effort to delay the trial, they entered a motion for a continuance and asked for time to prepare the necessary affidavit. Judge Zane granted the request but emphasized that in doing so he was departing from standard courtroom procedure; he warned Hamilton and Orendorff that if in the future they asked for a continuance in his courtroom, they had better have an affidavit ready.[22]

Hamilton and Orendorff wasted no time; within an hour they had a lengthy affidavit ready to show the judge. In it they argued that their clients could not go to trial, because none of the twenty-three witnesses the defense had subpoenaed had appeared in court. These witnesses were essential to the defense's case because they would testify that Mullen and Hughes had come to Springfield on November 7 on legitimate business, not to steal Lincoln's body; that Lewis Swegles was an unreliable witness, since he had once served time in the Wisconsin state penitentiary for what the trial transcript describes only as "an infamous crime"; that Swegles had approached Hughes's sister, Bridget Lewis, with an offer to win an acquittal for her brother if she would pay him $2,000; and that Patrick D. Tyrrell, chief of the Chicago District Office of the Secret Service, had hatched this plot in order to frame Mullen and Hughes. All of these points were secondary to the defense's main argument—that the plot to steal Abraham Lincoln's body and hold it for ransom had not been concocted in October by Big Jim Kennally, Terence Mullen, and Jack Hughes in the Hub but had been cooked up entirely by Lewis Swegles. The affidavit went on to assert that witnesses for the prosecution would give false testimony that Mullen and Hughes had been present at Swegles's house on November 5 to firm up the last details of the plot to rob the tomb, but the defense had three witnesses who would swear (if they ever showed up in court) that on that date they had spent the entire evening with Mullen and Hughes. In other words, Mullen and Hughes were the victims of a conspiracy, or, as the Chicago low-lifes liked to call it, a put-up job.[23]

After reading the affidavit, Judge Zane stated that the central issue was the allegation by the attorneys for the defense of a conspiracy to frame their clients. Now he turned to Reed, the prosecutor. Would the prosecution's witnesses testify, under oath, that no conspiracy to rob Abraham Lincoln's grave had been hatched at Swegles's house on November 5, 1876? Reed said they would, whereupon Judge Zane disallowed the affidavit and the continuance and ordered jury selection to begin.[24]

Then Reed made an offer. The prosecution was willing to forgo a trial if Mullen and Hughes pleaded guilty to petty larceny and accepted a jail sentence. Hamilton and Orendorff rejected the offer with the assertion that their clients, like George Washington, "could not tell a lie."[25]

The next day the trial resumed with jury selection. The lawyers went through a pool of seventy-seven men before agreeing on twelve jurors, including two farmers, two clerks, two schoolteachers, a stonemason, a stonecutter, a pump dealer, an ironworker, a coal dealer, and a coal miner. They were sworn in at the outset of the afternoon session; then Reed made the opening statement for the prosecution. In detail, he described the origin of the plot, the desecration of Lincoln's tomb, and the evidence that weighed so heavily against Mullen and Hughes. Hamilton responded by claiming that his clients were the victims of a conspiracy hatched by Elmer Washburn, Patrick Tyrrell, and Lewis Swegles, who had invented this fantastic scheme to enhance their personal reputation and add to the luster of that of the Secret Service.[26]

Next came the witnesses. The undertaker Thomas C. Smith testified that the remains in the sarcophagus were those of Abraham Lincoln and that the coffin that held the president's body was worth seventy-five dollars—the price for which he had sold it to the Lincoln Monument Association.

Thomas Keagle and John Dixon, the farmers who had encountered the bedraggled and travel-stained Mullen and Hughes on the morning of November 8, repeated the implausible story the accused had told them that day about being officers of the law pursuing black men who had started a race riot in Springfield and killed a white man.

Frederick Schlitt, who operated the St. Charles House, identified Mullen and Hughes as the travelers who had arrived at his hotel near dawn on the morning on November 7, asked for rooms, and registered as T. Durnan and James Smith. As proof, Schlitt had brought to court the hotel register and pointed out the false names Mullen and Hughes had written in the book.[27]

Charles Elkin, the streetcar conductor on Springfield's Oak

Ridge line, testified that he had been near the cemetery on the night of the break-in. He had heard gunfire, then saw two men running in a northeasterly direction. One of the men was bellowing, as the reporter for the *Illinois Daily Journal* put it, "a fearful volley of oaths."

The prosecution's next witness was Elmer Washburn, who testified that his active part in the case had begun only on November 6, although Tyrrell, Swegles, and Robert Todd Lincoln, among others, had discussed it with him at an earlier date. Washburn stated that he had encouraged Swegles to do everything he could to keep Mullen and Hughes's confidence and instructed him to go with them down to Springfield and out to the tomb on election night. Washburn said he had been at the train station in Chicago the night before the crime and had seen Swegles, Mullen, and Hughes board the train to Springfield. Hamilton tried to get Washburn to admit under cross-examination that the day after the attempted grave robbery he had confessed to a Springfield resident named John Bunn that the whole break-in at the tomb had been a scam and Washburn wished he had never had anything to do with it. Washburn denied ever saying such a thing. What he had expressed regret about to Bunn was that the police presence at the tomb had been badly managed; the police should have posted some officers beside the tomb door, to seize Mullen and Hughes as they ran out.[28]

Of all the witnesses for the prosecution, Swegles gave the most damning testimony. Under Reed's questioning, he covered in detail every stage of the plot, from the time Mullen and Hughes had first approached him at the Hub up to the night they broke into the Lincoln tomb and tried to lift the coffin from its sarcophagus. Hamilton put the witness through a withering cross-examination, but as the reporter covering the trial for the *Illinois State Register* put it, Swegles "was not shaken in the least and when he left the stand it was quite clear a conviction would result."[29]

But the prosecution had not finished. The attorneys introduced into evidence two letters written by Mullen while he was in the Sangamon County jail, one of which was addressed to Thomas Sharp, the Lincoln, Illinois, newspaper publisher whose boozy boast to a Springfield prostitute had derailed the Logan County gang's scheme to steal Lincoln's body. By coincidence, on November 14, 1876, exactly one week after Mullen and Hughes had bungled the Lincoln job, Sharp himself was arrested on a charge of passing some of Big Jim Kennally's counterfeit money. Mullen's second letter was to William O. Birdsall, or Burtsall, another counterfeiter locked up in the Sangamon County jail, who in all probability was also a member of Kennally's counterfeiting ring. In the letters Mullen appealed to Sharp and Birdsall to furnish him with an alibi.

The letter to Sharp is the most interesting to read. Sharp, the newspaper publisher, a man of letters, was the brains of Kennally's Logan County operation. In his letter to Sharp, Mullen went to enormous lengths to impress Sharp with a catalog of all the witnesses his pals were collecting in Wisconsin, Indiana, and Illinois, who would stream down to Springfield to testify to Swegles's "bad caracter and vileney [*sic*]." Mullen says that among the witnesses "we are going to have the Chief and the assistant Chief off [*sic*] Police and Detectives" from Chicago. And Swegles is not the only one who will be exposed in court as a scoundrel. "Tyrell's wife is coming to show up his bad caracter and prove that he has left her and is now living with his own sons wife [*sic*]." Mullen estimates that about twenty witnesses will stand up to prove his and Hughes's inno-cence.[30]

Then came the catch.

The man assembling all these witnesses was William O'Brien of the Chicago law firm of O'Brien and Kettelle (the letter had been written before O'Brien abandoned the case). Accord-ing to Mullen, O'Brien said, "He will have no truball to beat the case but he will have to get all those witeness here from Diferend parts of the country."[31]

One cannot help marveling over Mullen's bravado. He claims that twenty witnesses, including Chicago's chief of police and Detective Tyrrell's supposedly outraged wife, are ready to march up to the witness stand on his behalf, and that a crowd of wit-nesses from Wisconsin, Indiana, and Illinois is prepared to swear that he is innocent. Yet, Mullen concedes, attorney O'Brien has his doubts whether such a preponderance of tes-timony will be enough to overcome the "bad caracter and vileney" of the Washburn-Tyrrell-Swegles cabal. To reassure O'Brien and persuade him to take the case, Mullen needs a rock-solid alibi; he wants Sharp to persuade a man named "Lightning Rod" Curtis to supply that alibi for the night Mul-len and Hughes were supposed to be on the train from Chi-cago to Springfield.

"I want to prove by him," Mullen wrote, "that we missed the train that night [November 6, the night before the attempted grave robbery] and stayed at his house that night . . . and had brackfast the next morning—left after brackfast." Just to be on the safe side, Mullen asks Sharp to have Curtis come see him in jail, so he can "give me the location of his house and discription of the house and how maney in the famley."[32]

The next issue was to secure an alibi for November 7, the

night of the Lincoln tomb break-in. Mullen appealed to Birdsall directly to cover for him and Hughes, and even spelled out everything he should say on the witness stand. Birdsall was to claim that he had known Hughes for about two years but had never met Mullen. He would say that about eight o'clock on the night of the attempted grave robbery, he was driving his wagon home when he saw two men walking along the old Peoria road, about four miles outside Springfield. When he pulled up to offer them a ride, he recognized Hughes, who introduced him to his traveling companion, Terence Mullen. Birdsall was to explain that the two men had missed their train, so he took them to his house for the night. The next morning he dropped off Mullen and Hughes on the road to Gilman—a story that would dovetail nicely with John Dixon and Thomas Keagle's testimony about meeting Mullen and Hughes early on the morning of November 8. Mullen urged Birdsall to "get things fixed solid so you can prove that we stayed with you all night. I think you can do it if you only use your head a little." Then, to sweeten the deal, Mullen added, "I think we can raise you $35 cash."[33]

"The introduction of these letters created a decided sensation," wrote the reporter for the *Illinois Daily Journal*, "and manifestly moved the jury. The defense did not seek to rebut them."[34] Of course, at the trial neither Birdsall nor Curtis put in an appearance. Nor did the Chicago chief of police, Mrs. Tyrrell, or any of the other witnesses who supposedly were well acquainted with Swegles's wickedness. With no one else to testify on their behalf, Mullen and Hughes took the witness stand one after the other, both telling substantially the same story. Hughes said that back in Chicago, Swegles had told him about his plot to steal Lincoln's body, but Hughes had paid no attention to the story because Swegles was drunk at the time. On November 7 he and Mullen had traveled together to Springfield, Hughes on business, Mullen on the off chance of meeting his brother, whom he had not seen for some time. They had run into Swegles in Springfield and agreed to join him on a tour of the Lincoln tomb at Oak Ridge Cemetery. Later in the day, Swegles showed Mullen and Hughes a collection of burglar's tools, which he said he would use that night to break into the tomb. Considering that they had been seen around Springfield in the company of Swegles, Hughes had suggested to Mullen that they ought to get out of town before they were suspected of being accessories to the crime. They went back to Chicago and had heard nothing more about the robbery until they were arrested.[35] Writing to the chief of the Secret Service, James Brooks, Tyrrell dismissed Mullen and Hughes's testimony as "a long and untruthful statement."[36]

After Hughes and Mullen testified, the court adjourned for supper. At 7:30 that evening, the court reconvened. The chamber was "crowded to its utmost capacity," to hear the attorneys' closing statements; and both the defense and prosecution put on a good show. Hamilton and Orendorff tried one last time to convince the jury that Mullen and Hughes were the victims of a vast conspiracy that extended from Elmer Washburn to the Secret Service agents to the reporters and editors of the *Chicago Tribune* (the newspaper had never been shy about asserting that Mullen and Hughes were guilty of trying to steal Abraham Lincoln's body). Later that same day, Orendorff admitted to a *Tribune* reporter that the statements he and Hamilton had made about Washburn, Tyrrell, Swegles, and other witnesses for the prosecution—calling them conspirators, scoundrels, and even horse thieves—may have been excessive, but that that was what their clients had wanted them to say and they felt obligated to do so. "In other words," the *Tribune* reporter explained to his readers, "their clients paid them for lying about decent people in the hope of prejudicing the jury in favor of the thieves." Incensed by the final volley of slurs and insults from the defense, Reed returned fire. In his statement to the jury, he branded Hamilton and Orendorff "shysters."[37] Then Reed went on to deliver a summation so impressive that he was interrupted two or three times by spontaneous bursts of applause.[38] It was after midnight when the jury retired to deliberate on a verdict.

Early the next morning, the jury rendered its decision—Mullen and Hughes were guilty on both counts of larceny and conspiracy and would serve a one-year sentence at the penitentiary in Joliet. The reporter covering the case for the *Chicago Times* wrote, on the issue of the prison sentence, "On the first ballot four were for five years,—the extent of the law,—two were for two years and four for six months, in the penitentiary. Those who were in favor of the shorter term expressed themselves to the effect that the accused were not the original devisers of the plot, but they had been led into it by Sweagles [*sic*]." The jury's intuition that Mullen and Hughes were not the ones who had dreamed up the grave robbery scheme was correct, of course. But their conclusion that the mastermind was Swegles reveals that in some respects the lawyers for the defense had managed to undermine Swegles's credibility—although not enough to get their clients off. The reporter for the *Chicago Times* came to a similar conclusion, although he did not think Swegles was the mastermind. Summing up the newspaper coverage of the trial, the reporter closed by saying, "There is reason to believe that the actual extent of the plot is not yet exposed and many think that Mullins and Hughes, though really guilty of complicity in the plot, did not contrive it, but are really the tools of smarter men."[39] If Big Jim Kennally read that summation, he must have smiled.

Hamilton and Orendorff moved for a new trial, but Judge Zane denied their request. In Tyrrell's opinion, a new trial would have been a pointless exercise; the outcome would have been the same because "the evidence [against Mullen and Hughes] is too strong."[40]

Ten days later, Tyrrell wrote to James Brooks asking, "Chief, I have the Tools captured by me on the night of November 7, 1876, in the Monument, which were used as evidence in the Trial of Terrence Mullen and Jack Hughes, what shall I do with them, I learn that the Lincoln Monument Association wishes to have them in exhibition in Memorial Hall, but they have said nothing to me about them personally, the true facts, of that night will be more interesting in years hence than at present."[41]

After the reading of the jury's verdict and the sentence, the court adjourned. Later that morning, Judge Zane received a message from Charles Kern, the sheriff of Cook County. His men had rounded up some of the subpoenaed defense witnesses; the sheriff wanted to know, should he send them to Springfield? Zane replied that there was no longer any need for witnesses and ordered their release.[42]

On June 21, 1877, Robert Lincoln invited Tyrrell to his home. Lincoln thanked Tyrrell for saving his father's remains from desecration; and as a token of his gratitude, Robert presented Tyrrell with a large portrait of Abraham Lincoln.[43]

That next day, under a column entitled "Hazlett's Harvest," the *Illinois State Register* reported that Mullen and Hughes had been taken on the noon train from Springfield to the prison in Joliet along with fifteen other felons successfully prosecuted by State Attorney Hazlett and, of course, Reed. The two Lincoln grave robbers traveled to the state penitentiary in the company of a murderer, a bigamist, a forger, a rapist, two common thieves—one of whom had stolen a suit of clothes, the other a team of mules with wagon and harness—a horse thief, several burglars, and an embezzler.[44]

7

The Lincoln Guard of Honor

During summer 1877, two large bronze sculptural groups honoring the men who had served the Union in the infantry and the navy during the Civil War were installed on the base of the Lincoln Monument obelisk. A man named H. W. Cole superintended the job. About the same time, John Carroll Power hired an assistant, John Harrison, to help him at the tomb a few hours every day. The installation of the sculptures required that part of the outside walls of the monument be taken down and rebuilt. Of necessity, Cole would have to go into the basement to ensure that the new work was not compromising the foundation, and once he was down there, he was certain to find the crate that held Lincoln's coffin. Rather than let Cole and Harrison make the sensational discovery on their own, Power decided to reveal the secret himself. He took the two men aside and asked them to swear, on their honor, not to disclose to anyone what he was about to tell them.[1] The men gave the custodian their word, swearing in such a solemn manner that Power was convinced that anyone "with the smallest particle of manhood" would have sacrificed his right arm rather than break such an oath. He was wrong. Within forty-eight hours Springfield was buzzing with the news that since the attempted grave robbery, Abraham Lincoln's body had been stashed away in the airless, dank basement of his monument. Mortified by the betrayal, Power sought out John Todd Stuart. Power imagined that Stuart would summon all the members of the Monument Association, that they would go into the basement of the tomb and find some solution to the problem of how to safeguard Lincoln's body. But the custodian was in for another disappointment. Stuart, now seventy years old, reminded Power that carrying Lincoln's coffin had disabled him for months, that almost all the gentlemen of the Monument Association were elderly, that the heat of summer was upon them, and that the air in the unventilated cellar was very bad. The question of what do with Lincoln's body would have to wait.[2]

Another year went by. Now Power discovered that his assistant was not only a gossip but also a thief who had been pocketing a portion of the twenty-five-cent entrance fee to the tomb as well as skimming profits from the sales of books and postcards in the gift shop. About the same time, the newspapers were reporting that the body of A. T. Stewart, the New York City department store tycoon, had been stolen from its grave in the churchyard of St. Mark's in the Bowery and was being held for ransom. The date was November 18, 1878, two years and eleven days since Mullen and Hughes had made their attempt on Lincoln's remains. Fearful of experiencing a repetition of that old nightmare, Power hurried off to see Stuart once again. This time Stuart authorized Power to do whatever he thought best and to solicit the help of discreet, trustworthy men. Wisely, Power recruited men who were young enough for the job—Gustavus S. Dana, aged thirty-nine, a commission merchant who traded in futures; Jasper N. Reece, thirty-seven, assistant secretary of state for Illinois; Joseph P. Lindley, thirty-six, a railroad ticket agent and telegraph operator; James F. McNeill, thirty-seven, a bank clerk; and Edward S. Johnson, thirty-five, co-owner with his father, Joel Johnson, of the Revere House hotel in Springfield. At eight o'clock that evening, they all took the Fifth Street trolley out to Oak Ridge Cemetery, where Power was standing by with a supply of lamps, spades, and shovels.[3]

Down in the basement on the east side of the tomb Power showed his recruits Lincoln's coffin concealed behind a pile of old boards and still encased in the wooden crate the marble dealer Adam Johnston had built for it. Abraham Lincoln was exactly where Power, Stuart, and the others had left him two years earlier. The new team of gravediggers decided to shift the crate to the north end of the basement, where the water table was not so high. They did not dig deep, just down far enough that the crate would rest a few inches below the surface of the dirt floor. The space was cramped, the air stifling; by the time the men lowered the box containing the coffin into the shallow grave, it was midnight and they were utterly exhausted. Power urged his helpers to go home: he would fill in the hole the next day.

On the trip back into town, someone in the party had the morbid thought that if some calamity carried off all of them at once, posterity would never know where Lincoln's body was hidden. That night, before going to bed, Gustavus Dana sat down and drew a diagram of the Lincoln tomb showing the spot where the coffin was buried. Then he wrote a memorandum explaining that he, Power, and their four associates "did this night remove the remains of Abraham Lincoln from the place they had been secreted since the attempt to steal them, to a place of greater safety and buried them about six inches deeper than the depth of the case." Dana sealed the diagram and the memo inside an envelope, locked it inside his safe, and went to bed.[4]

The next day, Springfield was overrun by at least a thousand delegates for a convention of the Odd Fellows. When Power arrived at the Lincoln tomb that morning, a large crowd of conventioneers was waiting for him to open up. There was not a moment during the next four days, while the convention was in town, when Power was not occupied giving tours. Meanwhile, down in the basement, the crate containing Lincoln's body lay exposed in its open grave. If Power was worried, the rush of an endless stream of visitors compelled him to put all thought of the coffin out of his head. About ten o'clock at night on November 21, as he was on his way to bed, Power paused to flip through his mail. In the pile was a postcard from Chicago that read, "Be careful. Do not be alone, particularly Thursday night, Nov. 21st." The card was dated "Nov. 18, '78" and signed "C." The custodian panicked. It was Thursday the twenty-first. Were thieves breaking into the tomb at this moment? Did they know that the body was not in the burial chamber but in the cellar? Frightened by what might happen to Lincoln's remains, but also nervous about what might happen to him if he went out to the cemetery alone at this hour of the night, Power decided he would have to wait until morning.

At dawn, after a long, restless night, Power arrived at the Lincoln Monument, hours before any Odd Fellow would turn up asking for a tour. There were no signs of forced entry. Hurrying downstairs, Power found the crate exactly as he and his friends had left it. He felt relieved, but the message on the postcard still worried him. "Is there real danger?" he asked himself. "Is there another scheme to capture the remains of Lincoln? Or is someone trying to play a joke?" Power's anxiety level rose again. He could not gamble with Lincoln's body; the hole had to be filled in and all trace of activity in the basement erased that day. For what must have been the first time in his career as custodian, Power left the tourists to find their own way around the monument, while he hurried back to town. There, he persuaded Dana and Reece to come out to the cemetery and finish the business in the basement.[5]

Down in the cellar, Dana and Reece had a terrible scare themselves. Spooked by Power's postcard, they convinced themselves that they detected signs of recent excavation around the crate, as if something had been buried there. They dug into the spot and about a foot down struck an iron coffin. Their imaginations racing, they supposed that grave robbers had found the crate in the cellar, transferred Lincoln's body into this iron box, then buried it, with the intention of retrieving it later. It was a wild scenario. Suppressing their impulse to run upstairs to tell Power, Dana and Reece agreed instead to investigate the matter more closely. The iron coffin was empty. Then, for their own complete peace of mind, they pried the lid off the crate. Inside was Lincoln's cedar coffin, undisturbed, "no signs of screws having been removed and the fungus on the corners, where it would have been parted by taking off the cover, was intact." So the two men nailed down the lid of the crate, filled in the shallow grave, and smoothed the dirt over, so that no sign remained that anyone had ever been down there; then, for good measure, they scattered some debris and bricks over Lincoln's grave, to create the appearance that the spot had been left untouched ever since the builders had laid the foundation of the monument.

The mystery of the empty iron coffin continued to trouble Dana and Reece until John Todd Stuart resolved it for them. Lincoln's body had lain in the iron coffin while his monument was being built, Stuart explained. When the monument was finished, the coffin proved too long for the marble sarcophagus, so Lincoln's remains were transferred to a lead casket, which was enclosed in the cedar coffin. Dana, who was becoming the group's unofficial historian, recorded all these facts in another memorandum, sealed it up in an envelope, and deposited it in his safe.[6]

The mystery of the postcard, however, has never been solved. The only source for the story is Power himself, and he told it in his book about the plot to steal Abraham Lincoln's body. If it were any man other than John Carroll Power, one might suspect that the postcard never existed, that the story was a bit of melodrama dreamed up by the custodian to attract a little extra attention to himself and remind his neighbors of his importance as the guardian of the remains of the martyred president. But Power was not that kind of man. Everything we know about him suggests that he was scrupulously honest. Furthermore, he saw himself as a historian, and he was a very good one. The books he wrote on the first settlers of Springfield and Sangamon County, not to mention the Lincoln tomb robbery, are invaluable. Tragically, many of the documents that Power used have been lost or destroyed. In his book on the Lincoln grave robbery, for example, Power included what appears to be the complete text of the transcript of Mullen and

Hughes's trial. Clearly, he must have had access to the original transcript, but since then that document has disappeared. Very likely the postcard with the ominous message was lost or destroyed, too.

In the days after the burial of Lincoln's coffin, Power's friends found themselves reflecting on the seriousness of what they knew and what they had done. Unlike Cole, the foreman, and Harrison, the sticky-fingered assistant custodian, Dana, Reece, Lindley, McNeill, and Johnson could keep a secret. In consultation with Power, the men agreed to organize themselves formally into a secret society of guardians of the remains of Abraham Lincoln. If they advertised themselves as such, however, they would be issuing a general invitation to would-be vandals to try their hand at carrying off the president's body. Instead, the guardians would declare to the world that they had dedicated themselves to leading memorial services on the anniversaries of Lincoln's birth and death, "to aid," as Power put it, "in keeping green the laurel wreath on the brow of his fame." Furthermore, they all agreed to invite three new members into their exclusive circle. The attorney Clinton L. Conkling was the scion of a prominent Springfield political family; his mother, Mercy Levering Conkling, was Mary Lincoln's lifelong friend and confidante.[7] Horace Chapin was an editor of the *Illinois Daily Journal* and a hero of the Civil War who had lost a leg at the Battle of Chickamauga.[8] Noble B. Wiggins had risen from steward to become co-owner of Springfield's Leland and Wiggins Hotel, reputed to offer the finest accommodations in Illinois outside the city of Chicago.[9] Counting John Carroll Power, that made nine in all. They called themselves the Lincoln Guard of Honor, and the nine held their first formal meeting at the monument in Memorial Hall on Abraham Lincoln's birthday, February 12, 1880.[10]

It is typical of their times that Power and his companions did not look into hiring security guards or installing a sophisticated alarm system or, at the very least, buying better and stronger locks to safeguard the monument; instead, they formed an exclusive club dedicated to keeping the secret of Lincoln's grave. Today such an idea seems odd, but in the America of the 1870s, the formation of a select brotherhood would have been regarded as unexceptional, even sensible.

The last third of the nineteenth century was the golden age of secret societies and fraternal organizations in America, with the high-water mark coming in 1897, when, out of a population of 19 million adult males in the United States, 5.5 million belonged to at least one such organization. The Odd Fellows led the pack, with 810,000 members, followed by the Freemasons with 750,000 members and the Knights of Pythias in third place with 475,000.[11] A study of the phenomenon published that year concluded that members found in these societies "a charm of deep potency in the unrestricted, out-of-this-world atmosphere which surrounds the scenes where men are knit together by the closest ties, [and] bound by the most solemn obligations to maintain secrecy."[12]

Almost fifty years later, when the glory days of secret societies and fraternal organizations were past, Arthur M. Schlesinger, Sr., explained their appeal. "The plain citizen sometimes wearied of his plainness," he wrote, "and, wanting rites as well as rights, hankered for ceremonials, grandiloquent titles and the exotic costumes of a mystic brotherhood."[13] Such ceremonies, titles, and costumes, by lending dignity and legitimacy to the societies, accounted for a good part of their appeal in the nineteenth century. A man might be a butcher, a store clerk, or a farmer during the working day, but one night a week at his lodge or hall or temple he was someone noble and exalted.

And new organizations sprang up all the time. In 1893, a group of men approached General Lew Wallace, author of the best-selling novel *Ben-Hur*, to ask his permission to found a new secret society whose rituals would be inspired by scenes from the general's epic. They intended to call themselves the Knights of Ben-Hur. A stickler for historical accuracy, Wallace felt obliged to point out that there had been no knights in the first century. Instead, he suggested that the men call themselves the Supreme Tribe of Ben-Hur. And so a new fraternal organization was born, and thousands of American men signed up. As one would expect, the tribe's most solemn ritual was a reenactment of the novel's famous chariot race.[14]

While the pageantry and the mystery of the Odd Fellows or the Freemasons were, in part, the inspiration for the Lincoln Guard of Honor, one important factor set Power's group apart—they actually had a secret worth keeping. They communicated their intention to Robert Lincoln, and he gave his approval to the men whose "one and all controlling thought, was to guard the precious dust of Abraham Lincoln, from vandal hands."[15]

As for the general public, it took the Lincoln Guard of Honor at face value. When the gentlemen organized their first memorial service for April 15, 1880, the fifteenth anniversary of Lincoln's death, a crowd of three hundred braved rain and the early hour to assemble at the Lincoln Monument in Oak Ridge Cemetery by 7:22 in the morning, the precise moment when Abraham Lincoln had breathed his last. The program was designed to please: the eighty-one-year-old Rev. Albert Hale, a retired Presbyterian pastor, read Lincoln's 1861 farewell speech to the people of Springfield, Springfield's YMCA Quintette sang the *Battle Hymn of the Republic*, and Lincoln Guard of Honor member Clinton L. Conkling read Lincoln's second inaugural address.[16] Although visitors to the Lincoln Monument continued to pester John Carroll Power with their doubts about the sarcophagus—whether it truly held the remains of Abraham Lincoln—no one appears to have suspected that the Lincoln Guard of Honor existed for any other purpose than to mount memorial services. Then, in 1882, its members received an unexpected request.

After years of wandering in France, Mary Todd Lincoln had sailed home to America in October 1880. A telling incident from her return voyage has come down to us, thanks to an eyewitness. Mary had been walking on deck and was about to descend a steep staircase when the ship lurched and she lost her balance. A woman who happened to be standing behind her grabbed Mary's voluminous skirt. "You might have been killed, madame," the stranger said, "down that horrible staircase!"

"Yes," Mary replied, with a sigh, "but it was not God's will."

The stranger took the liberty of introducing herself; she was Sarah Bernhardt, the celebrated actress. Mary introduced herself as "the widow of President Lincoln."

Reflecting on this chance meeting in her autobiography, Bernhardt wrote, "[I had] just done this unhappy woman the only service that I ought not to have done her—I had saved her from death."[17]

When the ship docked in New York, Mary's favorite nephew, Lewis Baker, was waiting to meet her and escort her back to Springfield. There she moved in with her sister Elizabeth and her brother-in-law Ninian Edwards. It was in the Edwardses' parlor that Mary Todd had married Abraham Lincoln on November 4, 1842. Now she spent most of her time alone in her upstairs bedroom, where she kept the shades drawn day and night. The homecoming was not a happy one; the two sisters quarreled a great deal. Mary, insisting that she was an invalid, demanded Elizabeth's constant attention. Elizabeth countered that Mary was a hypochondriac who would feel better if she left her gloomy room now and again to enjoy some natural light and fresh air and to spend some time in the company of her family and old friends.[18]

Mary had been in Springfield for seven months when she received an unexpected visitor—Robert appeared with his eleven-year-old daughter Mary, or Mamie, as the family called her. He wanted to be reconciled with his mother, and Mary did not resist. Robert agreed with his Aunt Elizabeth that Mary's illnesses were imaginary, but Mary ignored her son.

A year later Mary was indeed ill. A strange creeping paralysis overtook her limbs; she suffered from boils, and her eyesight was almost entirely gone. The end came quietly at 8:15 in the evening of July 15, 1882. At the time of her death, Mary Todd Lincoln was sixty-four years old.[19]

The funeral was splendid. The mayor of Springfield called on all businesses in the city to close, out of respect for their old neighbor and former First Lady. The city newspapers, the *State Register* and the *Journal*, framed their columns inside a dense black border. Thousands of spectators lined the streets to watch the funeral procession that carried Mary's coffin from the Edwardses' house to the Presbyterian Church and then to Oak Ridge Cemetery. Among the many floral arrangements that filled the church was a cross of flowers, as tall as Mary had been in life, with her name spelled out in forget-me-nots.[20]

All nine members of the Lincoln Guard of Honor turned out to escort Mary Lincoln to the grave. Inside the monument they slid her double lead-lined coffin into the crypt prepared for it beside the bodies of her sons Edward, William, and Thomas. But the stone panels were not cemented in place. That night, at the request of Robert Lincoln, the Guard removed Mary's coffin from its crypt and carried it down to the basement. There they dug a shallow grave beside the place where Abraham Lincoln's body was concealed and lowered the box into place. Once again the bad air and stifling heat of the cellar—worse because it was July—almost overcame the men of the Guard. They did not finish until two in the morning, long after the last streetcar had made its final run from the cemetery gates back to the city. No one had thought to bring a carriage or even a wagon out to Oak Ridge, so eight bone-weary men (for Power's house was very near the cemetery) walked the two or three miles back to their homes. It was an especially painful ordeal for Horace Chapin, who limped along on a wooden leg that replaced the one he had lost at Chicka-mauga.[21]

Four months after Lincoln's assassination, Mary had written to her friend Elizabeth Blair Lee that time would not ease the pain she felt over the murder of her husband. "I [will never] be reconciled to my loss," she said, "until the grave closes over the remembrance and I am again reunited with *him*."[22] After seventeen wretched, often humiliating years, Mary was united with her husband once again.

A few days after the funeral, Clinton Conkling received a letter from Robert Lincoln.[23]

Washington, July 26, 1882

Clinton L. Conkling, Esq.:

My Dear Friend

On my return here I find a letter from Major [John Todd] Stuart advising me that you and the other gentlemen of The Guard of Honor, have laid me under a great obligation by carrying out the wish I expressed to him that my mother's body should be placed beside my father's so that there can be no danger of a spoliation. It is a great satisfaction to know that such an act is now impossible and I think it will be best that no change should be made for a long time to come.

I cannot adequately thank you and the other gentlemen for personally doing this, so that the object should be fully attained, but I beg you and them to be assured that I appreciate the kind act.

Believe me to be
Sincerely yours,
Robert T. Lincoln

While Power and the Guard kept careful watch over the Lincoln Monument, Patrick Tyrrell kept his eye on Terence Mullen, Jack Hughes, and Big Jim Kennally. Mullen and Hughes were scheduled to be released from the state penitentiary in Joliet at noon on May 22, 1878. On that day Tyrrell and a deputy U.S. marshal took the train from Chicago down to Joliet. At the prison Tyrrell dropped in on the men who, he wrote, figured "among the most prominent of my cases since I entered the Secret Service." He found Nelson Driggs, "looking very well," working as a nurse in the prison hospital. He did not mention what work Ben Boyd did at the prison, but Tyrrell did notice that although Boyd "enjoys good Health [he] is some what thin in flesh."[24]

The real object of Tyrrell's visit to Joliet, however, was Jack Hughes. At ten in the morning, two hours before Hughes expected to walk out of the penitentiary a free man, Tyrrell informed him that "there was another case against him, that he would have to come to Chicago." Tyrrell had discovered an old charge against Hughes for passing phony five-dollar bills in 1875. Now he planned to indict him and send him back to prison to serve another term.[25] Mullen, however, left the Joliet prison that same day, a free man.

Unlike the Lincoln grave-robbery case, the counterfeiting case against Hughes moved swiftly. On June 19, 1878, less than a month after his release from Joliet and rearrest, Hughes stood trial in Chicago. Before the judge pronounced sentence, he asked Hughes whether he had anything to say. And the man did. Standing before the bench, he characterized himself as "a child of Misfortune." He claimed that bad luck had been following him for three years. He swore he was not guilty of passing counterfeit money, that he was a victim of mistaken identity. And then he brought up Lewis Swegles, spinning a wild story of how Swegles had tried to sell him a gold watch that had belonged to a murdered man named Nathan. It was yet another put-up job, another plot against the long-suffering Hughes. If he had been so foolish as to buy the watch, Hughes assured the court, Swegles would have had him arrested and the gold watch in his pocket would have been enough to indict Hughes falsely on the charge of murdering Nathan.

The judge endured it all patiently. Then, when Hughes was finished, he delivered a little lecture to the prisoner itemizing the evidence against him, which left no doubt in the judge's mind that he was guilty of passing bad money. The judge sent Hughes back to Joliet for three years at hard labor.[26]

As for Terence Mullen, he may have walked out of prison a free man, but he was also an impoverished one. While he had been incarcerated, Kennally had sold the Hub and vanished with the proceeds. Not long after Mullen got out, Elmer Washburn ran into him on the street in Chicago. What with his saloon sold out from under him and Kennally nowhere to be found, Mullen was "dead broke." Soon thereafter, he too disappeared. Lewis Swegles, by February 1880, was at the state penitentiary in Joliet serving a twelve-year sentence for burglary.[27]

On March 20, 1880, Tyrrell was in St. Louis and packing for a trip to Washington, D.C., to see the chief of the Secret Service, James Brooks, when he was interrupted by a visit from an operative named Hall. He had Terence Mullen in custody for passing counterfeit currency—would Tyrrell like to see him? Tyrrell dropped what he was doing and at once went with Hall to the jail. There Mullen made the Secret Service men an offer. They had been chasing Kennally for some time now without success—Mullen was ready to turn in his "old Pal." At first, Tyrrell could not believe that Mullen meant what he said. But the more they talked, the more Tyrrell understood that Mullen was willing to cut a deal for two reasons; first, because Kennally had robbed Mullen of his living when he sold the

Hub; and second, because Mullen knew "his own neck [was] in the halter." Seeing Mullen prepared to turn informer and Kennally almost within his grasp, Tyrrell could not imagine leaving town on a long trip to Washington. He sent his excuses to Brooks, explaining, "The importance of these parties with my personal Knowledge of the men Mullen and Kinnelly [*sic*] renders my presence here at present of some value." On April 14, acting on information from Mullen, Secret Service operatives in St. Louis found and arrested Kennally.[28] Big Jim went to prison, but he was out again within two years. The last reference to Kennally in Tyrrell's daily reports is dated November 18, 1882. Tyrrell notes that Kennally was one of several prisoners appearing in court that day and that he was sentenced to a year at the penitentiary in Chester, Illinois. Tyrrell doesn't mention the charge, but it is a safe assumption that Kennally was sent up for counterfeiting.[29]

Back in Springfield, something always seemed to be amiss at the Lincoln Monument. Before dawn on February 5, 1884, Power arrived at the monument. It was not his usual hour to start work, but delegates from a state organization known as Mutual Aid had arrived in Springfield the night before; years of experience had taught Power to expect a steady stream of visitors as long as the convention was in town. He was just writing the heading for the day in the visitors' register when he heard a tremendous crash from the corridor on the east side of the building that led to the Lincoln burial chamber. Seizing a lamp, he hurried down the hallway, where he found that one of the brick arches that supported the terrace above the Memorial Hall and the tomb chamber had collapsed. Directly above the wreckage he could see the paving stones of the terrace still in place, with nothing supporting them save force of habit. They were sure to give way as soon as someone stepped on the terrace pavement.[30]

With the first visitors of the day likely to arrive at any moment, the frantic custodian began hauling wooden boards out to the exterior of the monument, to block the entrance to the terrace staircase. (It is odd, but in every emergency during Power's long administration of the Lincoln Monument, it appears there was always a cache a spare lumber at hand.) Three-quarters of an hour later he finished the job, just as the first streetcar full of conventioneers came through the cemetery gates.

Bad as the collapse of the arch was, it could have been worse. Power shuddered to think what might have happened if visitors had been strolling on the terrace at the time or walking through the passageway en route to the Lincoln burial chamber. But relief soon gave way to anger. "I never think of the events of that morning," Power wrote, "without a feeling of astonishment that the people of our State do not demand legislation holding any and all architects, contractors and superintendents guilty of man-slaughter who, through ignorance, incompetence or greed of gain, constructs a building that falls and causes loss of life."[31] The editors of the *Chicago Inter-Ocean* agreed with Power. Outraged that the Lincoln Monument was "already falling into ruin," the editors denounced the "unscrupulous contractor" who had committed such "a fraud" on the American people.[32]

It took all summer long in 1884 for workmen to rebuild the collapsed portion of the monument. While they were on hand, Power and the members of the Monument Association had them open a ventilation shaft into the basement of the tomb. It was heavy work cutting through the monument's three-and-a-half-foot-thick brick foundation, and the fastidious Power must have found the noise, dust, and disruption irritating. Much more troubling was the knowledge that day after day workmen were trampling over the graves of Abraham and Mary Lincoln and Power could not do or say anything, without drawing attention to the secret burial place.

Rumors that the president was not resting in the handsome marble sarcophagus in the burial chamber had been circulating since 1876, when the foreman of work crew and Power's own assistant had betrayed his trust and spread the word around Springfield that Abraham Lincoln's coffin was hidden in the basement of the monument. Those rumors had never dissipated. As the *Illinois Daily Journal* put it, "in Springfield it has been well understood that [Abraham Lincoln's remains] are not in the marble sarcophagus always shown to visitors in the north hall of the monument and where the public supposes they are."[33] Out-of-town visitors were not quite so well informed. Whenever one of them asked John Carroll Power whether Abraham Lincoln's body was truly inside the sarcophagus, he solemnly assured them that it was. In other words, he lied; and not just occasionally, but as he himself confessed, "many times a day, for weeks and months and years." He had no choice. The admission that Lincoln and his wife were lying in shallow graves in a mildewed cellar would have scandalized the nation and brought shame on the gentlemen of the Monument Association and the city of Springfield, and, in the public outcry that would undoubtedly have followed, might even cost Power his job. It would also have tipped off potential copycat grave robbers about the exact location of their prize.[34]

To soothe his conscience, he came up with a pat reply to anyone who asked whether Lincoln's body was indeed in the sarcophagus: "We put it back there," he would say, "the second day after the attempt to steal it." And indeed, Power and his helpers had returned the coffin to the sarcophagus two days after the break-in. Granted, he made no mention of what they had done with the body later, but if that was a sin, it was a sin of omission.

Some visitors were more persistent in their interrogation of the custodian than others, and for them Power had another pat answer. "I suppose you wish to know if there is not further danger [to Lincoln's body]," he would say. "If so, I can assure you that it is absolutely safe." He even had a prepared follow-up answer for visitors who wanted to know more about security at the monument. "If I was to explain what precautions have been taken to make it safe," he would say, "it would not be so any longer and I would prove myself unworthy of the confidence reposed in me."[35]

There was one kind of visitor, however, who could make Power lose his composure and work him into a white-hot fury. He loathed "upstart" journalists who, eager for a sensational scoop, wheedled and hectored and abused the custodian, hoping he would lose his temper and disclose some secret about the tomb.[36] Power never did take any journalist's bait; nonetheless, the shabby burial of Abraham and Mary Lincoln weighed on him. He lobbied the members of the Monument Association to find some new, dignified, yet completely secure method of interring Lincoln's remains—and he believed he had the solution. Power suggested transferring Lincoln's body to a steel casket "so hard and strong and ponderous that it could not be broken [into] or removed." For a brief time the Monument Association adopted Power's idea, but then it let it languish until February 1887, when Power took it upon himself to consult a contractor named Joseph O. Irwin about what might best be done to safeguard the president's body. The sarcophagus was the problem, Irwin said, and as long as the coffin was kept in the sarcophagus, there was no way to make it secure. He suggested in-ground burial, but with improvements. In his bid for the job, Irwin proposed to dig a vault in the catacomb chamber "five feet wide, seven and a half feet long and six feet deep." The vault would be lined with an eighteen-inch-thick wall of "hard-burned brick laid in good cement mortar." Once the Lincoln coffin was in place in the new vault, the space around it would be filled up to the coffin lid with wet cement. After it dried, a final layer of wet cement would be poured on top, completely sealing the coffin. Actually, *coffins*, for Mary Todd Lincoln would be buried in the same vault, beside her husband.[37] Power and the members of the Monument Association gave their approval to the plan.

It took Irwin and his work crew only three days to excavate and build the brick vault in the catacomb of the Lincoln Monument. The members of the Lincoln Guard of Honor set April 14, 1887—the twenty-second anniversary of the day Abraham Lincoln had been shot at Ford's Theatre—as the day for the exhumation and reburial of Abraham and Mary Lincoln. The Guard thought it proper to invite the members of the Monument Association to the ceremony, so Power sent out notes asking them to assemble in the catacomb at nine in the morning on the appointed day. The ceremony would not be open to the general public—on this point Power's note was emphatic. "It is thought best that it be strictly private," he wrote. "Do not, on any account, let a reporter know it."[38]

But someone leaked the story to the Springfield press anyway.

On the morning of April 14, the two Springfield newspapers ran stories on the new vault at the Lincoln Monument and confirmed what citizens of the town had suspected and whispered to one another for eleven years—that since the grave robbery in 1876 the white marble sarcophagus in the catacomb had been empty; Abraham Lincoln's body had been concealed in a secret location somewhere inside the monument. The newspapers also disclosed that the Lincoln Guard of Honor's annual observances in Lincoln's honor were a front—they were not a memorial association but an actual guard "devoted to the security of the martyr's remains and . . . bound together by oath, to keep their knowledge in regard to [Lincoln's] resting place a profound secret."[39]

The secret was out. Yet that realization vexed John Carroll Power less than the newspaper's assertion that a formal oath obliged the members of the Lincoln Guard of Honor to keep the secret of Lincoln's grave. Bristling a bit, Power insisted, "We were never bound by any oath, but something much stronger—our own sense of honor—for to a man who will not be bound by that, an oath is a mere cord of sand."

Surprisingly, the sensational revelation about the Lincoln burial place did not draw a crowd of curious spectators to Oak Ridge Cemetery. A small handful of gawkers came out, enough to create an annoyance, as Power put it, but far fewer than the Guard had feared.[40] Among the first to show up at the Lincoln Monument was a reporter from the *Illinois Daily Journal*, who arrived at the cemetery by streetcar at eight o'clock in the morning. We do not know the reporter's identity; the story he wrote for his newspaper bore no byline, for it was not common practice in nineteenth-century journalism to include one.

Like any other tourist, he paid his twenty-five cents and

asked to be shown around the monument, but no one came out to give the newspaperman a tour. Meanwhile, he watched as in pairs or small groups all the members of the Lincoln Guard of Honor pulled up in carriages before the tomb. Joseph Irwin, the contractor, along with his brother Wash and several workman, were busy around the place, collecting tools. Then all the invited guests went inside Memorial Hall; the reporter heard the click as someone locked the door. Standing outside the door were the reporter and a black hack driver. "The latter did not want in," the reporter wrote, "but the former did." A few minutes later Power came outside and tried to get the reporter to leave, but "he did not go." Disgusted, Power went back inside. Through the locked the door the reporter heard the custodian say, "I guess we might as well go to work."

It was quiet for a time; then, suddenly, Jacob Bunn, the Lincoln family's banker, emerged from Memorial Hall. "He looked sick," the reporter said, "and wanted fresh air."

Then George N. Black, a member of the Lincoln Monument Association, came to the door and beckoned to his son, who was waiting some distance from the tomb. That was all the excuse the reporter needed. Arguing that the rules had just been broken, that someone without a proper invitation had been allowed to enter the tomb, the newspaperman insisted that he should be admitted too. The dignitaries relented and let him in.[41]

In addition to seven members of the Guard besides Power (their president, Gustavus Dana, was out of town) and the six members of the Monument Association, other invited guests included Joseph Irwin, the contractor, with several workmen; Meredith Cooper, the sexton of Oak Ridge Cemetery; Power's assistant, George W. Trotter; Springfield undertaker Thomas

Smith; and Leon Hopkins, a plumber. The anonymous newspaperman was the only journalist present. In the presence of these witnesses, the coffins of Abraham and Mary Lincoln were brought up from the basement and laid on trestles in Memorial Hall. Then the vice president of the Guard, Jasper Reece, made a little speech addressed to the members of the Monument Association. "The Lincoln Guard of Honor has never assumed that it is their province to examine and decide upon the identity of the remains," he said; "[it] belongs exclusively to your Association to do that. Having exhumed the bodies, we hereby certify that they are in the identical enclosures in which we received them and that the enclosures have never been broken except as stated in our historical account. In this condition we turn them over to your Association, thus terminating what has been to us a labor of love and veneration."[42]

According to Power, once Reece had concluded his speech, the members of the Monument Association, "by mutual agreement, decided that in order to satisfy the reasonable expectations of the people, after so many changes, it was indispensably necessary to identify the body of the President."[43] The decision was not as impulsive or ad hoc as Power suggests. The members of the Guard and the Monument Association had planned to open Abraham Lincoln's coffin—that was why Hopkins the plumber had been invited to the ceremony. What is odd is the choice of witnesses. Power says, "Of the eighteen or nineteen persons present, nearly all had personally seen the President in life." Seen, yes; known—well, that was something else. Two of the guests in Memorial Hall that morning had been acquainted with the Lincolns. James C. Conkling had served as mayor of Springfield while the Lincolns lived in town and had been a staunch Lincoln man during the elections of 1860 and 1864.

John Williams's son George had played with the Lincoln's boy Tad.[44] But if the Guard and the Monument Association wanted absolute, incontrovertible verification of the remains, why had they not invited more people like the Lincoln family's banker and financial adviser, Jacob Bunn, who had not merely "seen the President," but been close to him?

It would not have been hard to round up reliable witnesses. Springfield in 1887 was filled with Lincoln relatives, friends, acquaintances, and political allies, including Ann Todd Smith, Mary's sister and one of Abraham's favorite in-laws; Frances Todd Wallace, Mary's youngest sister and a witness at the Lincolns' wedding; Ninian and Elizabeth Todd Edwards, who had hosted the Lincoln wedding and had given Mary a home during the last two years of her life; James Matheny, Lincoln's best man; Mary Remann, the Lincolns' favorite neighbor; Ozias Hatch, perhaps the Lincolns' closest friend in Springfield; and William Herndon, Abraham's law partner and Mary's nemesis.[45] Most conspicuous by his absence was Robert Lincoln. He was still living in Chicago in 1887 and could have made the train trip to Springfield easily.[46] Why the Guard and the Monument Association did not invite the Lincolns' sole surviving child remains a mystery.

As Smith, the undertaker, removed the lid of the cedar coffin, the exclusive little group in Memorial Hall gathered around Abraham Lincoln's coffin. They watched as Hopkins the plumber made three cuts into the lead inner coffin—across the top and then three feet down along each side. Carefully, he peeled back the soft metal, revealing the face and upper chest of the corpse within. The remains were "somewhat shrunken," but none of the onlookers doubted that they were looking upon the face of Abraham Lincoln. Power described Lincoln's features as "almost as perfect as they are in the bronze statue on the Monument and the color is about as dark as the statue." The dark color, of course, was the result of the contrecoup bruising caused by John Wilkes Booth's bullet.[47]

The reporter for the *Journal* concurred. "The remains were a remarkable case of preservation," he wrote. "Those who stood around and had known Lincoln when alive easily discerned the features. They were very distinct."[48]

The coffin of Mary Lincoln was not opened for identification. For fifteen or twenty minutes, Abraham Lincoln lay exposed to view. Then Hopkins rolled the lead back in place and soldered it shut.[49]

As Lincoln's body lay in state in the New York city hall, Jeremiah Gurney took this photograph. It is the only surviving image of Lincoln in death—Secretary of War Edwin Stanton ordered all other such photographs destroyed. (Courtesy of the Abraham Lincoln Presidential Library)

In Union Square in New York City the Lincoln funeral procession passed the house of Cornelius Roosevelt (seen on the left). The two small figures looking out the second story corner window are six-year-old Theodore Roosevelt and his four-year-old brother Elliott. (Courtesy of the Theodore Roosevelt Collection, Harvard College Library)

In preparation for the funeral, virtually every building in Springfield, Illinois, was draped in mourning. The commercial building pictured here housed Lincoln's law office. (Courtesy of the Abraham Lincoln Presidential Library)

While a grand monument was being built at Oak Ridge Cemetery, Lincoln and his sons Eddie and Willie lay within this small temporary tomb. This engraving depicts Mary Todd Lincoln at her husband's resting place with her sons Tad and Robert in December 1865. It is the only time she visited Lincoln's grave. (Library of Congress)

This stereopticon photograph depicts the Lincoln Monument as it appeared in 1883, when the president's body lay hidden in a shallow grave in the basement. (Courtesy of the Abraham Lincoln Presidential Library)

In 1872 Mary Todd Lincoln visited the Boston studio of William Mumler, a "spirit photographer" who specialized in portraits that included the ghostly image of the sitter's deceased love one. (Courtesy of the Abraham Lincoln Presidential Library)

Terence Mullen made counterfeiters welcome at the Hub, the Chicago saloon and billiard parlor he owned with Big Jim Kennally. (Courtesy of the Abraham Lincoln Presidential Library)

A notorious passer of counterfeit money, Jack Hughes was also a first-rate con man who spun an elaborate tale of how he and Mullen were the innocent victims of a conspiracy hatched by the Secret Service and the Chicago police. (Courtesy of the Abraham Lincoln Presidential Library)

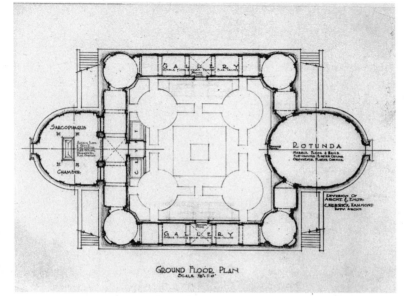

GROUND FLOOR PLAN
SCALE 16'=1'-0"

In the original design of the Lincoln Monument, there was no direct access from the Rotunda to the tomb chamber. In 1876 visitors to Lincoln's grave walked around to the back of the monument, where a steel door opened into the room known as the catacomb. There Lincoln's remains lay aboveground inside a white marble sarcophagus. (Courtesy of the Abraham Lincoln Presidential Library)

Technically, Secret Service detective Patrick D. Tyrrell's job was to hunt down counterfeiters. Because the grave robbers in this case were involved in counterfeiting, however, Tyrrell's superiors authorized him to take on the case. (Courtesy of R. Emmett Tyrrell, Jr.)

During his two-year stint as chief of the Secret Service, Elmer Washburn put an end to corruption within the bureau, held all detectives to a high ethical standard, and improved its performance. (Courtesy of the U.S. Secret Service)

The attempt to steal Lincoln's body traumatized the custodian of the Lincoln Monument, John Carroll Power. For the rest of his life he went to enormous lengths to keep the president's body secure. (Courtesy of the Abraham Lincoln Presidential Library)

Within hours of the break-in, Power had an artist draw the Lincoln tomb chamber as it appeared after Mullen and Hughes had fled. The sarcophagus lid leans against the rear wall. The front panel of the sarcophagus, bearing the inscription "LINCOLN," has been sawed off, and the president's coffin has been dragged out just a few inches—all that the grave robbers could manage, given the weight of the box. (Courtesy of the Abraham Lincoln Presidential Library)

When they ran from Oak Ridge Cemetery, Mullen and Hughes left their tools in the tomb chamber. Tyrrell confiscated them as evidence, but after the trial he presented them to Power, who put them on display in his little Lincoln museum in Memorial Hall. (Courtesy of the Abraham Lincoln Presidential Library)

Robert Todd Lincoln's emotional response to the assault on his father's body is unknown. His surviving letters discuss the business of the upcoming trial but offer no hint of what he may have felt about the attempted grave robbery. (Courtesy of the Abraham Lincoln Presidential Library)

Judge David Davis was among the most dependable of Abraham Lincoln's political allies. After the president's assassination the Lincoln family asked Davis to settle the estate, and in 1877 Robert Lincoln asked Davis for help in collecting from the U.S. treasury the money already paid out to witnesses in the grave robbery trial. (Library of Congress)

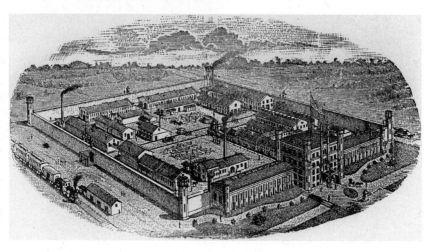

The Illinois State Penitentiary in Joliet, where the crime boss Big Jim Kennally, the grave robbers Terence Mullen and Jack Hughes, and the counterfeiters Benjamin Boyd and Nelson Driggs all did time. (Courtesy of the Abraham Lincoln Presidential Library)

The bitter dispute over which candidate had won the Hayes-Tilden presidential election, depicted here in a cartoon by Thomas Nast, dominated the national news and in many cases drove the story of the Lincoln grave robbery from the front pages. (Library of Congress)

George M. Pullman intended his company town to be a model community, complete with this beautifully landscaped park. During an acrimonious labor dispute Pullman took a hard line that not only lost him the goodwill of his workers but made him the most hated man in America.

Before his death Pullman instructed his family to make his body absolutely secure by burying it in concrete—an unusual request that became the inspiration for the final burial of Abraham Lincoln. (Library of Congress)

THE LINCOLN GUARD OF HONOR.

Photo by Pittman.

Publicly, the Springfield businessmen and shopkeepers who formed the Lincoln Guard of Honor described themselves as an organization dedicated to honoring the memory of Abraham Lincoln. Privately, they were a select band who kept the secret of where they had buried the martyred president. (Courtesy of the Abraham Lincoln Presidential Library)

On September 26, 1901, a crane lifted the coffins of the Lincoln family from their temporary vault for reburial in the reconstructed Lincoln Monument. (Courtesy of the Library of Congress)

Without ceremony, workmen carried the coffin of Abraham Lincoln into Memorial Hall. All the men in suits and ties are members of the Lincoln Guard of Honor, except the man at the far right of the photo. He is Will Colvin, a reporter for the *Chicago Inter-Ocean*, who was furious when he was told he would not be permitted to witness the final identification of Lincoln's remains. (Courtesy of the Abraham Lincoln Presidential Library)

Inside the Lincoln Monument individual crypts were prepared for each member of the family. Seen here, from left to right, are the coffins of Eddie and Mary Todd Lincoln, an empty vault, and Tad's coffin. In the foreground is the old white marble sarcophagus that held Abraham Lincoln's coffin on the night of the break-in. (Courtesy of the Abraham Lincoln Presidential Library)

Two Springfield plumbers, Leon P. Hopkins (right), and his brother-in-law, Charles L. Willey, were hired to cut through the lead sheath that sealed Lincoln's coffin and then to resolder it after the body was identified. (Courtesy of the Abraham Lincoln Presidential Library)

After the final identification of the body of Abraham Lincoln, the sixteen invited witnesses posed outside the tomb for a group portrait. The only two women witnesses were Mrs. Clara Kern Bayliss, wife of one of the trustees of the Lincoln Monument, and Mrs. Laura Clinton Johnson, wife of the custodian of the tomb. (Courtesy of the Abraham Lincoln Presidential Library)

At the last minute Joseph Lindley had his thirteen-year-old son Fleetwood released from school, so that he could be present when Lincoln's coffin was opened. Fleetwood Lindley survived until 1963, the last person to have looked upon the face of Abraham Lincoln. (Courtesy of the Abraham Lincoln Presidential Library)

8

A Pullman-Style Burial

It was Larkin G. Meade, a young sculptor and architect from New Hampshire who had studied in Florence, who designed the Lincoln Monument that visitors to Oak Ridge Cemetery see today. The placement of the tomb chamber at the north end of the monument and the Memorial Hall at the south end; the soaring obelisk; the four dramatic sculptures representing the men of the cavalry, infantry, artillery, and navy who had fought for the Union in the Civil War; the bronze statue of Lincoln proclaiming emancipation—they are all the work of Meade and a tribute to his genius. Far less satisfactory, however, was the construction of the monument itself.

The collapse of one of the monument's supporting arches back in 1884 was a tip-off that worse was to come. By 1900 the Lincoln Monument was in precarious condition. The foundation was unstable and the seepage of water between the inner and outer walls of the tomb had caused tremendous damage to the fabric of the building. The only option was to disassemble the monument, dig down to bedrock, and lay a new foundation, then rebuild the entire structure. Of course, the bodies of the Lincoln family would have to be removed from the monument and placed in a secure location—again.[1]

The project was a tremendous undertaking and an expensive one; the Illinois state legislature appropriated a hundred thousand dollars for the reconstruction. The toughest part would be removing the coffins of Abraham and Mary Lincoln. Since 1887 they had been sealed in concrete beneath the floor of the catacomb. It took a dozen workmen a week to hack their way through the solid cement before they reached the wooden outer coffins. Water damage had reached here, too, rotting the wood; a few more years and the moisture would have seeped into the Lincolns' lead coffins. Barely attached to the decaying wooden lid of one box, the workmen found a silver plate, eight inches square, inscribed,

Abraham Lincoln
Born February 12, 1809
Died April 15, 1865

For safekeeping, a workman handed the plate up to Edward S. Johnson, one of the original members of the Lincoln Guard of Honor and by that time the custodian of the Lincoln Monument.[2]

Twenty-four years had passed since Terence Mullen and Jack Hughes had broken into the Lincoln tomb chamber with the intention of carrying off the president's body, but the people of Springfield had not forgotten. While the workmen chipped through the concrete, guards were posted at the tomb round the clock and the general public was not allowed near the monument. As for the Lincoln family's temporary vault, it sounds like something built for a pharaoh. The chamber was twelve feet square with solid concrete walls a foot thick. Once the coffins were inside, the vault would be sealed with four stone slabs, each weighing two tons. Over that the contractors intended to pile a mound of earth thirty feet high.[3] Before the transfer to the temporary vault, Abraham Lincoln's and Mary Lincoln's lead coffins were encased in fresh wooden crates, exactly like the crate Adam Johnston had built in 1876 to shield the president's coffin.[4] Wooden crates were also on hand for the coffins of the Lincoln children and grandson.[5]

The transfer took place at eleven in the morning on Saturday March 10, 1900. About fifty spectators had come out to the cemetery to watch as a big crane lifted the ponderous lead coffins of the president and the First Lady, swung them over to the vault, then lowered them into the temporary tomb. Over the coffins the crane dropped in place two of the massive stone slabs. On top of those slabs, the coffins of the Lincolns' three youngest sons and grandson were placed; they too were sealed beneath two stone slabs. A reporter for Springfield's *Journal* assured readers: "A dozen vandals working all night, with a clear field, could not remove the bodies or any one of them from the depository. No chances will be taken, however, and until a mound of debris and earth is built over the vault, a guard will be on watch every minute of the day and night."[6]

Lying in the temporary vault with Abraham and Mary Lincoln were not only the remains of their sons Edward, William, and Thomas, but also the body of their only grandson, Abraham Lincoln II, Robert Lincoln's boy. In 1889 Jack, as the family called him, had been sixteen years old. As part of his preparations to enter Harvard the following year, Jack had enrolled at a school in Versailles, France, where he hoped to polish up his French language skills. That November the boy noticed a carbuncle on the underside of his arm. A French physician convinced him to submit to an operation to remove the multi-headed boil. But the surgery did not go well; the incision refused to heal. Jack Lincoln was suffering from blood poisoning.

His parents moved Jack to London, where Robert Lincoln was serving as the United States ambassador to Great Britain, but the British doctors were no more successful than their French colleagues in reversing the infection. After four months of useless treatments, Abraham Lincoln II died on March 5, 1890. In a letter to his father's old secretary John Nicolay, Robert, for once, opened his heart. "Our boy's life was very precious to us," he said, "and as his character & ability became year by year more assured, I had good reason for setting no limit in our hopes for him. Now that there is nothing left but a memory, the loss is very hard to bear."[7] Robert Lincoln escorted his son's body from London to Springfield, where it was entombed in the family crypt.[8]

The six Lincolns remained in the temporary vault for eighteen months while a construction crew rebuilt the Lincoln Monument. When the reconstruction was complete, in September 1901, a work crew cleared away the great mound of earth, a crane removed the heavy stone slabs, and the contractor's men, serving as impromptu pallbearers, carried the coffins of the Lincoln family into the monument. Crypts had been prepared in the wall facing the catacomb chamber for Mary, her three sons, and her grandson. Incredibly, Abraham Lincoln's coffin would be placed in the old aboveground marble sarcophagus—the exact box that Mullen and Hughes had vandalized twenty-five years earlier.

When word of this arrangement reached Robert Lincoln, he sent a telegram to Illinois governor Richard Yates to say he was coming, and boarded a train to Springfield. Yates was waiting on the platform when the train pulled into the Springfield depot at four in the afternoon on May 23, 1901. He escorted Robert through the depot to his private carriage, and together they drove out to Oak Ridge Cemetery. Edward Johnson, the custodian, was waiting to receive them and show Robert Lincoln and the governor around the rebuilt monument. When they got to the catacomb, Robert spoke candidly about his objections—his father's remains were in the same spot where they had been in 1876 and were just as vulnerable to desecration. Johnson tried to reassure Robert by pointing out the new heavy steel door at the back of the tomb chamber and reminding the president's son that now the custodian lived in a handsome stone house right next door to the monument. But Robert Lincoln was not satisfied. Nothing was resolved that afternoon, not least of all because as the three men wrestled with the problem, a messenger arrived with word that John Riley Tanner, former governor of Illinois, had just died. Yates was obliged to leave at once, to pay a call on the Tanner family.[9]

One wonders how much thought Robert devoted to the problem of security at his family's tomb once he was back home in Chicago. He was a busy man by then; in 1897 he had been named permanent president of the Pullman Company, succeeding the company founder, George M. Pullman. Robert was not a surprise candidate for the job; he had a head for business, and he had learned a great deal about the palace car industry during the years when he had served as George Pullman's attorney. In fact, Robert was Pullman's attorney during the infamous Pullman Strike; and the advice he appears to have given his client at the time did nothing to enhance Robert's reputation, either in his own day or at any time since.[10]

George Pullman belonged to the nineteenth century's bumper crop of entrepreneurs who saw something the American public needed, delivered it, and made a fortune from it. Pullman's contribution to American life was luxury sleeper cars. Before Pullman, passengers who tried to sleep on long-distance trains were in for a foretaste of purgatory. The compartments had no ventilation; the berths were cramped; the mattresses and pillows were rough and lumpy; and sheets and blankets, if they were supplied at all, were soiled. Railroad owners conceded that their sleepers were dreadful, but since the cars were dirt cheap to build—only five thousand dollars each—and no company was offering anything better at a competitive price, the railroads felt no incentive to improve their service.

In the early 1860s, George Pullman took aim at the sleeper car industry, by producing a sleeper car that would transform long-distance rail travel. He called his prototype the Pioneer and modeled it on the comforts provided by fine hotels. The cars were paneled in gleaming wood, the floors covered with thick, expensive carpets; the beds were soft, comfortable, and spotlessly clean; and each well-ventilated car featured its own immaculate washroom. The only problem with Pullman's magnificent new Pioneer car was the cost—eighteen thousand dollars.[11] Railroad owners refused to buy anything so outrageously expensive. But Pullman insisted that his cars would pay for themselves if the railroad magnates charged every passenger who wanted a berth on a Pullman sleeper an extra fifty cents. Pullman's instincts were correct—the American traveler was happy to pay fifty cents for a restful night in a luxurious Pullman car.[12]

And Pullman's innovations kept coming. He added restaurant cars and parlor cars to his product line, until three-quarters of the railroad lines in the United States made use exclusively of Pullman's luxury railway cars.[13] By the end of the 1892–93 fiscal year, the Pullman Palace Car Company showed tremendous growth—it employed fifty-five hundred men and women, had assets valued at $62 million, and showed a profit that year of $6.5 million.[14] George Pullman's profits, however, were not limited to sales of deluxe train cars.

In 1880 Pullman purchased five hundred acres of prairie south of Chicago and built on it a model town where his employees would live in close proximity to the company workshops.[15] Pullman hired a twenty-seven-year-old architect from New York, Solon Spencer Beman, to build his utopia—and Pullman intended it to be a utopia. Most of the homes in Pullman (as he named the town) were constructed of red brick; they were airy and laid out on broad tree-shaded streets, and they received plenty of natural light. Gas and water were supplied to all the homes. There were stores, offices for doctors and lawyers, a library, a theater, a bank, a hotel (which housed the only bar in town—for the use of hotel guests, not Pullman residents), a park, an athletic field, an ornamental lake, a vegetable farm, and stables. There was nothing cheap or ugly about the place.[16] Pullman, however, was not giving all of this away for free—the profit motive underlay his paternalism. He sold the gas he supplied to every home in town at the rate of $2.25 per thousand cubic feet; in Chicago, the rate was $1.25. The rent for homes in Pullman—George Pullman adamantly refused to permit anyone to buy property in his town—averaged 20 to 25 percent higher than the going rate in surrounding communities.[17] When it came to churches, initially Pullman would not permit any religious denomination to build one in his town. Congregations were welcome to hold religious services in any of the town community halls, and for the privilege, Pullman charged them rent, on average about five hundred dollars a year. In most cases the congregations of laborers could not raise the sum required and had to rely on the charity of their fellow Catholics, or Lutherans or Methodists, outside Pullman, in order to pay the rent for a place to worship.[18] As for the library, Pullman charged borrowers an annual fee of three dollars—about half a week's wages for many Pullman employees. Consequently, out of the town's 4,000 or 5,000 residents, only about 250 had paid for the privilege of borrowing books from the library.[19]

George Pullman saw himself as a man who not only provided the best for his employees but also knew what was good for them. Since elections were a tricky business—you could never tell what candidate the people would vote into office—the Pullman Company appointed all town officials. The residents of Pullman elected the members of the school board, but they all worked for the company and took their cues from upper management. Even in national and city elections (the town of Pullman was considered part of Chicago), George Pullman tried to exert his influence. Pullman handpicked one of his own employees, James Chasey, to run for alderman, then sent his managers into the factories and shops to campaign for him. During their campaign tours of the shop floor, Pullman's men made veiled threats about what might happen to any worker who did not support the Pullman candidate. When three Pullman employees were foolish enough to say they were supporting Chasey's rival, they were fired. During the presidential campaign of 1892, Pullman held a mass meeting for his workers and delivered a speech in which he warned them that if they did not vote against the Democrat, Grover Cleveland, he would not be responsible for anything that might follow. In defiance of their boss, the men of Pullman voted overwhelmingly for Cleveland.[20]

Then in 1893 the Reading Railroad, bogged down by debts, went into receivership. The collapse of one of the major railway lines in the eastern United States had a ripple effect that brought down hundreds of banks and other businesses that had relied on the Reading as an important client. The resulting economic turmoil created an economic depression that lingered for four years.

The Pullman Company did not go unscathed by the downturn in business: orders for new cars dried up, and pending orders were canceled. Operating on the principle that it was necessary to be hard and realistic to succeed in business, George Pullman personally made the decision to reduce the wages of all his employees. Under the new wage scale, freight car builders experienced the worst decline, as their salaries dropped by 41 percent. Painters were the best off—they saw "only" a 17.5 percent reduction in their pay.[21] Under the circumstances, one might have expected Pullman to make comparable cuts in the fees he charged for gas heat and in the rent he demanded for employee housing. This he did not do, arguing there was no connection between what he paid his workers and what he charged for rent. Many Pullman workers, however, judged otherwise. With their drastically reduced wages, Pullman employees faced a grim choice—they could feed their families, or they could pay their rent; they could not do both. As more and more workers fell into arrears, the company adopted a new strategy. Workers' salaries were sent directly to the town bank. On payday the workers lined up at the tellers' windows, where they were informed how much they had made, how much they owed for rent, and how much, if anything, was left over. The town's Methodist pastor, Rev. William Carwardine, recorded pathetic scenes of skilled working men weeping because they had only one dollar or less on which to feed their families until the next payday, two weeks away.[22] As for the Pullman fore-men, superintendents, and upper managers, their salaries remained untouched. George Pullman defended this policy by arguing that if he reduced the salaries of such able, experienced managers, they would leave him to find work elsewhere.[23]

In May 1894 the workers sent a delegation of forty-six men to lay their grievances before George Pullman. They asked that their old salary levels be restored or that the rents be reduced. Pullman rejected both requests. The next day, three men who had presented the workers' grievances to Pullman were fired. The day after that, May 11, 1894, three thousand Pullman employees walked off the job.[24]

For the next month both strikers and Pullman Company executives remained entrenched. No acts of anarchy or violence took place in the town of Pullman; the situation of the workers was tragic, but they kept the peace. In its report to the United States Senate on the Pullman Strike, the members of the U.S. Strike Commission said of the strikers, "Such dignified, manly and conservative conduct in the midst of excitement and threatened starvation is worthy of the highest type of American citizenship."[25] As for George Pullman, he remained unmoved, refusing even to accept arbitration in the crisis. "Arbitration," he said, "always implies acquiescence."[26]

By coincidence, one month after the Pullman workers walked off the job, the members of the American Railway Union gathered in Chicago for their first convention. The situation in Pullman was on everyone's mind, and some of the delegates made the short trip to the company town to learn about the workers' grievances firsthand. The stories they brought back to the convention fired up the conventioneers—so much so that on June 26 the union voted for a nationwide boycott of any train that carried Pullman cars.[27] Suddenly the Pullman Strike was no longer a local dispute between labor and management; it was a national transportation crisis. Chicago alone was the hub for twenty-six different railroad lines; the disruption of rail service could paralyze the city's economy and affect businesses, consumers, and travelers all over the United States. Operating on the flimsy premise that the railroad boycott was an illegal obstruction of the U.S. mail, President Grover Cleveland sent federal troops to Chicago to ensure—at gunpoint if necessary—that the trains would run. Some fourteen thousand U.S. troops and Illinois National Guardsmen were deployed to Chicago.[28]

As the troops took up position around the city, the mood of Chicagoans turned ugly. On July 6 an angry mob of approximately six thousand entered the train yards, setting fires that consumed seven hundred railroad cars. The next day, a train guarded by men of the National Guard tried to make its way out of town. At Loomis Street, several thousand people blocked the tracks, showering the train with stones, while those in the crowd who had guns took potshots at the train crew and the guardsmen. The commanding officer ordered his

men into formation for a bayonet charge, a tactic that succeeded in scattering the crowd, but not before several rioters
were severely wounded. As the train tried once again to move
out, the mob renewed its attack. This time the troops were ordered to open fire. They kept firing into the crowd until the
streets were clear. The casualties for the day were four dead
and more than twenty wounded among the rioters; four soldiers and a lieutenant wounded on the other side. As for the
town of Pullman, troops stationed there had not a single violent incident to report.[29]

By July 10, the military had restored order to Chicago; and
by July 13 the trains were running freely again.[30] It was a death
knell for the strike. The end came on July 18, when the Pullman Company issued a statement that it was ready to reopen
its shops and factories. Leaders of the strike and other Pullman
employees who had been active in the labor agitation were
barred from applying for work. All others were welcome back,
as long as they surrendered their American Railway Union
membership cards and signed a statement never to join a
union. The terms of employment were the same as before the
strike—no raise in pay, no reduction in rent.

The Pullman Strike had cost the U.S. economy eighty million dollars, but it had done nothing to alleviate the hard-
ships of the Pullman workers.[31] If anything, for many strikers and their families, it had made their lives worse. Illinois
governor John Peter Altgeld visited the company town and
found out-of-work former Pullman employees who were on
the verge of starvation.[32] Governor Altgeld made a personal
appeal to George Pullman: "The State of Illinois has not the
least desire to meddle in the affairs of your company, but it
cannot allow a whole community within its borders to perish of

hunger." But the tycoon, in a rebuff to the governor, placed the blame on the blackballed ex-workers. So the governor called upon the people of Illinois to open their hearts and wallets. Almost overnight, a thousand bags of flour and four thousand pounds of rice arrived in Pullman. And the relief kept coming.[33]

In January 1895 labor activist Eugene V. Debs went on trial for his part in the Pullman Strike; the charge was conspiracy. Debs's attorney, Clarence Darrow, subpoenaed George Pullman to testify.[34] When the deputy marshal arrived at the Pullman Building with the writ, he was told, after some delay, that Mr. Pullman was not in the office. In fact, Pullman had been in the office; when he learned that the deputy marshal was waiting for him, he left the building and left Chicago. Pullman did not return to Chicago until the trial had ended. Then, accompanied by his attorney, Robert Lincoln, he called on the presiding judge of the Debs trial, Peter S. Grosscup. In the comfort of the judge's home, Robert Lincoln worked out an amicable agreement by which his client was excused for dodging a subpoena.[35]

During the last two years of his life, George Pullman had the dubious distinction of being one of the most despised men in America. He received death threats, and at least two attempts were made on his life. In November 1895, a janitor who worked at the Pullman Building threatened to shoot Pullman. A month later a pipe bomb arrived in the mail at Pullman's house.[36]

After Pullman died of a massive heart attack on October 18, 1897, his family found written instructions regarding the manner in which he wanted to be buried. Pullman knew that counterfeiters had tried to steal Abraham Lincoln's body and that grave robbers had held the body of the New York department store tycoon A. T. Stewart for ransom. During the last months of his life, George Pullman feared that his former employees, still nursing an intense hatred of him over the strike, would open his grave and desecrate his body. To frustrate any would-be grave robbers, Pullman gave elaborate orders regarding his burial.

He wanted his body placed in a lead-lined casket. After the viewing, the casket was to be wrapped in tar paper, then coated with asphalt an inch thick. His grave must be thirteen feet long, nine feet wide, and eight feet deep. At the bottom of the grave he wanted an eighteen-inch-thick concrete slab. Once the casket was lowered onto the slab, workmen would construct a steel cage of eight T-rails around the box, then fill the grave with wet cement, sealing George Pullman forever within a massive block of concrete and steel.[37] When the acid-tongued satirist and writer Ambrose Bierce heard of Pullman's burial arrangements, he is reported to have said, "It is clear the family in their bereavement was making sure the sonofabitch wasn't going to get up and come back."[38]

A Pullman-style burial is precisely what Robert Lincoln wanted for his father. It was the Culver Construction Company that had rebuilt the Lincoln Monument. Now Robert invited J. S. Culver, the president of the company, to Chicago to discuss the final disposition of Abraham Lincoln's body. Robert wanted Culver to excavate a vault ten feet deep below the floor of the catacomb chamber at the north end of the monument. He wanted his father's coffin encased in a new wooden box. This chest would be entirely enclosed in a cage of heavy steel bars. When the coffin in its cage was lowered into the vault, Robert wanted it aligned as closely as possible with the dead center of the catacomb. Then the vault would be filled with Portland cement. The steel cage served a dual purpose—it would be one last obstacle to grave robbers and would protect the coffin from being crushed by the weight of the concrete. Robert declared that he would not attend the final burial of his father, but he gave strict instructions that the interment was to be as private as possible. There was to be neither an announcement to the public nor a religious or civil ceremony.[39]

Thursday, September 26, 1901, was chosen as the date for the burial. Twenty-two individuals were selected as witnesses. Among them were the last four surviving members of the Lincoln Guard of Honor—Jasper Reece, Joseph P. Lindley, Clinton L. Conkling, and Edward S. Johnson, who was also custodian of Lincoln Monument. Culver the contractor was there, along with the company superintendent, Arthur L. Meriam, who left a brief account of the final burial. Leon Hopkins the plumber was there, too. There were only two women present—Laura Clinton Johnson, wife of the custodian, and Clara Kern Bayliss, who was standing in for her husband, Alfred Bayliss, one of the trustees of the Lincoln Monument.[40] There was also a thirteen-year-old boy, Fleetwood Lindley, son of Joseph P. Lindley.

Fleetwood was a tall, good-looking boy with light brown hair and a high forehead. He was in school when his teacher told him that she had received an urgent message from his father. Fleetwood was to jump on his bicycle and pedal as fast as he could out to the Lincoln tomb in Oak Ridge Cemetery. As the boy raced through town, he wondered what could be so critical that his teacher would excuse him from class. It was almost noon when he dashed through the cemetery gates, rode his bicycle right up to Memorial Hall, leaped off, and parked the bike against the wall. Inside, as the heavy door swung shut behind him, Fleetwood noticed how dark the room was. The glass in the door had been covered with newspaper, and the chamber was lit by a single lightbulb. In one corner a small electric fan labored without success to dispel the hot, muggy air inside the monument. A small group of people in the chamber were all looking at a coffin resting on two wooden sawhorses in the middle of the hall. All at once, Fleetwood Lindley realized what he was about to see.[41]

It was Robert Lincoln's express wish that his father's coffin not be opened before burial. He felt it was unnecessary, given that the remains had been identified in 1887 and since that time the coffin had never been tampered with. Whether it was a return of the old anxiety about the safety of the president's remains or a desire to see Abraham Lincoln's face one last time, the four members of the Lincoln Guard of Honor, Culver, and the various state officials present agreed to disregard Robert's instructions and open the coffin.

Leon Hopkins cut the lead seal he had made at the conclusion of the last viewing fourteen years earlier and once again peeled back the metal. In later years Fleetwood Lindley would recall that a sharp, unpleasant odor filled Memorial Hall, yet in spite of that, everyone pressed forward to look inside the casket. There, unmistakably, was Abraham Lincoln, perfectly preserved—the wart on his cheek, the tuft of beard on his chin, the unruly black hair. Some of the white chalky makeup that Thomas Lynch, the undertaker, had applied to the president's face in 1865 was still visible; but where the makeup had fallen away, Fleetwood and his fellow witnesses could see that Lincoln's skin was the color of bronze. Lincoln looked like any of the sculptures of him that stood in so many city parks around the country.

Lincoln's black broadcloth suit was flecked with tiny mounds of yellow mold, as well as bits of red fabric, perhaps the remnants of a small American flag that had been laid on the president's chest and that had since disintegrated, just like the fraying remnants of kid gloves they could see on Lincoln's large, powerful hands. The identification complete, Hopkins closed the coffin lid and resoldered the lead. Then, six workmen who had been waiting outside with the newspaper reporters and other spectators were called into Memorial Hall.[42] Under the supervision of Arthur Meriam, the work crew enclosed the coffin in the steel cage, lowered it into the vault, and covered it with wet cement, just as Robert Lincoln had directed.[43]

Fleetwood Lindley never forgot that day in the Memorial Hall, or what he had seen. On January 29, 1963, he was seventy-five years old, a patient in St. John's Hospital in Springfield, preparing for a gall bladder operation, when a reporter for *Life* magazine interviewed him in his hospital room. "I was allowed to hold one of the leather straps as we lowered the casket for the concrete to be poured," he told the reporter. "I was not scared at the time, but I slept with Lincoln for the next six months." Three days after that interview, Fleetwood Lindley, the last person to look upon the face of Abraham Lincoln, died. His family buried him in Oak Ridge Cemetery.[44]

Epilogue:
Safe and Secure at Last

In 1930 the Lincoln tomb required yet another round of repairs. This time the coffins stayed put; but before the contractors went to work, everything else fragile or valuable was cleared out of the tomb. Perhaps because of its size and weight, the white marble sarcophagus that had once held Lincoln's coffin was not locked away in a storage shed but was left exposed outdoors. C. Herrick Hammond, supervising architect for Illinois, felt that the sarcophagus ought to be preserved and was considering where and how to display it, but before Hammond could come to a decision, vandals entered Oak Ridge Cemetery after dark and smashed the sarcophagus to pieces. Some of the bits were carried off, probably as souvenirs.[1]

Like the Lincoln Monument, Ford's Theatre had a rough history. That unhappy, interrupted performance of *Our American Cousin* on April 14, 1865, put the theater out of business. Secretary of War Edwin Stanton issued an order closing the building and barring any future theatrical productions there. As for the owner of the theater, John Ford, he was out of town visiting relatives in Richmond, Virginia, the night of Lincoln's assassination. Four days after his return to Washington, Ford was arrested on suspicion of complicity in the plot against the president. After thirty-nine days in prison, Ford was cleared and released.

In July 1865, a relieved Ford received permission from the government to reopen his theater. He advertised a gala evening of entertainment, but the public turned on him. Deluged with hate mail and threats to burn his theater to the ground, Ford did not know what to do. Once again, Stanton stepped in and seized the property. This time Ford took legal action, demanding that the government at least pay him a fair price for the building. Recognizing the justice of his claim, federal officials wrote Ford a check for a hundred thousand dollars. Of course, the government had no use for a theater, so the interior was gutted, divided into three stories, and converted into office and warehouse space. Between 1867 and 1887 the third floor housed the Army Medical Museum, where the "must-see" exhibit displayed several vertebrae of John Wilkes Booth. In 1964 the building was closed again, as part of an intensive project to restore it to its assassination night appearance. In 1968 Ford's Theatre opened again, with a performance of Stephen Vincent Benet's *John Brown's Body*, the first play staged in the building in 103 years.[2]

As for Henry P. Cattell, who had embalmed Lincoln's body, he gave up the funeral trade in 1869 to become a lithographer. In 1880 he changed careers again and joined the Washington, D.C., police force, where he served until 1914, the year before his death.[3]

The judge who had presided over Mullen and Hughes's trial, Charles S. Zane, left Springfield in 1884 for Utah Territory, where President Chester A. Arthur had appointed him chief justice of the Utah Supreme Court and a judge for the Third Judicial District, which encompassed Salt Lake City. Zane was part of a flood of federal officials sent to Utah for the express purpose of enforcing the Edmunds Act of 1882, which outlawed polygamy in the territory and banned unrepentant polygamists from voting and even from serving on juries.

Although Zane denounced multiple marriage partners as "a scandal to society and a menace to . . . lawful marriage," on the bench he was no more rigid in his enforcement of the Edmunds Act than any other judge in Utah. Nonetheless, Zane became a lightning rod among Mormons because he presided over the notorious Rudger Clawson case.[4] In the courtroom Zane the skeptic squared off against Clawson the Mormon traditionalist. "I much regret that the laws of my country should come in conflict with the laws of God," Clawson said, "but whenever they do, I shall invariably choose the latter." Zane replied, "The constitution of the United States . . . does not protect any person in the practice of polygamy," adding, "the civilized world recognizes [polygamy] as a mere superstition."[5]

Zane spent the rest of his long life in Salt Lake City, where he died of an attack of apoplexy in 1915 at the age of eighty-four.[6] His family brought the judge's body back to Springfield for burial at Oak Ridge Cemetery. Lloyd F. Hamilton, who had argued Mullen and Hughes's case before Judge Zane, served as an honorary pallbearer.[7]

Lloyd Hamilton made a career of defending difficult clients—and usually got them acquitted. When Hamilton died in

1917 at the age of seventy, the *Illinois Daily Journal* eulogized him as "Sangamon County's best lawyer."[8]

In later life Hamilton's co-counsel in the Mullen and Hughes case, Alfred Orendorff, became an inveterate "joiner." He kept up his law practice in Springfield and served as chairman of the Democratic State Central Committee, but he also became vice president of the German-American Loan Association and vice president of the Franklin Life Association, an insurance company. He was one of the civic-minded founders of the Springfield Improvement Association. He was president of the Illinois State Historical Society and president of the Sangamon County Bar Association. And like so many men of his time, Orendorff joined fraternal organizations. He became a leader of the Odd Fellows in Springfield,[9] and he rose in the ranks of the Masons to become a representative to the Sovereign Grand Lodge of the World.[10] Alfred Orendorff died in his bed in 1909 at sixty-four.

After Charles H. Reed successfully prosecuted the Lincoln grave robbery case in 1877, his law practice and his reputation went into decline. At a time when the temperance movement was gaining ground in the United States and reform-minded citizens of Chicago were insisting that saloons be closed on Sundays, Reed became the defense attorney for an unsavory group of distillers and saloon owners known in Chicago as the Whisky Ring. He even traveled to Washington to lobby on behalf of his clients. From that point on, Reed's life could be described as in free fall. In 1880 he was serving as executor of the estate of the late S. Addison Irving when the dead man's heirs charged him with failing to report twenty thousand dollars of the estate's money. Reed sat in jail until he and the Irving heirs agreed that he would repay a portion of the missing cash. With his reputation in tatters in Illinois, Reed moved to New York, where he opened a new law office. In 1882 Reed was one of two attorneys defending Charles Guiteau, the assassin of President James A. Garfield. Although the defense lost and Guiteau was hanged, the case ended happily for Reed. He fell in love with a Miss Daniels, a young woman who had been an almost daily spectator at the trial. In spite of Reed's precarious reputation and his two previous marriages, both of which had ended in divorce, Miss Daniels became the third Mrs. Reed. The lady lived to regret it. Reed got involved in investment fraud, lost his law practice, and died an alcoholic in 1892, at fifty-eight.[11]

William O'Brien, the Chicago lawyer who dropped Mullen and Hughes when he realized that their case was unwinnable, continued his career as one of the city's most flamboyant and successful defense attorneys. In 1878 O'Brien, a forty-four-year-old widower, married nineteen-year-old Sarah Gillien. O'Brien had recently converted to Catholicism, and the two were married by Bishop Thomas Foley. Shortly after the birth of their only child, a boy, the O'Briens' marriage turned sour. Sarah Gillien O'Brien divorced her husband, citing his persistent alcoholism. In 1884, having just returned to his office from court, O'Brien complained of severe abdominal pains and collapsed. He died two days later of peritonitis.[12]

In 1879 Patrick Tyrrell moved his family to Topeka, Kansas, which fell under the jurisdiction of the St. Louis District of the Secret Service. His marriage with Kate had always been rocky, and in 1899 they divorced. That same year, Tyrrell's fine brick house was seized when the owner didn't pay his taxes.[13] He retired from the Secret Service and moved back to Chicago.

There, on April 3, 1920, Patrick Tyrrell died; he was eighty-nine years old. His children, Frank and Anna, arranged a solemn High Requiem Mass for their father at his parish church, St. Elizabeth's, on the South Side. After the Mass, Tyrrell's body was taken to Chicago's Calvary Cemetery for burial.[14]

Elmer Washburn never returned to law enforcement work. He struck out in a new direction, by starting his own business, Washburn, Shale & Washburn, an engineering firm that among other projects built the Marlboro Reservoir for the city of Boston and the Carmel Dam, to channel water into the New York City's Croton Aqueduct. For a time he was president of the Chicago livestock exchange, and then he became president of the National Live Stock Bank. In 1891 Washburn was one of five candidates to run for mayor of Chicago; he lost to Hempstead Washburne (no relation). Elmer Washburn died at age eighty-four in his home in Chicago on November 23, 1918.[15]

The day after Washburn's obituary was published in the *Chicago Tribune*, the newspaper ran a follow-up article under the headline, "A Story of 1879, Still Big News. Plot to Steal Lincoln's Body Can Be Revealed at Last." The crux of the story was that for thirty-nine years Elmer Washburn and the editors and reporters of the *Chicago Tribune* had kept secret "one of the most astounding stories to develop in years." Now that Washburn was dead, the *Tribune* felt free to disclose how, decades earlier, four villains had tried to steal the body of Abraham Lincoln from its tomb. The newspaper had the inside track on the story from the very beginning because one of its reporters, Percy English, had been with Washburn in the Springfield cemetery on the night of the break-in. It was a tremendous scoop, but the *Tribune* had never published it, out of respect for a promise Washburn had made to Robert Lincoln to keep the attempted desecration of the Lincoln tomb secret.[16]

Whoever wrote this article—there is no byline—got almost everything wrong. The grave robbery took place in 1876, not 1879; the robbers were not relatives of the counterfeiter locked up in Joliet; there were two grave robbers (plus Swegles), not four; Washburn, English, and the Secret Service operatives were not scattered around the grounds risking frostbite, but safe and warm inside the monument; the tomb robbers did not smash open the sarcophagus—the lid came off easily; they planned to hide the body in Indiana, not Canada; and the *Chicago Tribune* never kept the story a secret but gave it prominent (usually front-page) coverage, beginning the day after the break-in.

The only secret revealed at last in the November 26 *Tribune* piece was the name of the reporter—Percy English. It turns out that English had been Washburn's private secretary during his term as Chicago chief of police. It was Washburn who told English that a plot was afoot to kidnap Lincoln's body and invited him to come down to Springfield, to cover the story firsthand.

John Carroll Power continued as custodian of the Lincoln Monument until his death in 1894. In Memorial Hall, the main entry into the Lincoln Monument, he established a small museum of Lincoln relics.[17] Prominent among the displays was a piece of actress Laura Keene's costume, stained with the president's blood. Keene was starring in *Our American Cousin* the night the Lincolns came to Ford's Theatre. After Booth shot Lincoln, Keene grabbed a pitcher of water and rushed to the presidential box, where she knelt, cradling the dying man's head in her lap.[18] Powers also exhibited the tools Mullen and Hughes had used to break into the tomb.[19] When the Monument Association began charging a twenty-five-cent entrance fee to Oak Ridge Cemetery, Power made it his personal crusade to have the fee decision revoked, on the grounds that nothing should prevent visitors from paying their respects at the grave of Abraham Lincoln. Power would have been pleased to learn that during its first fifty years, one million visitors came to the Lincoln Monument and that a million more made their way to Oak Ridge Cemetery between 1920 and 1932.[20] Today the tomb receives over four hundred thousand visitors annually, making Oak Ridge the second-most-visited cemetery in the United States; only Arlington National Cemetery, across the Potomac River from Washington, D.C., receives more visitors.[21]

In 1890 Power published his *History of the Attempt to Steal the Body of Abraham Lincoln.* Although long out of print and usually kept in the rare book room of libraries lucky enough to own a copy, Power's narrative remains an invaluable resource. Not only was he himself an eyewitness and participant in the events he describes, but he had access to documents that disappeared long ago.

On January 11, 1894, Power was waiting for the streetcar that would take him out to Oak Ridge, when he suffered what appeared to be a stroke. Friends carried him to his home, an apartment above the Smith Bros. Funeral Parlor, where he died two hours later; he was seventy-four years old. He lies buried in Oak Ridge Cemetery, a short walk from the Lincoln Monument.[22] John Carroll Power's headstone records that he was "on duty the night of Nov. 7, 1876, when ghouls attempted to steal the body of President Lincoln."

Time and again, prominent men in the Republican Party had tried to cajole Robert Lincoln into running for office, but always he declined. Nonetheless, when President James A. Garfield appointed him secretary of war, Robert felt obligated to accept. He set out for Washington and by some awful irony arrived at the train station in the capital just in time to witness the assassination of President Garfield. The new president, Chester A. Arthur, persuaded Robert Lincoln to remain in office under the new administration, but it was not a happy time for Lincoln. He did not have the temperament to endure the relentless sniping, half-truths, and sly innuendos that fed the Washington gossip mills and often found their way into the newspapers.[23]

In 1888, three years after he had left office, a story broke about some Confederate flags captured during the Civil War that had been boxed up and, it was said, were going to be returned to the Southern states. The persistent rumor that Robert Lincoln had given the order to return the flags dredged up once again the old charge that, given how many Todds had fought for the Confederacy, the Lincoln family's loyalty to the Union had always been shaky at best. When newspaper reporters asked Robert about the flags, he lost his temper. "Well, what of it?" he snapped. "If the flags were boxed and anybody wants to insinuate that they were boxed for the purpose of returning them to the Southern States, it is all poppycock. The thing was never once spoken of, nor even thought of while I was in the [War] Department. We had more important things to think about when I was there than the disposition that should be made of a few, rotten old rebel flags."[24]

Whatever the press thought of him, official Washington still considered Robert a prime asset. In 1889 President Benjamin

Harrison sent Robert to England as his ambassador to the Court of St. James—then as now the most prestigious assignment in the diplomatic service. During his three years of service Robert came to hate the protocol of the British court, which he regarded as an enormous waste of his time. His impatience and frustration led Theodore Roosevelt to comment that "all of our envoys to London have been pro-British except Bob Lincoln."[25]

Back in the United States Robert gave up the law permanently to take up a new career in finance. In 1897 he became president of the Pullman Company, and by 1902 he was a millionaire. He bought several hundred acres in the mountains outside Manchester, Vermont, where he built an English-style estate, complete with formal gardens; he named the place Hildene. The estate became the family's spring and summer home; they spent autumn and winter in Washington, D.C.[26]

In 1909, when Springfield celebrated in high style the hundredth anniversary of the birth of Abraham Lincoln, Robert attended but refused to give a speech. Robert chose, however, not to attend the dedication of the so-called Lincoln Cabin on the Kentucky farm where his father had been born. Perhaps he didn't care to be reminded that only one generation back, the Lincolns had been an obscure frontier family, poverty-stricken and barely literate.[27]

Robert died at Hildene on July 26, 1926. A servant entered his room that morning to rouse him for breakfast, only to find that Robert Todd Lincoln had passed away peacefully in his sleep. If he had survived just six more days, he would have reached his eighty-third birthday. Robert had expected to be buried in the Lincoln tomb in Springfield. Young Jack was already there. But Robert's widow, Mary Harlan Lincoln, decided to bury her husband in Arlington National Cemetery instead. In 1930, she had her son Jack's remains removed from Springfield and buried in the Arlington plot, too.[28]

Leon Hopkins, the plumber who had twice opened and resealed Abraham Lincoln's coffin, waited fifty-two years for payment for the 1887 job. Power had promised him $3 for his work, but Hopkins had neglected to submit a bill. On February 11, 1939—the eve of Lincoln's birthday—a Chicago attorney, Francis Garvey, presented Hopkins with a check for $22.76, to cover the original debt, plus more than half a century of interest.[29] Hopkins died in Springfield on June 18, 1946, less than a month shy of his ninety-fifth birthday.[30]

As for the Lincoln grave robbers, Terence Mullen and John Hughes, the counterfeiter Big Jim Kennally, and the informant Lewis Swegles, they all disappeared from the historical record.

In 1879 the Illinois state legislature revised its statute on robbing graves. Under the old 1845 law, grave robbers and their accomplices were sentenced to a year in the county jail. Under the new provision—undoubtedly inspired by the 1876 Lincoln grave robbery—the penalty was increased to up to ten years in the state penitentiary.[31]

As for the Lincoln tomb on the Mather Block, although it was never used, it was never dismantled, either. Construction of the new state capitol complex began in March 1868, and at some point the tomb Mary Lincoln had rejected became buried. In August 1930, during the course of some routine maintenance, a work crew discovered the tomb about forty feet north of the capitol driveway. They covered it over, but the vault was discovered again in the early 1970s, when workmen were digging a trench on the north side of the statehouse. Mal Hildebrand, director of the Office of the Capitol Architect, was there at the time and remembers seeing the "red, vitreous clay brick" of the tomb chamber. How much of the Lincoln tomb has survived intact is unknown, because the state of Illinois has never ordered a thorough excavation.[32]

Eventually, the Secret Service won its war on counterfeiters. In 1903 agency chief John E. Wilkie sent a survey to bankers asking them to estimate how much counterfeit currency was in circulation. The bankers replied that about one dollar in every hundred thousand dollars of paper money was counterfeit and that three dollars out of every hundred thousand dollars of silver coins were bogus. That reduction in the number of counterfeit dollars represented a remarkable achievement, considering that when the Secret Service had been created forty years earlier, about half of all the paper currency in the United States was counterfeit.[33]

In spite of its reconstructions, the exterior of the Lincoln Monument in Oak Ridge Cemetery has not changed since 1876. All the players in the grave-robbing drama—John Carroll Power, Patrick Tyrrell, Robert Todd Lincoln—would recognize it immediately. As for the monument's interior, well, that's a different story. Memorial Hall is no longer a minimuseum of Lincoln relics and curiosities; today it serves as the vestibule or lobby where two or three members of the helpful, well-informed monument staff are always on hand to answer a visitor's questions and tell the story of the Lincoln family tomb. The old labyrinth of passageways was cleared away in 1930 and replaced with a single circular corridor that leads from Memorial Hall to the tomb chamber, then back to Memorial Hall again.

It is the tomb chamber that has changed the most. The rear steel door with its single padlock is gone, and the doorway has been bricked up, except for a small opening that contains a stained glass window. The original white marble sarcophagus that held Abraham's Lincoln's body is gone, too. Since 1901 the president's remains have rested ten feet below the monument floor, encased in a steel cage, sealed permanently in a solid block of concrete. Above Lincoln's grave stands a massive headstone of red marble.

It made good, practical sense to clear out the clutter from Memorial Hall; at a historical site that receives hundreds of thousands of visitors every year, the display cases were in the way. And the direct route that has been built to and from the Lincoln family graves keeps the foot traffic moving through the monument.

Practicality had nothing to do with the reburial of Abraham Lincoln, of course. In that case the motivation was fear. For twenty-five years John Carroll Power, the members of the Lincoln Monument Association, and the men of the Lincoln Guard of Honor were tormented by the possibility that a smarter, better-organized, more skillful gang of thieves would break into the monument and this time succeed in carrying off the sacred remains of Abraham Lincoln. In 1901 Robert Lincoln buried those fears, along with his father, in a ten-foot-deep, concrete-filled vault. Abraham Lincoln's body has lain there, safe and secure, ever since.

Notes

Bibliography

Index

Notes

Prologue

1. Charles A. Leale, *Lincoln's Last Hours* (New York: 1909), 12.

2. Edward Steers, Jr., *Blood on the Moon: The Assassination of Abraham Lincoln* (Lexington: University Press of Kentucky, 2001), 133–134.

3. Dorothy Meserve Kunhardt and Philip B. Kunhardt, *Twenty Days: The Authoritative Account of Lincoln's Assassination, The Conspiracy and Aftermath* (North Hollywood, Calif.: Newcastle, 1985), 56–57, 80.

4. Steers, *Blood on the Moon*, 133.

5. Jean H. Baker, *Mary Todd Lincoln: A Biography* (New York: Norton, 1987), 245.

6. Steers, *Blood on the Moon*, 268.

7. Ibid., 269.

8. Kunhardt and Kunhardt, *Twenty Days*, 93–95.

9. Edward C. Johnson, "Civil War Embalming," unpublished, undated article, Edward C. and Gail R. Johnson Collection, Springfield, Ill., Museum of Funeral Customs, 6.

10. Robert W. Habenstein and William M. Lamers, *The History of American Funeral Directing*, 3rd rev. ed. (Brookfield, Wisc.: Burton & Mayer, 1995), 199.

11. Robert G. Mayer, *Embalming: History, Theory, and Practice*, 2nd ed. (Stamford, Conn.: Appleton & Lange, 1996), 436–437.

12. Edward C. Johnson, "Henry P. Cattell," unpublished, undated ar-

ticle, Edward C. and Gail R. Johnson Collection, Springfield, Ill., Museum of Funeral Customs, 4.

13. "Funeral of Willie Lincoln," *Sunday Morning Chronicle*, Washington, D.C., February 23, 1862.

14. Johnson, "Henry P. Cattell," 7.

15. Kunhardt and Kunhardt, *Twenty Days*, 95.

16. Johnson, "Henry P. Cattell," 9.

17. Steers, *Blood on the Moon*, 271–272.

18. Elizabeth Keckley, *Behind the Scenes: Thirty Years a Slave and Four Years in the White House* (New York: Arno/New York Times, 1968), 191.

19. Ruth Painter Randall, *Lincoln's Sons* (Boston: Little, Brown, 1955), 215.

20. Baker, *Mary Todd Lincoln*, 220, 219, 221.

21. Susan Krause, Kelley A. Boston, and Daniel W. Stowell, *Now They Belong to the Ages: Abraham Lincoln and His Contemporaries in Oak Ridge Cemetery* (Springfield: Illinois Historic Preservation Agency, 2005), 78–80, 54–56.

22. Steers, *Blood on the Moon*, 272.

23. Wayne C. Temple, *Abraham Lincoln: From Skeptic to Prophet* (Mahomet, Ill.: Mayhaven, 1995), 315–331.

24. Ibid., 331–332, 335.

25. Steers, *Blood on the Moon*, 274.

26. Victor Searcher, *Farewell to Lincoln* (New York: Abingdon, 1965), 79–81.

27. Leale, *Lincoln's Last Hours*, 15.

28. Searcher, *Farewell to Lincoln*, 84–85.

29. Temple, *Abraham Lincoln*, 332.

30. Searcher, *Farewell to Lincoln*, 85.

31. Kunhardt and Kunhardt, *Twenty Days*, 132.

32. Temple, *Abraham Lincoln*, 335–336.

33. Scott D. Trostel, *The Lincoln Funeral Train: The Final Journey and National Funeral for Abraham Lincoln* (Fletcher, Ohio: Cam-Tech, 2002), 37, 150.

34. David Herbert Donald, *Lincoln* (New York: Simon & Schuster, 1995), 378.

35. Trostel, *The Lincoln Funeral Train*, 64.

36. Ibid., 72–73, 87.

37. David McCullough, *Mornings on Horseback* (New York: Simon & Schuster, 1981), 64.

38. Trostel, *The Lincoln Funeral Train*, 188.

39. Searcher, *Farewell to Lincoln*, 240.

40. Ibid., 241, 290.

41. Trostel, *The Lincoln Funeral Train*, 197–198.

42. Kunhardt and Kunhardt, *Twenty Days*, 256.

43. Carl Lewis Barnes, *The Art and Science of Embalming: Descriptive and Operative* (Chicago: Embalmers' Monthly, n.d.), 273.

44. *Chicago Tribune*, May 2, 1865.

45. Mark A. Plummer, *Lincoln's Rail-Splitter: Governor Richard J. Oglesby* (Urbana: University of Illinois Press, 2001), 109.

46. David Charles Sloane, *The Last Great Necessity: Cemeteries in American History* (Baltimore, Md.: Johns Hopkins University Press, 1991), 45.

47. Ibid., 44.

48. Ibid., 52.

49. Ibid., 46, 53–54.

50. Krause, Boston, and Stowell, *Now They Belong to the Ages*, 2–3.

51. Isaac N. Arnold, *The Life of Abraham Lincoln*, 6th ed. (Chicago: A. C. McClurg, 1893), 435.

52. Papers of the National Lincoln Monument Association, box 1, Collection of the Abraham Lincoln Presidential Library.

53. *Illinois Daily Journal*, April 18, 1865.

54. John Carroll Power, *Abraham Lincoln: His Life, Public Services, Death and Funeral Cortege, with a History and Description of the National Lincoln Monument* (Chicago: H. W. Rokker, 1889), 224.

55. Newton Bateman and Paul Selby, eds., *Historical Encyclopedia of Illinois and History of Sangamon County*, vol. 2, pt. 1 (Chicago: Munsell, 1912), 654.

56. Deed: Hannah G. Mather to the State of Illinois, January 18, 1867, case no. 27, file no. 55, acc. no. 96, Illinois State Archives, Springfield, Illinois.

57. Power, *Abraham Lincoln*, 224.

58. Papers of the National Lincoln Monument Association, box 1. Collection of the Abraham Lincoln Presidential Library.

59. Randall, *Lincoln's Sons,* 220.

60. *Illinois Daily Journal,* May 1, 1865.

61. *Illinois State Register,* May 5, 1865.

62. Steers, *Blood on the Moon,* 291.

63. Kunhardt and Kunhardt, *Twenty Days,* 285.

64. Temple, *Abraham Lincoln,* 356.

65. Kunhardt and Kunhardt, *Twenty Days,* 301–302.

66. *Illinois Daily Journal,* May 13, 1865.

67. Paul M. Angle, "The Building of the Lincoln Monument," *Journal of the Abraham Lincoln Association,* 1926, 24.

68. Ozias M. Hatch Papers, box 7, folder 6, Fundraising Correspondence, April–August, 1865, Collection of the Abraham Lincoln Presidential Library, Springfield, Illinois.

69. Mary Todd Lincoln Letters, Letter to Governor Richard J. Oglesby, June 5, 1865, Collection of the Abraham Lincoln Presidential Library, Springfield, Illinois.

70. Angle, "The Building of the Lincoln Monument," 25.

71. Mary Todd Lincoln Letters, Letter to Governor Richard J. Oglesby, June 10, 1865.

72. Papers of the National Lincoln Monument Association, box 1, June 15, 1865.

73. Ibid., June 19, 1865.

1. The World of the Counterfeiters

1. Lynn Glaser, *Counterfeiting in America: The History of an American Way to Wealth* (Philadelphia: Clarkson N. Potter, 1960), 11.

2. Ibid., 12.

3. Ibid., 12, 13, 16, 18.

4. Kenneth Scott, *Counterfeiting in Colonial America* (New York: Oxford University Press, 1957), 7.

5. Glaser, *Counterfeiting in America,* 15, 36.

6. Ibid., 19.

7. Ibid., 22.

8. Scott, *Counterfeiting in Colonial America,* 242.

9. Glaser, *Counterfeiting in America,* 37–39.

10. Ibid., 40–41.

11. Ibid., 47.

12. Ibid., 66.

13. Ibid., 82.

14. George P. Burnham, *Three Years with Counterfeiters, Smugglers and Boodle Carriers, with Accurate Portraits of Prominent Members of the Detective Force in the Secret Service* (Boston: J. P. Dale, 1875), 418–422.

15. David Johnson, *Illegal Tender: Counterfeiting and the Secret Service in Nineteenth-Century America* (Washington, D.C.: Smithsonian Institution Press, 1995), 43, 46.

16. Ibid., 12, 39.

17. Bray Hammond, *Sovereignty and an Empty Purse: Banks and Politics in the Civil War* (Princeton, N.J.: Princeton University Press, 1970), 134.

18. Robert P. Sharkey, *Money, Class, and Party: An Economic Study of Civil War and Reconstruction* (Baltimore, Md.: Johns Hopkins University Press, 1995), 18.

19. Hammond, *Sovereignty and an Empty Purse,* 125–126.

20. Sharkey, *Money, Class, and Party,* 18–19.

21. Irwin Unger, *The Greenback Era: A Social and Political History of American Finance, 1865–1879* (Princeton, N.J.: Princeton University Press, 1964), 14.

22. Sharkey, *Money, Class, and Party,* 22–23.

23. Unger, *The Greenback Era,* 14.

24. Wesley Clair Mitchell, *A History of the Greenbacks, with Special Reference to the Economic Consequences of Their Issue: 1862–65* (Chicago: University of Chicago Press, 1903), 40, 44.

25. Sharkey, *Money, Class, and Party,* 46.

26. Johnson, *Illegal Tender,* 66.

27. Hammond, *Sovereignty and an Empty Purse*, 245–246.

28. Glaser, *Counterfeiting in America*, 103.

29. Ibid., 105.

30. Johnson, *Illegal Tender*, 70.

31. Glaser, *Counterfeiting in America*, 105–106.

32. Johnson, *Illegal Tender*, 76.

33. General Register of the Secret Service: Description and Information of Criminals, 1863–1906, National Archives, College Park, Md., vol. 1, 441.

34. Johnson, *Illegal Tender*, 77.

35. Glaser, *Counterfeiting in America*, 106.

36. Johnson, *Illegal Tender*, 76.

37. Glaser, *Counterfeiting in America*, 106–107.

38. Ibid., 108.

39. Ibid., 108–109.

40. Ibid., 110–111.

41. Johnson, *Illegal Tender*, 79–80.

42. General Register of the Secret Service, vol. 1, 28.

43. *Peoria Transcript*, April 9, 1870.

44. Convict Register, State Penitentiary, Joliet, Illinois, May 7, 1870.

45. United States Census 1870, Joliet, Will County, Illinois, 35.

46. *Chicago City Directory*, 1876.

47. General Register of the Secret Service, vol. 1, 20, 75.

48. John Carroll Power, *History of the Attempt to Steal the Body of Abraham Lincoln (Late President of the United States of America) including a History of the Lincoln Guard of Honor, with Eight Years Lincoln Memorial Services* (Springfield, Ill.: H. W. Rokker, 1890), 29.

49. General Register of the Secret Service, vol. 10, 331–333; Convict Register, February 16, 1876.

50. Burnham, *Three Years with Counterfeiters*, 45.

51. Glaser, *Counterfeiting in America*, 133.

52. Burnham, *Three Years with Counterfeiters*, 63–64.

53. General Register of the Secret Service, vol. 1, 92.

54. Burnham, *Three Years with Counterfeiters*, 68.

55. Power, *History of the Attempt*, 30.

56. General Register of the Secret Service, vol. 10, 334.

57. Power, *History of the Attempt*, 31.

58. Burnham, *Three Years with Counterfeiters*, 47–48.

59. Glaser, *Counterfeiting in America*, 135.

60. Johnson, *Illegal Tender*, 88.

61. Herbert Asbury, *The Gangs of Chicago: An Informal History of the Chicago Underworld* (New York: Knopf, 1940), 43.

62. Johnson, *Illegal Tender*, 88.

63. Ibid., 87.

64. Ibid., 89.

65. Ibid., 94.

66. State of Illinois Department of Public Health—Division of Vital Statistics, Standard Certificate of Death, Registration No. 13237, April 3, 1920.

67. E. Robinson and Roger H. Pidgeon, *Robinson's Atlas of the City of Chicago, Illinois: Compiled and Published from Official Records, Private Plans, and Actual Surveys* (New York: Robinson, 1886).

68. Chicago Fact Book Consortium, *Local Community Fact Book: Chicago Metropolitan Area* (Chicago: University of Illinois at Chicago, n.d.), 18.

2. Big Jim's Kennally's Big Idea

1. Dominic A. Pacyga and Ellen Skerrett, *Chicago, City of Neighborhoods* (Chicago: University of Chicago Press, 1986), 457.

2. Lawrence J. McCaffrey, Ellen Skerrett, Michael F. Funchion, and Charles Fanning, *The Irish in Chicago* (Urbana: University of Illinois Press, 1987), 2.

3. Ibid., 3.

4. Rev. Msgr. Harry C. Koenig, *A History of the Archdiocese of Chicago* (Chicago: New World Publishing, 1980), 578, 580.

5. McCaffrey et al., *The Irish in Chicago*, 7.

6. Charles Fanning, Ellen Skerrett, and John Corrigan, *Nineteenth-*

Century Chicago Irish: A Social and Political Portrait (Chicago: Loyola University of Chicago, 1980), 2.

7. Harvey Strum, "Famine Relief from the Garden City to the Green Isle," *Journal of the Illinois State Historical Society* 93 (Winter 2000–2001): 391.

8. Pacyga and Skerrett, *Chicago, City of Neighborhoods*, 38.

9. Ibid., 39.

10. Strum, "Famine Relief," 392, 394–395.

11. Ibid., 403.

12. Richard Shaw, *Dagger John: The Unquiet Life and Times of Archbishop John Hughes of New York* (New York: Paulist Press, 1977), 141–142.

13. Perry R. Duis, *The Saloon: Public Drinking in Chicago and Boston, 1880–1920* (Urbana: University of Illinois Press, 1999), 154.

14. Iver Bernstein, *The New York City Draft Riots: Their Significance for American Society and Politics in the Age of the Civil War* (New York: Oxford University Press, 1990), 5.

15. Strum, "Famine Relief," 409.

16. See   *www.chipublib.org/004chicago/mayors/speeches/boone55.html* (Mayors' Inaugural Speeches, accessed August 20, 2006).

17. McCaffrey et al., *The Irish in Chicago*, 8.

18. Herbert Asbury, *The Gangs of Chicago: An Informal History of the Chicago Underworld* (New York: Knopf, 1940), 142–143.

19. Ibid., 150.

20. Ibid., 142.

21. Fanning, Skerrett, and Corrigan, *Nineteenth-Century Chicago Irish*, 15.

22. Ibid., 15–16.

23. Ibid., 16.

24. Asbury, *The Gangs of Chicago*, 278.

25. Fanning, Skerrett, and Corrigan, *Nineteenth-Century Chicago Irish*, 14–15.

26. Ibid., 2.

27. Ibid., 3.

28. McCaffrey et al., *The Irish in Chicago*, 62.

29. Ibid., 8.

30. Fanning, Skerrett, and Corrigan, *Nineteenth-Century Chicago Irish*, 3.

31. Ibid., 17.

32. David Johnson, *Illegal Tender: Counterfeiting and the Secret Service in Nineteenth-Century America* (Washington, D.C.: Smithsonian Institution Press, 1995), 12, 25, 61.

33. Convict Register, Illinois State Penitentiary at Joliet, 1870–1877, February 16, 1876; Johnson, *Illegal Tender*, 50.

34. General Register of the Secret Service: Description and Information of Criminals, 1863–1906, National Archives, College Park, Md., vol. 6, 153, and vol. 9, 88.

35. Johnson, *Illegal Tender*, 50.

36. General Register of the Secret Service, vol. 6, 153.

37. Johnson, *Illegal Tender*, 51.

38. John Carroll Power, *History of the Attempt to Steal the Body of Abraham Lincoln (Late President of the United States of America) Including a History of the Lincoln Guard of Honor, with Eight Years Lincoln Memorial Services* (Springfield, Ill.: H. W. Rokker, 1890), 31.

39. Patrick D. Tyrrell, Daily Reports of U.S. Secret Service, Records of the U.S. Secret Service, National Archives, College Park, Md., roll 282, October 21, 1875.

40. Ibid., December 3, 1875.

41. Power, *History of the Attempt*, 33.

42. Tyrrell, Daily Reports, roll 282, October 21, 1875.

43. Power, *History of the Attempt*, 34.

44. Johnson, *Illegal Tender*, 51.

45. Power, *History of the Attempt*, 35.

46. Tyrrell, Daily Reports, roll 282, October 26, 1875.

47. Ibid.

48. Ibid., October 27, 1875.

49. John J. Lalor, ed., *Cyclopædia of Political Science, Political Economy, and the Political History of the United States by the Best American and European Writers* (New York: Maynard, Merrill, 1899), 314.

50. Tyrrell, Daily Reports, roll 282, November 11, 1875.

51. Power, *History of the Attempt*, 35.

52. Tyrrell, Daily Reports, roll 282, November 21, 1875.

53. Ibid., December 24, 1875.

54. Power, *History of the Attempt*, 36.

55. Tyrrell, Daily Reports, roll 282, January 21, 1876.

56. Ibid., February 9, 1876.

57. General Register of the Secret Service, vol. 9, 88.

58. Tyrrell, Daily Reports, roll 282, January 13 and 30, 1876.

59. Convict Register, February 16–18, 1876.

60. Kenneth T. Jackson, ed., *The Encyclopedia of New York City* (New Haven, Conn.: Yale University Press, 1995), 1006.

61. Ruth Richardson, *Death, Dissection and the Destitute*, 2nd ed. (Chicago: University of Chicago Press, 2000), 133–137.

62. Norman Adams, *Dead and Buried? The Horrible History of Body-snatching* (New York: Bell, 1972), 99.

63. Linden F. Edwards, "The Famous Harrison Case and Its Repercussions," *Bulletin of the History of Medicine* 31 (1957): 162–168.

64. Papers of Harrison H. Dodge, Collection of Mount Vernon Library, George Washington's Mount Vernon Estate and Gardens, Mount Vernon, Virginia.

65. Charles W. Stetson, *Washington and His Neighbors* (Richmond, Va.: Garrett and Massie, 1956), 149.

66. Papers of Harrison H. Dodge.

67. Ibid.

68. Ibid.

69. Power, *History of the Attempt*, 12–13.

70. Ibid., 18–19.

71. Bonnie Stahlman Speer, *The Great Abraham Lincoln Hijack: 1876 Attempt to Steal the Body of President Lincoln* (Norman, Okla.: Reliance, 1997), 8.

72. Tyrrell, Daily Reports, roll 283, November 21, 1876.

73. Power, *History of the Attempt*, 15.

74. Tyrrell, Daily Reports, roll 283, November 23, 1876.

75. Power, *History of the Attempt*, 16.

76. Ibid., 14.

77. Ibid., 17.

3. The Boss Body Snatchers of Chicago

1. General Register of the Secret Service: Description and Information of Criminals, 1863–1906, National Archives, College Park, Md., vol. 3, 84, and vol. 5, 387.

2. Dominic A. Pacyga and Ellen Skerrett, *Chicago, City of Neighborhoods* (Chicago: University of Chicago Press, 1986), 160.

3. *The Carriers' Improved Business Directory of Chicago* (Chicago: Franklin, 1873).

4. Perry R. Duis, *The Saloon: Public Drinking in Chicago and Boston, 1880–1920* (Urbana: University of Illinois Press, 1999), 152–154.

5. *Chicago Tribune*, November 18, 1876.

6. Duis, *The Saloon*, 154, 232.

7. Ibid., 72.

8. *Chicago City Directory*, 1876.

9. General Register of the Secret Service, vol. 3, 52.

10. Ibid., vol. 6, 79.

11. *Chicago Tribune*, November 18, 1876.

12. Patrick D. Tyrrell, Daily Reports of U.S. Secret Service, Records of the U.S. Secret Service, National Archives, College Park, Md., roll 283, October 26, 1876.

13. *Chicago Tribune*, November 18, 1876.

14. Ibid.

15. *Chicago Times*, May 31, 1877.

16. *Chicago Tribune*, November 18, 1876.

17. *Commemorative Biographical Record of the Upper Wisconsin Counties of Waupaca, Portage, Wood, Marathon, Lincoln, Oneida, Vilas, Langlade and Shawano* (Chicago: J. H. Beers, 1895), 387.

18. *The Bench and Bar of Chicago: Biographical Sketches* (Chicago: American Biographical Publishing Company, 1883), 626–627.

19. Ellis Baker Usher, *Wisconsin—Its History and Biography, 1848–1913* (Chicago: Lewis, 1914), 946.

20. Tyrrell, Daily Reports, roll 282, January 22, 1876.

21. Ibid., roll 283, August 30, 1876.

22. *Chicago Tribune*, November 18, 1876.

23. Lloyd Lewis, *Myths after Lincoln* (New York: Grosset & Dunlap, 1957), 310.

24. *Chicago Tribune*, November 18, 1876.

25. Tyrrell, Daily Reports, roll 283, October 26, 1876.

26. Robert S. Eckley, "Lincoln's Intimate Friend: Leonard Swett," *Journal of the Illinois State Historical Society* (Autumn 1999): 275.

27. Ibid.

28. Ibid., 277.

29. David Herbert Donald, *Lincoln* (New York: Simon & Schuster, 1995), 248–250.

30. Eckley, "Lincoln's Intimate Friend," 279.

31. Ibid., 280–283.

32. Jean H. Baker, *Mary Todd Lincoln: A Biography* (New York: Norton, 1987), 316–322, 327.

33. Tyrrell, Daily Reports, roll 283, October 27, 1876.

34. *Chicago Tribune*, November 18, 1876.

35. Tyrrell, Daily Reports, roll 283, October 31, 1876.

36. Ibid., November 6, 1876.

37. Ibid.

38. *Chicago Tribune*, November 18, 1876.

39. Tyrrell, Daily Reports, roll 283, November 6, 1876.

40. Ibid.

41. Ruth Painter Randall, *Lincoln's Sons* (Boston: Little, Brown, 1955), 327–330.

42. Baker, *Mary Todd Lincoln*, 327.

43. Tyrrell, Daily Reports, roll 283, November 7, 1876.

4. "The Devils Are Up Here"

1. *Springfield City Directory*, 1876.

2. Patrick D. Tyrrell, Daily Reports of U.S. Secret Service, Records of the U.S. Secret Service, National Archives, College Park, Md., roll 283, November 7, 1876.

3. *Chicago Tribune*, November 18, 1876.

4. Tyrrell, Daily Reports, roll 283, November 8, 1876.

5. *Illinois Daily Journal*, January 12, 1894.

6. National Lincoln Monument Association Papers, Custodian Reports 1876–1878, Collection of the Abraham Lincoln Presidential Library, Springfield, Illinois.

7. Tyrrell, Daily Reports, roll 283, November 7, 1876.

8. *Chicago Tribune*, November 18, 1876.

9. Tyrrell, Daily Reports, roll 283, November 8, 1876.

10. John Carroll Power, *History of the Attempt to Steal the Body of Abraham Lincoln (Late President of the United States of America) Including a History of the Lincoln Guard of Honor, with Eight Years Lincoln Memorial Services* (Springfield, Ill.: H. W. Rokker, 1890), 49.

11. Tyrrell, Daily Reports, roll 283, November 8, 1876.

12. *Chicago Tribune*, November 26, 1918.

13. *Chicago Inter-Ocean*, November 20, 1876.

14. Tyrrell, Daily Reports, roll 283, November 8, 1876.

15. *Chicago Tribune*, November 9, 1876.

16. Power, *History of the Attempt*, 50.

17. *Chicago Tribune*, November 9, 1876.

18. Power, *History of the Attempt*, 49–51.

19. *Chicago Tribune*, November 18, 1876.

20. Ibid.

21. Ibid.

22. Tyrrell, Daily Reports, roll 283, November 7, 1876.

23. Ibid.

24. Ibid.

25. Ibid.

26. Power, *History of the Attempt*, 60.

27. *Chicago Tribune*, November 23, 1876.

28. Ibid.

29. Tyrrell, Daily Reports, roll 283, November 8 and 17, 1876.

30. Ibid.

31. *Chicago Times*, November 18, 1876.

32. Tyrrell, Daily Reports, roll 283, November 17, 1876.

33. Ibid., November 18, 1876.

34. *Chicago Tribune*, January 14, 1885.

35. Tyrrell, Daily Reports, roll 283, November 18, 1876.

36. *Chicago Inter-Ocean*, November 20, 1876.

37. Ibid.

38. Ibid.

39. Ibid., November 23, 1876.

40. Ibid., November 24, 1876.

5. The Body in the Basement

1. Roy Morris, Jr., *Fraud of the Century: Rutherford B. Hayes, Samuel Tilden, and the Stolen Election of 1876* (New York: Simon & Schuster, 2003), 164.

2. *Nashville Daily American*, November 9, 1876.

3. C. Vann Woodward, *Reunion and Reaction: The Compromise of 1877 and the End of Reconstruction* (Boston: Little, Brown, 1951), 17.

4. Morris, *Fraud of the Century*, 17.

5. Woodward, *Reunion and Reaction*, 17–18.

6. Morris, *Fraud of the Century*, 197–198.

7. Woodward, *Reunion and Reaction*, 18–19.

8. Morris, *Fraud of the Century*, 172–173.

9. *Chicago Inter-Ocean*, November 24, 1876.

10. Ibid., November 20, 1876.

11. *Charleston News and Courier*, November 14, 1876.

12. *New Orleans Daily Picayune*, November 16, 1876.

13. Ibid., November 14, 1876.

14. *Daily Memphis Avalanche*, November 23, 1876.

15. *Illinois State Register*, November 15, 1876.

16. *Chicago Tribune*, November 18, 1877.

17. Ibid., November 9, 1876.

18. John Carroll Power, *History of the Attempt to Steal the Body of Abraham Lincoln (Late President of the United States of America) Including a History of the Lincoln Guard of Honor, with Eight Years Lincoln Memorial Services* (Springfield, Ill.: H. W. Rokker, 1890), 77.

19. Caroline Goldthorpe, *From Queen to Empress: Victorian Dress, 1837–1877: An Exhibition at the Costume Institute, December 15, 1988–April 16, 1989* (New York: Metropolitan Museum of Art, 1988), 69–71.

20. Jean H. Baker, *Mary Todd Lincoln: A Biography* (New York: Norton, 1987), 246–247.

21. Daniel E. Sutherland, *The Expansion of Everyday Life, 1860–1876* (New York: Harper & Row, 1990), 129–130.

22. *Chicago Tribune*, November 18, 1876.

23. Lincoln Guard of Honor Records, 1880–1918, Collection of the Abraham Lincoln Presidential Library, Springfield, Illinois, 89–90.

24. Power, *History of the Attempt*, 79.

25. Patrick D. Tyrrell, Daily Reports of U.S. Secret Service, Records of the U.S. Secret Service, National Archives, College Park, Md., roll 283, November 18, 1876.

26. Candace Fleming, "A Fitful Night's Sleep," in "Lincoln Assassination and Aftermath," special issue, *America's Civil War, Civil War Times,* and *American History* (2005): 80–81.

27. M. Brayman, ed., *The Revised Statutes of the State of Illinois: 1845* (Springfield, Ill.: Walters and Weber, Public Printers, 1845), 370.

28. Ibid.

29. Professor James Carey, Loyola University Law School, Chicago, personal email of November 28, 2005.

30. *Chicago Tribune*, January 14, 1885.

31. *Illinois State Register,* May 31, 1877.

32. *Illinois Daily Journal*, March 13, 1877.

33. *Portrait and Biographical Album of Sangamon County, Illinois, Containing Full Page Portraits and Biographical Sketches of Prominent and Representative Citizens of the County Together with Portraits and Biographies of All the Presidents of the United States and Governors of the State* (Chicago: Chapman Bros., 1891), 719.

34. Joseph Wallace, *Past and Present of the City of Springfield and Sangamon County, Illinois* (Springfield, Ill.: S. J. Clarke, 1904), 285, 287.

35. *Portrait and Biographical Album*, 190.

36. *The United States Biographical Dictionary and Portrait Gallery of Eminent and Self-Made Men*, Illinois vol. (Chicago: American Biographical Publishing, 1876), 312–313.

37. John Carroll Power, *History of the Early Settlers of Sangamon County, Illinois* (Springfield, Ill.: Edwin A. Wilson, 1876), 366.

38. *History of Sangamon County, Illinois* (Chicago: Inter-State, 1881), 130.

39. Ibid., 120.

6. "The Tools of Smarter Men"

1. Ruth Painter Randall, *Lincoln's Sons* (Boston: Little, Brown, 1955), 320.

2. Justin G. Turner and Linda Levitt Turner, *Mary Todd Lincoln: Her Life and Letters* (New York: Knopf, 1972), 257.

3. Randall, *Lincoln's Sons*, 321.

4. Ibid., 319.

5. David Herbert Donald, *Lincoln* (New York: Simon & Schuster, 1995), 160.

6. Jean H. Baker, *Mary Todd Lincoln: A Biography* (New York: Norton, 1987), 267–268.

7. Mary Todd Lincoln Papers, Letters 1876–1877, Collection of the Abraham Lincoln Presidential Library, Springfield, Illinois.

8. Robert Todd Lincoln to David Davis, March 13, 1877, Robert Todd Lincoln Letterpress, vol. 3, Collection of the Abraham Lincoln Presidential Library, Springfield, Illinois.

9. Donald, *Lincoln*, 146.

10. David Davis Family Papers, Collection of the Abraham Lincoln Presidential Library, Springfield, Illinois, box 7, folder A-109.

11. Harry E. Pratt, *The Personal Finances of Abraham Lincoln* (Springfield, Ill.: Abraham Lincoln Association, 1943), 133–134.

12. Ibid., 141.

13. Turner and Turner, *Mary Todd Lincoln*, 458.

14. John S. Goff, *Robert Todd Lincoln: A Man in His Own Right* (Tulsa: University of Oklahoma Press, 1969), 72.

15. Robert Todd Lincoln to Charles F. Conant, March 13, 1877, Robert Todd Lincoln Letterpress, vol. 3, Collection of the Abraham Lincoln Presidential Library, Springfield, Illinois.

16. Randall, *Lincoln's Sons*, 219.

17. *Illinois Daily Journal*, May 18, 1877.

18. *Chicago Tribune*, May 18, 1877.

19. Ibid., May 22, 1877.

20. Ibid., May 23, 1877.

21. Ibid., May 28 and May 29, 1877.

22. Ibid., May 29, 1877.

23. John Carroll Power, *History of the Attempt to Steal the Body of Abraham Lincoln (Late President of the United States of America) Including a History of the Lincoln Guard of Honor, with Eight Years Lincoln Memorial Services* (Springfield, Ill.: H. W. Rokker, 1890), 71–72.

24. *Illinois Daily Journal*, May 29, 1877.

25. *Chicago Times*, May 30, 1877.

26. *Illinois Daily Journal*, May 30, 1877.

27. *Chicago Times*, May 30, 1877.

28. *Illinois Daily Journal*, May 30, 1877.

29. *Illinois State Register*, May 31, 1877.

30. Ibid.

31. Ibid.

32. Ibid.

33. Ibid.

34. *Illinois Daily Journal*, June 1, 1877.

35. *Illinois State Register*, May 31, 1877.

36. Patrick D. Tyrrell, Daily Reports of U.S. Secret Service, Records of the U.S. Secret Service, National Archives, College Park, Md., roll 283, May 30, 1877.

37. *Chicago Tribune*, June 1, 1877.

38. *Illinois Daily Journal*, June 1, 1877.

39. *Chicago Times*, June 1, 1877.

40. Tyrrell, Daily Reports, roll 283, May 31, 1877.

41. Ibid., June 10, 1877.

42. *Illinois State Register*, May 31, 1877.

43. Tyrrell, Daily Reports, roll 283, June 21, 1877.

44. *Illinois State Register*, June 22, 1877.

7. The Lincoln Guard of Honor

1. Lincoln Guard of Honor Records, 1880–1918, Collection of the Abraham Lincoln Presidential Library, Springfield, Illinois, 91.

2. John Carroll Power, *History of the Attempt to Steal the Body of Abraham Lincoln (Late President of the United States of America) Including a His-*

tory of the Lincoln Guard of Honor, with Eight Years Lincoln Memorial Services (Springfield, Ill.: H. W. Rokker, 1890), 80.

3. Lincoln Guard of Honor Records, 1880–1918, 92.

4. Power, *History of the Attempt*, 82.

5. Ibid., 83–84.

6. Ibid., 84–85.

7. Susan Krause, Kelley A. Boston, and Daniel W. Stowell, *Now They Belong to the Ages: Abraham Lincoln and His Contemporaries in Oak Ridge Cemetery* (Springfield: Illinois Historic Preservation Agency, 2005), 122.

8. Power, *History of the Attempt*, 87.

9. *History of Sangamon County, Illinois* (Chicago: Inter-State, 1881), 727, 703.

10. Lincoln Guard of Honor Records, 1880–1918, 98.

11. Mark C. Carnes, *Secret Ritual and Manhood in Victorian America* (New Haven, Conn.: Yale University Press, 1989), 1.

12. W. S. Harwood, "Secret Societies in America," *North American Review* 164 (May 1897): 622.

13. Arthur M. Schlesinger, Sr., "Biography of a Nation of Joiners," *American Historical Review* 50 (October 1944): 14.

14. Carnes, *Secret Ritual and Manhood in Victorian America*, 5.

15. Power, *History of the Attempt*, 108–109.

16. Ibid.

17. Quoted in Justin G. Turner and Linda Levitt Turner, *Mary Todd Lincoln: Her Life and Letters* (New York: Knopf, 1972), 704.

18. Ibid., 705.

19. Ibid., 716.

20. Jean H. Baker, *Mary Todd Lincoln: A Biography* (New York: Norton, 1987), 368–369.

21. Power, *History of the Attempt*, 87.

22. Turner and Turner, *Mary Todd Lincoln*, 717.

23. Lincoln Guard of Honor Records, 1880–1918, 138.

24. Patrick D. Tyrrell, Daily Reports of U.S. Secret Service, Records of the U.S. Secret Service, National Archives, College Park, Md., roll 283, May 22, 1878.

25. Ibid.

26. Ibid., June 19, 1878.

27. Ibid., roll 284, November 10, 1878, and February 4, 1880.

28. Ibid., March 20, 1880, and April 14, 1880.

29. Ibid., November 18, 1882.

30. Power, *History of the Attempt*, 88.

31. Ibid., 88–89.

32. *Chicago Inter-Ocean*, July 19, 1884.

33. *Illinois Daily Journal*, April 14, 1887.

34. Power, *History of the Attempt*, 89.

35. Ibid., 89–90.

36. Ibid., 89.

37. Ibid., 91.

38. Ibid., 92–93.

39. *Illinois Daily Journal*, April 14, 1887.

40. Power, *History of the Attempt*, 93.

41. *Illinois Daily Journal*, April 15, 1887.

42. Power, *History of the Attempt*, 94–95.

43. Ibid., 95.

44. Krause, Boston, and Stowell, *Now They Belong to the Ages*, 122, 110.

45. Ibid., 54, 58, 78, 98, 128, 163, 35, 151.

46. John S. Goff, *Robert Todd Lincoln: A Man in His Own Right* (Tulsa: University of Oklahoma Press, 1969), 151.

47. Power, *History of the Attempt*, 95–96.

48. *Illinois Daily Journal*, April 15, 1877.

49. Power, *History of the Attempt*, 95.

8. A Pullman-Style Burial

1. Herbert Wells Fay, *The Story of Lincoln's Tomb and Its Three Constructions* (Springfield, Ill.: Week by Week Press, 1932), 1.

2. *Illinois Daily Journal*, March 10, 1900.

3. Ibid.

4. Ibid., March 11, 1900.

5. *Chicago Tribune*, March 11, 1900.

6. *Illinois Daily Journal*, March 11, 1900.

7. Ruth Painter Randall, *Lincoln's Sons* (Boston: Little, Brown, 1955), 307–308.

8. John S. Goff, *Robert Todd Lincoln: A Man in His Own Right* (Tulsa: University of Oklahoma Press, 1969), 196.

9. *Illinois Daily Journal*, June 7, 1901.

10. Randall, *Lincoln's Sons*, 312, 328.

11. Liston Edgington Leyendecker, *Palace Car Prince: A Biography of George Mortimer Pullman* (Niwot: University Press of Colorado, 1992), 76.

12. Almont Lindsey, *The Pullman Strike: The Story of a Unique Experiment and of a Great Labor Upheaval* (Chicago: Phoenix Books/University of Chicago Press, 1942), 20–22.

13. Colston E. Warne, ed., *The Pullman Boycott of 1894: The Problem of Federal Intervention* (Boston: D. C. Heath, 1955), 9.

14. Lindsey, *The Pullman Strike*, 100, 96.

15. Warne, *The Pullman Boycott of 1894*, 9.

16. Leyendecker, *Palace Car Prince*, 169.

17. Lindsey, *The Pullman Strike*, 61–62.

18. Ibid., 53–54.

19. Warne, *The Pullman Boycott of 1894*, 9.

20. Lindsey, *The Pullman Strike*, 83–84.

21. Ibid., 98–99.

22. Ibid., 94.

23. Warne, *The Pullman Boycott of 1894*, 19–20.

24. Lindsey, *The Pullman Strike*, 122–123.

25. Warne, *The Pullman Boycott of 1894*, 21.

26. Leyendecker, *Palace Car Prince*, 230.

27. Lindsey, *The Pullman Strike*, 126–127, 130.

28. Ibid., 171, 175, 234.

29. Ibid., 207–209, 233.

30. Ibid., 233.

31. Ibid., 268, 335.

32. Leyendecker, *Palace Car Prince*, 230.

33. Lindsey, *The Pullman Strike*, 339–341.

34. Goff, *Robert Todd Lincoln*, 219.

35. Lindsey, *The Pullman Strike*, 303.

36. Leyendecker, *Palace Car Prince*, 243.

37. Ibid., 258.

38. *www.graveyards.com* (Cook County Cemeteries, Graceland, accessed December 10, 2005).

39. Arthur L. Meriam, "Final Interment of President Abraham Lincoln's Remains at the Lincoln Monument in Oak Ridge Cemetery, Springfield, Illinois," *Journal of the Illinois State Historical Society* (April 1930–January 1931): 171.

40. Ibid., 173.

41. Dorothy Meserve Kunhardt, "Strange History Brought to Light: Rare Photos of Lincoln Exhumation," *Life* (February 15, 1963): 88.

42. Ibid.

43. Meriam, "Final Interment of President Abraham Lincoln's Remains," 174.

44. Kunhardt, "Strange History Brought to Light," 88.

Epilogue

1. *Chicago Tribune*, September 19, 1930.

2. Victoria Grieve, *Ford's Theatre and the Lincoln Assassination* (Alexandria, Va.: Parks and History Association, 2001), 84–92.

3. Edward C. Johnson, "Henry P. Cattell," unpublished, undated article, Edward C. and Gail R. Johnson Collection, Museum of Funeral Customs, Springfield, Ill.

4. John A. Garraty and Mark C. Carnes, eds., *American National Biography* (New York: Oxford University Press, 1999) 24:217.

5. Jeffrey D. Nichols, *History Blazer*, September 1995, article 16.

6. *Illinois Daily Journal*, March 30, 1915.

7. Ibid., April 4, 1915.

8. Ibid., May 1, 1917.

9. Ibid., October 23, 1909.

10. *Portrait and Biographical Album of Sangamon County, Illinois, Containing Full Page Portraits and Biographical Sketches of Prominent and Representative Citizens of the County Together with Portraits and Biographies of All the Presidents of the United States and Governors of the State* (Chicago: Chapman, 1891), 719.

11. *Chicago Tribune*, April 26, 1892.

12. Ibid., January 14, 1884.

13. Bonnie Stahlman Speer, *The Great Abraham Lincoln Hijack: 1876 Attempt to Steal the Body of President Lincoln* (Norman, Okla.: Reliance, 1997), 173.

14. *Chicago Tribune*, April 5, 1920.

15. Ibid., November 25, 1918.

16. Ibid., November 26, 1918.

17. Papers of the National Lincoln Monument Association, box 5, Custodian Reports, 1876–1878.

18. Edward Steers, Jr., *Blood on the Moon: The Assassination of Abraham Lincoln* (Lexington: University Press of Kentucky, 2001), 121–122.

19. Papers of the National Lincoln Monument Association, box 5, Custodian Reports, 1876–1878.

20. Herbert Wells Fay, *The Story of Lincoln's Tomb and Its Three Constructions* (Springfield, Ill.: Week by Week Press, 1932), 4.

21. Interview with Nan Wynn, Lincoln Monument, Springfield, Illinois, June 9, 2005.

22. *Illinois Daily Journal*, January 12–13, 1894.

23. Ruth Painter Randall, *Lincoln's Sons* (Boston: Little, Brown, 1955), 299–301.

24. Ibid., 302.

25. Ibid., 306, 310.

26. Ibid., 312–313, 317–318.

27. John S. Goff, *Robert Todd Lincoln: A Man in His Own Right* (Tulsa: University of Oklahoma Press, 1969), 236.

28. Randall, *Lincoln's Sons,* 339–340.

29. Lincoln Grave Robbery File, Collection of the Lincoln Museum, Fort Wayne, Indiana.

30. *Illinois Daily Journal*, June 19, 1946.

31. Harvey B. Hurd, comp. and ed., *The Revised Statutes of the State of Illinois: 1880* (Chicago: Chicago Legal News, 1880), 378.

32. *The Cook-Witter Report* 20, no. 5 (November 14, 2005): 3.

33. Lynn Glaser, *Counterfeiting in America: The History of an American Way to Wealth* (Philadelphia: Clarkson N. Potter, 1960), 113.

Bibliography

Primary Documents

Chicago City Directory, 1875 and 1876

Chicago Mayors' Inaugural Speeches, *cpl.lib.uic.edu*

Convict Register, Illinois State Penitentiary at Joliet, 1870–1877

David Davis Family Papers, Collection of the Abraham Lincoln Presidential Library, Springfield, Illinois

Deed: Hannah G. Mather to the State of Illinois, January 18, 1867, case no. 27, file no. 55, acc. no. 96, Illinois State Archives, Springfield, Illinois

General Register of the Secret Service: Description and Information of Criminals, 1863–1906, 12 vols., National Archives, College Park, Maryland

Lincoln Guard of Honor Records, 1880–1918, Collection of the Abraham Lincoln Presidential Library, Springfield, Illinois

Mary Todd Lincoln Letters, 1865–1877, Collection of the Abraham Lincoln Presidential Library, Springfield, Illinois

National Lincoln Monument Association Papers, Collection of the Abraham Lincoln Presidential Library, Springfield, Illinois

National Lincoln Monument Association Papers, Custodian Reports, 1876–1878, Collection of the Abraham Lincoln Presidential Library, Springfield, Illinois

Bibliography

Ozias M. Hatch Papers, box 7, folder 6, Fundraising Correspondence, April–August 1865, Collection of the Abraham Lincoln Presidential Library, Springfield, Illinois

Papers of Harrison H. Dodge, Collection of Mount Vernon Library, George Washington's Mount Vernon Estate and Gardens, Mount Vernon, Virginia

Records of the U.S. Secret Service, Daily Reports of U.S. Secret Service Operative Patrick D. Tyrrell, July 1, 1875–June 30, 1886, rolls 282–286, National Archives, College Park, Maryland

Robert Todd Lincoln Letters, 1876–1877, Robert Todd Lincoln Letterpress, Collection of the Abraham Lincoln Presidential Library, Springfield, Illinois

Sangamon County Circuit Court Record, vol. 32, 1877, Collection of the University of Illinois at Springfield

Springfield City Directory, 1876 and 1877

United States Census, 1870

Newspapers

Chicago Tribune
Chicago Inter-Ocean
Chicago Times
Daily American (Nashville, Tenn.)
Daily Memphis Avalanche
Illinois Daily Journal (Springfield)
Illinois State Register (Springfield)
New Orleans Daily Picayune
News and Courier (Charleston, S.C.)
New York Times
Peoria Transcript

Books and Journals

Adams, Norman. *Dead and Buried? The Horrible History of Bodysnatching.* New York: Bell, 1972.

Alexander, Thomas G. *Things in Heaven and Earth: The Life and Times of*

Bibliography

Wilford Woodruff, a Mormon Prophet. Salt Lake City, Utah: Signature, 1993.

Angle, Paul M. "The Building of the Lincoln Monument." *Journal of the Abraham Lincoln Association* (1926): 17–59.

Arnold, Isaac N. *The Life of Abraham Lincoln*, 6th ed. Chicago: A. C. McClurg, 1893.

Asbury, Herbert. *The Gangs of Chicago: An Informal History of the Chicago Underworld.* New York: Knopf, 1940.

Baker, Jean H. *Mary Todd Lincoln: A Biography.* New York: Norton, 1987.

Barnes, Carl Lewis. *The Art and Science of Embalming: Descriptive and Operative.* Chicago: Embalmers' Monthly, n.d.

Bateman, Newton, and Paul Selby, eds. *Historical Encyclopedia of Illinois and History of Sangamon County*, vol. 2, pt. 1. Chicago: Munsell, 1912.

The Bench and Bar of Chicago: Biographical Sketches. Chicago: American Biographical Publishing Company, 1883.

Bernstein, Iver. *The New York City Draft Riots: Their Significance for American Society and Politics in the Age of the Civil War.* New York: Oxford University Press, 1990.

Bowen, Walter S., and Harry Edward Neal. *The United States Secret Service.* Philadelphia: Chilton, 1960.

Brayman, M., ed. *The Revised Statutes of the State of Illinois: 1845.* Springfield, Ill.: Walters and Weber, Public Printers, 1845.

Burnham, George P. *American Counterfeits: How Detected, and How Avoided.* Springfield, Mass.: W. J. Holland, 1875.

Burnham, George P. *Three Years with Counterfeiters, Smugglers and Boodle Carriers, with Accurate Portraits of Prominent Members of the Detective Force in the Secret Service.* Boston: J. P. Dale, 1875.

Carnes, Mark C. *Secret Ritual and Manhood in Victorian America.* New Haven, Conn.: Yale University Press, 1989.

The Carriers' Improved Business Directory of Chicago. Chicago: Franklin Printing, 1873.

Chicago Fact Book Consortium. *Local Community Fact Book: Chicago Metropolitan Area.* Chicago: University of Illinois at Chicago, n.d.

Commemorative Biographical Record of the Upper Wisconsin Counties of Waupaca, Portage, Wood, Marathon, Lincoln, Oneida, Vilas, Langlade and Shawano. Chicago: J. H. Beers, 1895.

Bibliography

The Cook-Witter Report. Volume 20, no. 5, November 14, 2005.

Donald, David Herbert. *Lincoln.* New York: Simon & Schuster, 1995.

Duis, Perry R. *The Saloon: Public Drinking in Chicago and Boston, 1880–1920.* Urbana: University of Illinois Press, 1999.

Eckley, Robert S. "Lincoln's Intimate Friend: Leonard Swett." *Journal of the Illinois State Historical Society* (Autumn 1999): 274–288.

Edwards, Linden F. "The Famous Harrison Case and Its Repercussions." *Bulletin of the History of Medicine* 31 (1957): 162–171.

Fanning, Charles, Ellen Skerrett, and John Corrigan. *Nineteenth-Century Chicago Irish: A Social and Political Portrait.* Chicago: Loyola University of Chicago, 1980.

Fay, Herbert Wells. *The Story of Lincoln's Tomb and Its Three Constructions.* Springfield, Ill.: Week by Week Press, 1932.

Fleming, Candace. "A Fitful Night's Sleep." In "Lincoln Assassination and Aftermath," special issue, *America's Civil War, Civil War Times,* and *American History* (2005): 76–83.

Flinn, John J. *History of the Chicago Police.* Chicago: Chicago Police Book Fund, 1887.

Gannal, J. N. *History of Embalming and of Preparations in Anatomy, Pathology, and Natural History Including an Account of a New Process for Embalming,* trans. R. Harlan, M.D. Philadelphia: Judah Dobson, 1840.

Garraty, John A., and Mark C. Carnes, eds. *American National Biography,* 24 vols. New York: Oxford University Press, 1999.

Gittings, Clare. *Death, Burial and the Individual in Early Modern England.* London: Croom Helm, 1984.

Glaser, Lynn. *Counterfeiting in America: The History of an American Way to Wealth.* Philadelphia: Clarkson N. Potter, 1960.

Goff, John S. *Robert Todd Lincoln: A Man in His Own Right.* Tulsa: University of Oklahoma Press, 1969.

Goldthorpe, Caroline. *From Queen to Empress: Victorian Dress, 1837–1877: An Exhibition at the Costume Institute, December 15, 1988–April 16, 1989.* New York: Metropolitan Museum of Art, 1988.

Good, Timothy S. *We Saw Lincoln Shot: One Hundred Eyewitness Accounts.* Jackson: University Press of Mississippi, 1995.

Bibliography

Grieve, Victoria. *Ford's Theatre and the Lincoln Assassination.* Alexandria, Va.: Parks and History Association, 2001.

Habenstein, Robert W., and William M. Lamers. *The History of American Funeral Directing,* 3rd rev. ed. Brookfield, Wisc.: Burton & Mayer, 1995.

Hammond, Bray. "The North's Empty Purse, 1861–1862." *American Historical Review* 67 (October 1961): 1–18.

Hammond, Bray. *Sovereignty and an Empty Purse: Banks and Politics in the Civil War.* Princeton, N.J.: Princeton University Press, 1970.

Harris, William C. *Lincoln's Last Months.* Cambridge, Mass.: Harvard University Press, 2004.

Harwood, W. S. "Secret Societies in America." *North American Review* 164 (May 1897): 620–623.

Hatfield, Marcus P. *The National Funeral Directors' Official Text Book.* Chicago: Donohue & Henneberry, 1886.

History of Logan County, Illinois. Chicago: Inter-State, 1886.

History of Sangamon County, Illinois. Chicago: Inter-State, 1881.

Hurd, Harvey B., comp. and ed. *The Revised Statutes of the State of Illinois: 1877.* Chicago: Chicago Legal News, 1877.

Hurd, Harvey B., comp. and ed. *The Revised Statutes of the State of Illinois: 1880.* Chicago: Chicago Legal News, 1880.

Jackson, Kenneth T., ed. *The Encyclopedia of New York City.* New Haven, Conn.: Yale University Press, 1995.

Johnson, David. *Illegal Tender: Counterfeiting and the Secret Service in Nineteenth-Century America.* Washington, D.C.: Smithsonian Institution Press, 1995.

Johnson, Edward C. "Civil War Embalming." Unpublished, undated article from the Edward C. and Gail R. Johnson Collection, Springfield, Ill., Museum of Funeral Customs.

Johnson, Edward C. "Henry P. Cattell." Unpublished, undated article from the Edward C. and Gail R. Johnson Collection, Springfield, Ill., Museum of Funeral Customs.

Keckley, Elizabeth. *Behind the Scenes: Thirty Years a Slave and Four Years in the White House.* New York: Arno Press/New York Times, 1968.

King, Willard L. *Lincoln's Manager: David Davis.* Cambridge, Mass.: Harvard University Press, 1960.

Bibliography

Knox, John Jay. *United States Notes: A History of the Various Issues of Paper Money by the Government of the United States.* New York: Scribner's, 1884.

Koenig, Rev. Msgr. Harry C. *A History of the Archdiocese of Chicago.* Chicago: New World, 1980.

Krause, Susan, Kelley A. Boston, and Daniel W. Stowell. *Now They Belong to the Ages: Abraham Lincoln and His Contemporaries in Oak Ridge Cemetery.* Springfield: Illinois Historic Preservation Agency, 2005.

Kunhardt, Dorothy Meserve, "Strange History Brought to Light: Rare Photos of Lincoln Exhumation." *Life* (February 15, 1963): 86–88.

Kunhardt, Dorothy Meserve, and Philip B. Kunhardt, Jr. *Twenty Days: The Authoritative Account of Lincoln's Assassination, the Conspiracy and Aftermath.* North Hollywood, Calif.: Newcastle, 1985.

Lalor, John J., ed. *Cyclopædia of Political Science, Political Economy, and the Political History of the United States by the Best American and European Writers.* New York: Maynard, Merrill, 1899.

Laws of the State of Illinois Enacted by the Seventieth General Assembly. Vol. 1. Printed by Authority of the General Assembly of the State of Illinois, March 3, 1958.

Leale, Charles A. *Lincoln's Last Hours* (pamphlet). Address delivered before the Commandery of the State of New York, Military Order of the Loyal Legion of the United States, at the regular meeting, February 1909, City of New York, in observance of the one hundredth anniversary of the birth of President Abraham Lincoln.

Lewis, Lloyd. *Myths after Lincoln.* New York: Grosset & Dunlap, 1957.

Leyendecker, Liston Edgington. *Palace Car Prince: A Biography of George Mortimer Pullman.* Niwot: University Press of Colorado, 1992.

Lindsey, Almont. *The Pullman Strike: The Story of a Unique Experiment and of a Great Labor Upheaval.* Chicago: Phoenix Books/University of Chicago Press, 1942.

Lossing, Benson J. *The Home of Washington, or Mount Vernon and Its Associations, Historical, Biographical, and Pictorial.* New York: Virtue & Yorston, 1871.

Mayer, Robert G. *Embalming: History, Theory, and Practice,* 2nd ed. Stamford, Conn.: Appleton & Lange, 1996.

Bibliography

McCaffrey, Lawrence J., Ellen Skerrett, Michael F. Funchion, and Charles Fanning. *The Irish in Chicago*. Urbana: University of Illinois Press, 1987.

Melandson, Philip H., with Peter F. Stevens. *The Secret Service: The Hidden History of an Enigmatic Agency*. New York: Carroll & Graf, 2002.

Mendelsohn, Simon. *Embalming Fluids: Their Historical Development and Formulation, from the Standpoint of the Chemical Aspects of the Scientific Art of Preserving Human Remains*. New York: Chemical Publishing, 1940.

Meriam, Arthur L. "Final Interment of President Abraham Lincoln's Remains at the Lincoln Monument in Oak Ridge Cemetery, Springfield, Illinois." *Journal of the Illinois State Historical Society* (April 1930–January 1931): 170–174.

Mitchell, Wesley Clair. *A History of the Greenbacks, with Special Reference to the Economic Consequences of Their Issue: 1862–65*. Chicago: University of Chicago Press, 1903.

Morris, Roy, Jr. *Fraud of the Century: Rutherford B. Hayes, Samuel Tilden, and the Stolen Election of 1876*. New York: Simon & Schuster, 2003.

Morrow, Raphael W., and Harriet I. Carter. *In Pursuit of Crime: The Police of Chicago. Chronicle of a Hundred Years, 1833–1933*. Sunbury, Ohio: Flats, 1996.

Moses, John, and Joseph Kirkland, eds. *The History of Chicago Illinois*. Vol. 2. Chicago: Munsell, 1895.

Nichols, Jeffrey D. "Justice Charles S. Zane and the Antipolygamy 'Crusade.'" *History Blazer*. September 1995, article 16.

Pacyga, Dominic A., and Ellen Skerrett. *Chicago, City of Neighborhoods*. Chicago: University of Chicago Press, 1986.

Peterson, Merrill D. *Lincoln in American Memory*. New York: Oxford University Press, 1994.

Plummer, Mark A. *Lincoln's Rail-Splitter: Governor Richard J. Oglesby*. Urbana: University of Illinois Press, 2001.

Plummer, Mark A. "A Tomb for All Time: Governor Richard J. Oglesby and the Battle over the Lincoln Gravesite." *Illinois Heritage* (May–June 2005): 10–14.

Portrait and Biographical Album of Sangamon County, Illinois, Containing

Full Page Portraits and Biographical Sketches of Prominent and Representative Citizens of the County Together with Portraits and Biographies of All the Presidents of the United States and Governors of the State. Chicago: Chapman, 1891.

Power, John Carroll. *Abraham Lincoln: His Life, Public Services, Death and Funeral Cortege, with a History and Description of the National Lincoln Monument.* Chicago: H. W. Rokker, 1889.

Power, John Carroll. *History of the Attempt to Steal the Body of Abraham Lincoln (Late President of the United States of America) Including a History of the Lincoln Guard of Honor, with Eight Years Lincoln Memorial Services.* Springfield, Ill.: H. W. Rokker, 1890.

Power, John Carroll. *History of the Early Settlers of Sangamon County, Illinois.* Springfield, Ill.: Edwin A. Wilson, 1876.

Pratt, Harry E. *The Personal Finances of Abraham Lincoln.* Springfield, Ill.: Abraham Lincoln Association, 1943.

Randall, Ruth Painter. *Lincoln's Sons.* Boston: Little, Brown, 1955.

Report of the General Superintendent of Police of the City of Chicago to the City Council for the Fiscal Year Ending December 31, 1876. Chicago: Clark & Edwards, 1877.

Richardson, Ruth. *Death, Dissection and the Destitute,* 2nd ed. Chicago: University of Chicago Press, 2000.

Robinson, E., and Roger H. Pidgeon. *Robinson's Atlas of the City of Chicago, Illinois: Compiled and Published from Official Records, Private Plans, and Actual Surveys.* New York: Robinson, 1886.

Schlesinger, Arthur M., Sr. "Biography of a Nation of Joiners." *American Historical Review* 50 (October 1944): 2–15.

Scott, Kenneth. *Counterfeiting in Colonial America.* New York: Oxford University Press, 1957.

Searcher, Victor. *Farewell to Lincoln.* New York: Abingdon, 1965.

Sharkey, Robert P. *Money, Class, and Party: An Economic Study of Civil War and Reconstruction.* Baltimore, Md.: Johns Hopkins University Press, 195).

Shaw, Richard. *Dagger John: The Unquiet Life and Times of Archbishop John Hughes of New York.* New York: Paulist Press, 1977.

Sievers, Harry J. *The Harrison Horror.* Fort Wayne, Ind.: Fort Wayne and Allen County Public Library, 1956.

Bibliography

Sloane, David Charles. *The Last Great Necessity: Cemeteries in American History*. Baltimore, Md.: Johns Hopkins University Press, 1991.

Speer, Bonnie Stahlman. *The Great Abraham Lincoln Hijack: 1876 Attempt to Steal the Body of President Lincoln*. Norman, Okla.: Reliance, 1997.

Steers, Edward, Jr. *Blood on the Moon: The Assassination of Abraham Lincoln*. Lexington: University Press of Kentucky, 2001.

Stetson, Charles W. *Washington and His Neighbors*. Richmond, Va.: Garrett and Massie, 1956.

Strum, Harvey. "Famine Relief from the Garden City to the Green Isle." *Journal of the Illinois State Historical Society* 93 (Winter 2000–2001): 388–414.

Sutherland, Daniel E. *The Expansion of Everyday Life, 1860–1876*. New York: Harper & Row, 1990.

Temple, Wayne C. *Abraham Lincoln: From Skeptic to Prophet*. Mahomet, Ill.: Mayhaven, 1995.

"The Tomb of George Washington: Historic Structure Report." Mesick Cohen Waite Architects, Albany, N.Y., February 1993.

Trostel, Scott D. *The Lincoln Funeral Train: The Final Journey and National Funeral for Abraham Lincoln*. Fletcher, Ohio: Cam-Tech, 2002.

Turner, Justin G., and Linda Levitt Turner. *Mary Todd Lincoln: Her Life and Letters*. New York: Knopf, 1972.

Turner, Thomas Reed. *Beware the People Weeping: Public Opinion and the Assassination of Abraham Lincoln*. Baton Rouge: Louisiana State University Press, 1982.

Unger, Irwin. *The Greenback Era: A Social and Political History of American Finance, 1865–1879*. Princeton, N.J.: Princeton University Press, 1964.

The United States Biographical Dictionary and Portrait Gallery of Eminent and Self-Made Men. Illinois vol. Chicago: American Biographical Publishing, 1876.

Usher, Ellis Baker. *Wisconsin—Its History and Biography, 1848–1913*. Chicago: Lewis, 1914.

Walker, Edwin S. *The Lincoln Monument, with Illustrations*. Springfield, Ill.: n.p., 1879.

Bibliography

Wallace, Joseph. *Past and Present of the City of Springfield and Sangamon County, Illinois.* Springfield, Ill.: S. J. Clarke, 1904.

Warne, Colston E., ed. *The Pullman Boycott of 1894: The Problem of Federal Intervention.* Boston: D. C. Heath, 1955.

Welles, Charles L. *Stories on Stone.* New York: Oxford University Press, 1954.

Woodward, C. Vann. *Reunion and Reaction: The Compromise of 1877 and the End of Reconstruction.* Boston: Little, Brown, 1951.

Index

Index